THE BOOK OF ENOCH THE PROPHET

THE BOOK OF ENOCH THE PROPHET:

AN APOCRYPHAL PRODUCTION,

SUPPOSED FOR AGES TO HAVE BEEN LOST;

BUT

DISCOVERED AT THE CLOSE OF THE LAST CENTURY IN ABYSSINIA;

NOW FIRST TRANSLATED FROM

AN ETHIOPIC MS. IN THE BODLEIAN LIBRARY.

BY

RICHARD LAURENCE, LL.D.

GYAN

Published by

Gyan Publishing House
5, Ansari Road
Daryaganj, New Delhi-110002
Phone: 011-47034999, 9811692060
E-mail: books@gyanbooks.com

Distribution Network
gyanbooks.com
India, USA, Canada, UK, Australia

ISBN: 978-93-6208-653-2 (PB)
First Published, 1821

2nd Impression 2024

Printed at: Gyan Press, Delhi.

THE BOOK OF ENOCH THE PROPHET
Translator: RICHARD LAURENCE

መጽሐፈ፡ ሄኖክ፡

ነቢይ።

THE BOOK OF ENOCH

THE PROPHET:

AN APOCRYPHAL PRODUCTION,

SUPPOSED FOR AGES TO HAVE BEEN LOST;

BUT

DISCOVERED AT THE CLOSE OF THE LAST CENTURY IN ABYSSINIA;

NOW FIRST TRANSLATED FROM

AN ETHIOPIC MS. IN THE BODLEIAN LIBRARY.

BY

RICHARD LAURENCE, LL.D.

ARCHBISHOP OF CASHEL,

LATE PROFESSOR OF HEBREW IN THE UNIVERSITY OF OXFORD.

SECOND EDITION, CORRECTED AND ENLARGED.

OXFORD,

J. H. PARKER;

J. G. AND F. RIVINGTON, LONDON.

MDCCCXXXIII.

PRELIMINARY DISSERTATION.

THE apocryphal Book of Enoch, in the last and the preceding century, proved a prolific subject for critical speculation and theological discussion. The circumstance of its having been quoted by an inspired writer of the New Testament [a] augmented the despair of recovering a supposed treasure, which had long been lost. It was known until the eighth century of the Christian æra; after which it seems to have sunk into complete oblivion.

A considerable fragment of it however was discovered by Scaliger in the Chronographia of Georgius Syncellus; a work which had not then been printed. He extracted the whole of this fragment, and published it in his notes to the Chronicus Canon of Eusebius [b]. Still however, as it did not contain the passage quoted by St. Jude, doubts were entertained whether the Apostle really referred to the same production as was cited by Georgius Syncellus, or derived his information respecting the prophecy of Enoch from some other source.

Since the discovery of Scaliger, much has been written, but very little, if any, additional information obtained, upon this subject. The fullest ac-

[a] Jude ver. 14, 15.

[b] P. 404, 405. ed. Amst. 1658.

count of the opinions entertained by the Fathers, and the quotations which they made from this celebrated apocryphal production, before it was lost, as well as what has since been conjectured respecting it by modern critics, are to be found in Fabricius's Codex Pseudepigraphus Vet. Testamenti, vol. i. p. 160—224 [a]; who also gives at length the Greek fragment of it, preserved by Georgius Syncellus: [which is reprinted in this edition, p. 181.]

But although the Greek copy of this book, itself perhaps nothing more than a mere translation from some Hebrew or Chaldee original, seems to have been irretrievably lost; yet an idea prevailed so early as at the commencement of the seventeenth century, that an Ethiopic version of it still existed in Abyssinia. Ludolf, in his Commentary upon his History of Ethiopia, remarks, that an Ethiopic tract, supposed to be the Book of Enoch, had been transmitted from Egypt, and purchased by Peiresc. His words are; "Gassendus in vita *Peireskii*, de Ægidio "Lochiensi Capucino, qui in Ægypto septennium "egerat, inter alia scribit; Quandoquidem inter cætera animadvertisse se dixit Mazakpha Enok, seu "prophetiam Enochi, declarantem ea, quæ ad finem "usque seculi eventura sunt; librum Europæ pridem invisum, illic autem charactere ac idiomate "Æthiopico seu Abyssinorum, apud quos is fuerat "servatus, conscriptum; ideo Peireskius *sic fuit ac-*

[a] In p. 222, 223, Fabricius refers to twenty different authors, who have more or less alluded to this book.

"*census ejus quoquo pretio comparandi studio, ut* "*nullis parcens sumptibus, ipsum denique sui fece-* "*rit juris.*" In consequence, he adds, of this report, he was advised by his learned friends to use every exertion in his power in order to procure at least a specimen of a book, respecting which so much literary but unsatisfactory discussion had taken place; to determine whether such a production ever really existed, or, admitting it to have existed, what its weight and authority were. Nor did he spare, he remarks, either expense or labour, until he obtained the wished-for specimen. "Igitur "et ego nullis neque sumptibus neque laboribus "peperci, donec specimen istius libri adipiscerer." At length likewise, completely to satisfy himself, he went to Paris, where the book was deposited in the Royal Library, and inspected the whole of it. But the result was, that the work alluded to was not, what report had made it, the Book of Enoch, but one of a very different description, replete with fable and superstition [a].

After the disappointment of Ludolf, every idea that the book in question existed in an Ethiopic version was altogether abandoned; until towards the conclusion of the last century, when our own enterprising countryman, Bruce, not only proved its existence, but brought over with him from Abyssinia three copies of it. The following is the account

[a] Commentarius ad Histor. Ethiopicam, p. 347.

which he himself gives of the manner in which he disposed of them—"Amongst the articles," he remarks, "I consigned to the library at Paris, was a "very beautiful and magnificent copy of the prophecies of Enoch, in large quarto; another is "amongst the books of Scripture, which I brought "home, standing *immediately before the Book of "Job, which is its proper place in the Abyssinian "Canon;* and a third copy I have presented to the "Bodleian Library at Oxford by the hands of Dr. "Douglas, the Bishop of Carlisle [a]." And shortly after he subjoins; "I cannot but recollect, that "when it was known in England, that I had presented this book to the library of the King of "France, without staying a few days to give me "time to reach London, when our learned countrymen might have had an opportunity of perusing "at leisure a copy of this book, Dr. Woide set out "for Paris, with letters from the Secretary of State "to Lord Stormont, Ambassador at that Court, desiring him to assist the Doctor in procuring access to my present, by permission from his most "Christian Majesty. This he accordingly obtained; "and *a translation of the work was brought over; "but, I know not why, it has nowhere appeared* [b]."

Whatsoever might have been the public curiosity and impatience upon this point at the period alluded to by Mr. Bruce, it seems to have long since

[a] Travels, vol. ii. p. 422. 8vo edit. [b] Ib. p. 425, 426.

subsided; as the copy deposited in the Bodleian Library has quietly slept there undisturbed to the present day. At length however I have ventured to break in upon its repose; and to employ myself in the subsequent translation of it. I have certainly spared neither time nor trouble in rendering it correct; but as the Bodleian Statutes, wisely in my judgment, preclude the use of books *out* of the library, I have been under the necessity of translating the work *in* it. This circumstance perhaps, if inaccuracies occur, may be admitted in mitigation of censure.

It is stated by Bruce, that Woide translated the whole of it at Paris, and brought his translation back with him to England, although he never published it. This however is certainly a mistake. Woide indeed *transcribed* the Ethiopic version, but did not *translate* it; for nothing like a translation is to be found among his papers, which since his death have all become the property of the Delegates of the University Press. Every scrap relative to the Book of Enoch has been carefully collected and preserved; but nothing more occurs than a slight attempt at literally rendering into Latin a few detached passages; an attempt which sufficiently evinces, that his knowledge of Ethiopic was too imperfect for the completion of such a task[a]. He seems only to have been then commencing his

[a] See also Magasin Encyclopédique, an. VI. tom. i. p. 375, 376.

studies in that language; studies, which his Coptic pursuits and publications interrupted, and which were finally arrested by the hand of death.

I had finished my translation of the Bodleian MS. before I was aware, that the Delegates of the Press possessed a transcript by Woide of the Paris MS. I have nevertheless since examined that transcript; and have noted some occasional and manifest variations between the two copies; but the latter is too incorrectly transcribed to be trusted in a minute comparison. That the public have hitherto reaped no advantage from the donation to the Bodleian Library, I have already remarked. This however has not been altogether the case with respect to the other MSS.; for Mr. Murray, the editor of the octavo edition of Bruce's travels, from that which the author reserved to himself, has given in a note a short summary of the contents of the book [a]; and the learned Silvestre De Sacy, in a

[a] "The translation from the Greek, which is found in the "Ethiopic Bible, under the name of Metsahaf Henoc, is divided "into 90 kefel, or chapters. It begins with this preface;—'In "the name of God, the merciful and gracious, slow to anger, and "of great mercy and holiness. This book is the book of Enoch "the prophet. May his blessing and help be with him who loves "him for ever and ever, Amen*.' Chap. i. 'The word of the "blessing of Enoch, with which he blessed the chosen and the "righteous, that were of old. And Enoch lifted up his voice and "spake, a holy man of God, while his eyes were open, and he saw "a holy vision in the heavens, which the angels revealed to him.

* This short preface, which occurs in both the others, is omitted in the Bodleian MS.

"Notice du Livre d'Enoch," (published in the Magasin Encyclopédique, an. VI. tom. i. p. 382.) has fa-

"And I heard from them every thing, and I understood what I "saw.'—After this follows the history of the angels, of their "having descended from heaven, and produced giants with the "daughters of men; of their having instructed these in the arts "of war and peace, and luxury. The names of the leading spirits "are mentioned, which appear to be of Hebrew original, but "corrupted by Greek pronunciation. The resolution of God to "destroy them is then revealed to Enoch. These topics occupy "about eighteen chapters, which Mr. Bruce had translated into "English, but weary of the subject proceeded no further. From "the eighteenth to the fiftieth chapter, Enoch is led by Uriel and "Raphael through a series of visions, not much connected with "the preceding. He saw the burning valley of the fallen angels, "the paradise of the saints, the utmost ends of the earth, the "treasuries of the thunder and lightning, winds, rain, dew, and "the angels who presided over these. He was led into the place "of the general judgment, saw the Ancient of days on his throne, "and all the kings of the earth before him. At the fifty-second "chapter, Noah is said to have been alarmed at the enormous "wickedness of mankind, and, fearing vengeance, to have im-"plored the advice of his great grandfather. Enoch told him, "that a flood of waters would destroy the whole race of man, "and a flood of fire punish the angels, whom the deluge could "not affect. Chap. lix. The subject of the angels is resumed. "Semeiza, Artukafu, Arimeen, Kakabael, Tusael, Ramiel, Dan-"del, and others, to the amount of twenty, appear at the head of "the fallen spirits, and give fresh instances of their rebellious dis-"positions. At kefel lxii. Enoch gives his son Mathusala a long "account of the sun, moon, stars, the year, the months, the winds, "and like physical phenomena. This takes up eight chapters, after "which the patriarch makes a recapitulation of what he had ut-"tered in the former pages. The remaining twenty chapters are "employed on the history of the deluge, Noah's preparations for "it, and the success which attended them. The destruction of all

voured us with a Latin translation of the first three chapters; of all between the sixth and sixteenth

" flesh, excepting his family, and the execution of divine venge- " ance on the angels and their followers, conclude this absurd " and tedious work." Vol. ii. p. 424, 425, 426. note. The reader will perceive that this account is imperfect and inaccurate, particularly that which is given of the last twenty chapters. Mr. Murray seems to have taken a hasty and prejudiced view of the book. He has since however spoken of it more favourably. For in a descriptive Catalogue of Mr. Bruce's Oriental MSS., which has been kindly communicated to me by their present possessor, Mr. Murray thus alludes to it:

" The Book of the prophet Enoch is in vol. iv. of the MSS., " and occupies thirty-two leaves, beautifully and closely written, " of the volume. It stands before the book of Job. It is divided " into ninety-six chapters, and also into nineteen sections, which " last have no connection with the chapters, and seem to be arbi- " trarily made, without regard to the subject of the work. *The " language is the purest Ethiopic; and the whole book has a pecu- " liar dignity of style and manner, which imposes on the reader, " and impresses on his mind ideas of its great antiquity.*

" The Book of Enoch was first brought into Europe by Mr. " Bruce; and three copies originally belonging to him, one of " which is in Paris, another in Oxford, and the third and most " original in this volume, are all that exist of it on our continent. " *It must be regarded as highly curious,* being the translation of a " Greek book long since lost, which was older than the appear- " ance of our Saviour, and the age of the Apostles. A passage " from the book of Enoch is found in the 14th and 15th verses " of the Epistle of Jude in our Scriptures. Some fragments of " the Greek original are given by Kircher, Œd. Egypt. vol. ii. " p. 69. The subject of the book is a series of visions, respecting " the fallen angels, their posterity the giants, the crimes which " occasioned the deluge, the mysteries of heaven, the place of the " final judgment of men and angels, and various parts of the uni- " verse seen by Enoch, and related by him to his son Mathusala.

chapters inclusively; and likewise of the twenty-second and thirty-second chapters, from the Paris manuscript. This translation I have republished at the end of my own: p. 169.

I understand also, that Dr. Gessenius of Halle in Saxony has been lately at Paris, and has transcribed the whole of the book, purporting hereafter to publish it in Ethiopic with a Latin version. If the freedom therefore of an English translation, or my own inattention, has any where betrayed me into error of conception, or into obscurity of expression, the public will possess the advantage of seeing them corrected in the Latin version.

Having thus considered the source from which the present translation was derived, I shall have little occasion to dwell upon the proof, that the Ethiopic version of the Book of Enoch contains precisely the same work as the Greek version, which was known to the Fathers. For if the account given of the descent, &c. of the angels in the former be compared with that contained in the latter, as extant in Georgius Syncellus, no doubt will arise upon the subject. The variations, I apprehend, will

" *The narrative is bold and fabulous, but highly impressive of the* " *sentiments and character of those speculative enthusiasts, who* " *blended the Chaldaic philosophy with the sacred history of the* " *Jews*. As a literary relic, it merits attention; and as an Ethi-* " *opic book, written in the purest Geez, and venerated by the Abys-* " *sinians, as of equal authority with the writings of Moses, it de-* " *serves to be laid before the public.*"

* This remark appears to me destitute of proof.

appear to be purely accidental. This might alone be sufficient to establish the fact. But from several quotations of the Fathers themselves, additional evidence may be obtained. Irenæus, in the second century, distinctly alluded to the embassy of Enoch to the angels, which is not contained in the fragment preserved by G. Syncellus: "Sed et Enoch," he says, "sive circumcisione placens Deo, *cum* "*esset homo, legatione ad angelos fungebatur*, et "translatus est, et conservatur usque nunc testis "justi judicii Dei; quoniam angeli quidem trans-"gressi deciderunt in judicium; homo autem pla-"cens, translatus est in salutem[a]." The account of this embassy occurs in the fourteenth and fifteenth chapters of the present translation. Tertullian also, who wrote in the same century, makes a direct and distinct quotation from chapter xcvii. 7, 8; "Et "rursus juro vobis peccatores, quod in diem sangui-"nis perditionis justitia parata est. Qui servitis la-"pidibus, et qui imagines facitis aureas, et argen-"teas, et ligneas, et lapideas, et fictiles, et servitis "phantasmatibus, et dæmoniis, et spiritibus infami-"bus, et omnibus erroribus non secundum scienti-"am, nullum ab iis invenitis auxilium[b]." This in

[a] Opera, p. 319. ed. Grabe.

[b] Opera, p. 87. ed. Paris 1664. Upon the word *infamibus* the following various readings are furnished by Rigalt; "In cod. Ful-"vii Ursini legitur *infanis*. At in cod. Agobardi *infanis*." Perhaps the true reading of the expression is *in fanis, in temples,* in conformity with the Ethiopic. This also might have been the reading of the two MSS. referred to in the note; Rigalt mistaking

the Ethiopic is thus expressed; "Again I swear to "you, ye sinners, that crime has been prepared for "the day of blood, which never ceases. They shall "worship stones, and engrave golden, silver, and "wooden images. They shall worship impure spi-"rits, demons, and every idol, in temples; but no "help shall be obtained from them." The identity of the two passages cannot, I conceive, be doubted; when a little allowance is made for the caprice of translation on one side, and for the freedom of quotation on the other.

To these testimonies I shall only subjoin one more; that of Anatolius, Bishop of Laodicea, cited by Eusebius. This, he remarks, (*viz.* that the first month among the Hebrews is about the equinox,) even the instructions contained in Enoch demonstrate[a]; referring to the account of the commencement of the year at the fourth gate given in chap. lxxi. 12. His previous argument, it should be added, goes to prove, that the computation of the year begins with the *vernal* equinox.

But indeed the evidence of their identity afforded

an *f* for an *ſ* in the first instance, and substituting an *m* for an *n* (both these letters being usually omitted in MSS., and expressed by the same horizontal mark over the word) in the second instance.

[a] Τοῦ δὲ τὸν πρῶτον παρ' Ἑβραίοις μῆνα περὶ ἰσημερίαν εἶναι, παραστατικὰ καὶ τὰ ἐν τῷ Ἐνὼχ μαθήματα. Ecclesiast. Histor. lib. vii. cap. 32. p. 235. The work of Anatolius here quoted was written in the year 276, according to Bucherius. See Tillemont's Mémoires d'Hist. Eccles. vol. iv. p. 127.

by the long fragment preserved by Georgius Syncellus is so complete in itself, as to require no corroboration. And that the Book of Enoch, extant for several centuries after the birth of Christ, was the source from which St. Jude derived his quotation, ver. 14, 15, every allusion of the early Commentators upon Scripture clearly evinces. The particular passage, it is true, was not pointed out; because, as the book was well known, that circumstance might have been deemed superfluous; but it occurs distinctly marked in the Ethiopic. In the Bodleian manuscript it occupies the whole of what is termed the second chapter; but in that of Paris it constitutes the last verse of the first chapter.

Admitting then that the book under consideration is precisely the same as that which was known to St. Jude and the Fathers of the Christian Church, we must not nevertheless hence conclude, that it was ever invested with canonical authority. It seems to have been always enumerated among the apocryphal books of Scripture. This is the station assigned to it in what are termed the Apostolical Constitutions[a]. Irenæus indeed[b], and Clemens of Alexandria[c], in the second century, refer to it without alluding to its apocryphal character; but Origen, in the commencement of the third, distinctly states, that the Church considers it not as an inspired production; ἐν ταῖς ἐκκλησίαις οὐ πάνυ φέρεται ὡς θεῖα[d].

[a] Lib. vi. cap. 16. [b] Opera, p. 319. [c] Opera, ed. Sylburgii, p. 801, et 808. [d] Contra Celsum, p. 267. ed. Spencer.

Yet, citing it on another occasion, he seems to imply, that there were some who deemed it canonical; for he prefaces his reference to it with the hypothetical remark, "if any be pleased to receive it as a sacred book," εἴ τῳ φίλον παραδέχεσθαι ὡς ἅγιον τὸ βιβλίον[a]. In the Synopsis of Scripture also, published with the works of Athanasius, it ranks as apocryphal. And a similar character is assigned to it by Jerome, who alludes to it more than once, in precisely the same point of view. "Manifestissimus liber est," he remarks in his Comment on Psalm cxxxii. 3, "et "inter apocryphos computatur, et *veteres* interpre- "tes de isto locuti sunt; nonnulla autem nos dixi- "mus, *non in auctoritatem sed in commemoratio-* "*nem*." Austin likewise speaks of it in the same manner[b]. And lastly, in the Catalogue of Nicephorus, Patriarch of Constantinople, written at the commencement of the ninth century, it is again classed among the apocryphal books[c].

Notwithstanding however that neither the Jewish nor Christian Church ever admitted it into the Canon of Scripture, a celebrated writer of the second century regarded it both as an inspired composition, and as the genuine production of him whose name it bears. Tertullian in his tract on Idolatry, says; "Hæc igitur ab initio *prævidens Spiritus* "*Sanctus*, etiam ostia in superstitionem ventura "*præcecinit per antiquissimum prophetam Enoch*[d];"

[a] In Joannem, p. 132. ed. Huetii. [b] De Civitate Dei, lib. xv. cap. 23. [c] Hody, De Bibl. Textibus, p. 648. [d] Opera, p. 95.

thus expressly asserting its inspiration, and ascribing it to the most ancient prophet Enoch. But in his tract *De Cultu Fœminarum*, after having alluded[a] to the intercourse of the angels with the daughters of men, and their consequent punishment, he directly adverts to the question of its rejection from the Canon of Scripture. "Scio," he remarks, "scripturam Enoch, quæ hunc ordinem angelis dedit, *non recipi a quibusdam*, quia *nec in armarium Judaicum admittitur*. Opinor non putaverunt illam ante cataclysmum editam; post eum casum orbis, omnium rerum abolitorem, salvam esse potuisse. Si ista ratio est, recordentur pronepotem ipsius Enoch fuisse superstitem cataclysmi Noë, qui utique domestico nomine et hæreditaria traditione audierat et meminerat de proavi sui penes Deum gratia, et de omnibus prædicatis ejus; cum Enoch filio suo Matusalæ nihil aliud mandaverit, quam ut notitiam eorum poste-

[a] "Nam et illi qui ea constituerunt, damnati in pœnam mortis deputantur: illi scilicet angeli, qui ad filias hominum de cœlo ruerunt, ut hæc quoque ignominia fœminæ accedat. Nam cum et materias quasdam bene occultas, et artes plerasque non bene revelatas seculo multo magis imperito prodidissent, (si quidem et metallorum operta nudaverant, et herbarum ingenia traduxerant, et incantationum vires provulgaverant, et omnem curiositatem usque ad stellarum interpretationem designaverant,) proprie et quasi peculiariter fœminis instrumentum istud muliebris gloriæ contulerunt? lumina lapillorum, quibus monilia variantur; et circulos ex auro, quibus brachia arctantur; et medicamenta ex fuco quibus lanæ colorantur; et illum ipsum nigrum pulverem, quo oculorum exordia producuntur." Opera, p. 150.

" ris suis traderet. Igitur sine dubio *potuit* Noë in " prædicationis delegatione successisse, vel quia et " alias non tacuisset, tam de dei conservatoris sui " dispositione, quam de ipsa domus suæ gloria. Hoc " si non tam expedite haberet, illud quoque asser- " tionem scripturæ illius tueretur; perinde potuit " abolefactam eam violentia cataclysmi in spiritu " rursus reformari; quemadmodum et Hierosolymis " Babylonia expugnatione deletis, omne instrumen- " tum Judaicæ literaturæ per Esdram constat re- " stauratum. Sed cum Enoch eadem scriptura et- " iam *de Domino* prædicavit, a nobis quidem nihil " omnino rejiciendum est, quod pertineat ad nos. " Et legimus omnem scripturam ædificationi habi- " lem *divinitus inspirari*. A Judæis potest jam vi- " deri propterea rejecta, sicut et cætera fere, quæ " Christum sonant. Nec utique mirum hoc, si scri- " pturas aliquas non receperunt de eo locutas, quem " et ipsum coram loquentem non erant recepturi. " Eo accedit, quod Enoch apud Judam Apostolum " testimonium possidet[a]."

From the preceding statement therefore of Tertullian, who lived at the conclusion of the second century, it appears, that in his time the Book of Enoch was not *universally* rejected, as an unauthentic and uninspired composition; although it was not admitted into the Jewish Canon. Not long however after the commencement of the third century, Origen expressly affirms, that it was not re-

[a] Opera, p. 151.

ceived *by the Church.* Indeed no trace is to be discovered of its having been ever enumerated among the canonical books of Scripture, either by Jews or Christians. With the arguments of Tertullian, in proof of its inspiration and authenticity, I have nothing to do; but I cannot help remarking, that they will not for a moment preponderate in the rigid balance of modern criticism. He *presumes* that the book was written by Enoch himself; and then concludes, that it might have *possibly* been preserved, or re-written, by Noah; a conclusion which is nothing more than a bare possibility, deduced from a mere presumption. Its allusions to the Lord, or rather to the Son of man, exalted on his throne of glory and of judgment by the Ancient of days, may demonstrate, that it was written *after the book of Daniel;* but not, surely, that it was the production of Enoch *before the flood.* Besides, the known fact of its having been never received into the Canon of Scripture seems an insuperable objection to its high antiquity. Nor will the quotation of a single passage from it by St. Jude prove his approbation of the whole book, more than the quotations of St. Paul from certain heathen poets prove that Apostle's approbation of every part of the compositions to which he referred. This is the reasoning of Jerome[a]; which has always appeared to me satisfac-

[a] "Putant quidam Apostolum reprehendendum, quod imprudenter lapsus sit, dum falsos doctores arguit, illorum versiculos comprobavit. Quibus breviter respondendum est. In eo quod

tory upon the point. St. Jude, it is true, uses the word *prophesied*, when speaking of apocryphal Enoch; but let it be also remembered, that St. Paul applies the equivalent term *prophet* even to a heathen poet. And as it was never doubted, before the book was lost, that St. Jude really alluded to it, so, I apprehend, since it is recovered, that fact will scarcely again be questioned.

From the preceding observations therefore it appears, that the Book of Enoch, now first published, contains precisely the same work as the Greek one of that title, known to the Fathers; that it was quoted by St. Jude; and that by the ancient Church, perhaps by every Church, ancient and modern, the Abyssinian alone excepted, it was always deemed apocryphal. By whom, and at what period, it was composed, are the next questions which naturally present themselves for discussion; but in attempting

" ait: *Corrumpunt bonos mores colloquia mala* (1 Cor. xv. 33.); " et in illo: *Ipsius et genus sumus* (Acts xvii. 28.); non statim *to-* " *tam Menandri* comœdiam, et *Arati* librum, præsenti loco (Titus " i. 12.*) non *totum* opus *Callimachi*, sive *Epimenidis*, quorum " alter laudes Jovis canit, alter de oraculis scripsit, per *unum* " *versiculum* comprobavit; sed Cretenses tantum mendaces vitio " gentis increpavit, non ob illam opinionem, qua sunt arguti a " poetis, sed ob ingenitam mentiendi facilitatem de proprio eos " gentis auctore confutans. Qui autem putant totum librum de- " bere sequi eum, qui libri usus sit versiculo, videntur mihi et " *apocryphum Enochi, de quo Apostolus Judas in Epistola sua* " *testimonium posuit, inter Ecclesiæ scripturas recipere.*" Comm. in Tit. i. 12.

* "One of themselves, even *a prophet* of their own, said, The Cretians " are always liars, evil beasts, slow bellies."

an investigation of this nature, I may be only thought, perhaps, to wander from conjecture to conjecture, without a clue, through a labyrinth of doubt and perplexity. This would indisputably prove to be the case, were I to raise an hypothesis upon conclusions derived from *external* evidence; but I have fancied, that something like an approximation towards fact may be extracted from evidence altogether *internal*.

With respect to the supposed *author*, if indeed it were the work of one and the same person, little more seems discoverable, than that he was a Jew, and wrote in his own language. Of this every passage in every part of it bears the most clear and distinct testimony. In proof that it was originally written in Hebrew, I shall refer to the opinion of Scaliger; who, I should likewise remark, formed that opinion from the *Greek* fragment which was preserved by Georgius Syncellus. Assigning his motives for transcribing and publishing what he contemplated as Jewish lies and disgusting fables, he says; "Sed quia *ex Hebraismo* conversa sunt, ut "*etiam mediocriter Hebraice perito constare potest*, "et *vetustissimus* est liber, et a Tertulliano ex eo "quædam adducuntur, quæ huc alludunt, et quod "caput est, locus, qui in Epistola Judæ de ange-"lis prævaricatoribus producitur, manifesto ex hoc "fragmento excerptus est, malui tædium descri-"bendi devorare, quam committere, ut illis bene-"voli lectores diutius carerent[a]."

[a] In Chron. Euseb. p. 405.

But other testimonies to the same point are not wanting. It is well known that the most ancient remains of the Cabala are contained in the Zohar; a species of philosophical commentary upon the Law, combining theological opinions with the allegorical subtleties of the mystical school. In this celebrated compilation, of what was long supposed to constitute the hidden wisdom of the Jewish nation, occasional references are made to the Book of Enoch, as to a book carefully preserved from generation to generation. The following passage from it will sufficiently demonstrate, that the Cabalists were acquainted with a written composition in their own language under the title of the Book of Enoch, not with a mere traditional record of such a composition; and that this book, in an important part at least, was the same as that which still exists in Ethiopic. "The holy and the blessed One," it is said, "raised him (Enoch) from the world to serve him, "as it is written, ***For God took him.*** From that "time a book was delivered down, which was called "the Book of Enoch. In the hour that God took "him, he shewed him all the repositories above; "he shewed him the tree of life in the midst of the "garden, its leaves and its branches. ***We see all in*** "***his book***[a]." But there is another passage in the

[a] מעלמ׳ נטיל ליה קדשי ברוך הוא לשמושיה · ההד כי לקח אותו אלהים · ומן דא אתמסר ספרא דאקרי ספרא דחנוך · בשעתא דאחיד ליה קב׳ה · אחמי ליה כל גינזי עלאי · אחמי ליה אילנא דחיי בגו מציעו׳ גנתא וטרפוי וענפוי · וכלא חמינן בספריה. Vol. i. Parashah בראשית p. 37. b. ed. Mantuæ et Amsterdam.

Zohar of a similar description, which has been before quoted, for a different purpose, by Manasseh Ben-Israel in his Latin tract *De Resurrectione Mortuorum*. Amsterdam, A.D. 1636. p. 335. It is this; "We find in the Book of Enoch, that after the "holy and blessed One had caused him to ascend, "and shewed him all the repositories of the superior "and inferior kingdom, he shewed him the tree "of life, and the tree respecting which Adam had "received a command; and he shewed him the habitation of Adam in the garden of Eden [a]."

These allusions of the Zohar to the repositories of the celestial and terrestrial kingdoms, and to the tree of knowledge in the garden of Eden, shewn to Enoch after his ascent into heaven, are distinctly stated to have been taken from a book, entitled the Book of Enoch; and the very same allusions will be found minutely detailed between the sixteenth and thirty-seventh chapters of the present version. The reference to the tree of knowledge in the garden of Eden occurs in the thirty-first chapter. Now the authors of the Cabalistical remains wrote or conveyed down their recondite doctrines in Chaldee. Scarcely therefore, I apprehend, will it be questioned, that the copy of the Book of Enoch

[a] אשכחנא בספרא דחנוך דלבתר דסליק ליה קדשא ברוך הוא ואחמי ליה כל גנזייא דמלכא עלאי ותתאי · אחמי ליה אילנא דחיי ואילנא דאתפקד עליה אדם · ואחמי ליה דוכתיה דאדם בגנתא דעדן. Vol. ii. Parashah בשלח p. 55. a. Manasseh Ben-Israel quotes this passage incorrectly; and gives no reference whatsoever to the place in which it occurs.

which they cited was written either in that language or in Hebrew. For they appear to have regarded it as the genuine work of him whose name it bore, and not as the spurious production of a later age. Had they been solely acquainted with a Greek copy, which is very improbable, they could never have contemplated it as an original; but they certainly seemed to invest that to which they referred with this high and distinguished character. The conclusion is obvious.

Presuming therefore that the book before us was the composition of some unknown Jew, under the borrowed name of Enoch, I shall next consider what criteria are afforded us to determine the period at which it may have been written. That this period was one antecedent to the commencement of the Christian æra, admits of no question, when we recollect, that it was quoted by St. Jude; not indeed as the indisputable production of Enoch himself, (for, notwithstanding Cabalistical testimony, it was never, as I have observed, received into the Canon of Scripture,) but as one ascribed to him. Here we are furnished with a proof respecting the time, *after* which it could not have been possibly written; and if we examine its contents minutely, we shall immediately recognize a time, *before* which it was equally as impossible to have been written. This time is clearly the *captivity of Babylon*. For the very expressions, as well as descriptive ideas, of Daniel are adopted by it, in the representation of the Ancient of days coming to judgment with the Son of man[a]. It could not therefore have been written *before* the captivity. This however is not all the certainty which we are capable of obtaining. For there exists internal evidence sufficient to demonstrate that it was written long subsequent to the commencement, and even to the conclusion, of the Babylonian captivity.

From the eighty-third to the ninetieth chapter an allegorical narrative of the leading events recorded in sacred history is given, too obvious in the outline to be misapprehended. Now in this allegory the government of the Jewish nation is carried down so low as to the rule of seventy princes, under the character of seventy shepherds superintending the flock. Saul, David, and Solomon are first distinctly alluded to[b]. Then these seventy princes or shepherds are said to be appointed over the sheep[c]; thirty-seven of whom are classed together as superintending them in their respective periods[d]; afterwards twenty-three[e]; and last of all twelve[f]. But here a little mistake in the figures seems to have been committed; as the three numbers 37, 23, and 12, taken together, make seventy-*two*, not seventy. Instead therefore of 37, in the first instance, we should probably read 35; for when the *twenty-three* are enumerated, it is remarked, that

[a] Compare Daniel vii. 9, &c. with chap. xlvi. 1. xlvii. 3. lix. 1. lxix. 12, and 16. [b] Chap. lxxxviii. 67—82. [c] Ib. ver. 92. [d] Chap. lxxxix. 1. [e] Ib. ver. 7. [f] Ib. ver. 25.

they "completed in their respective periods *fifty-"eight* periods;" 35 and 23 making 58. Computing then *thirty-five* as the first class of rulers after Solomon, we shall find that to be the precise number of the kings of Judah and Israel combined together, until the captivity; if we omit those who only held their power for a few months, or even a less period, in unsettled times.

The thirty-five kings of Judah and Israel are these. Of Judah, 1. Rehoboam, 2. Abijam, 3. Asa, 4. Jehoshaphat, 5. Jehoram, 6. Ahaziah, 7. Athaliah, 8. Jehoaash, 9. Amaziah, 10. Azariah, or, as he is called in Chronicles, Uzziah, 11. Jotham, 12. Ahaz, 13. Hezekiah, 14. Manasseh, 15. Amon, 16. Josiah, 17. Jehoiakim, 18. Jehoiakin, 19. Zedekiah. Of Israel, 1. Jeroboam, 2. Nadab, 3. Baasha, 4. Elah, 5. Omri, 6. Ahab, 7. Ahaziah, 8. Joram, 9. Jehu, 10. Jehoahaz, 11. Jehoash, 12. Jeroboam II. 13. Menahem, 14. Pekaiah, 15. Pekah, 16. Hosea. In this list Jehoahaz, the son of Josiah, is omitted among the kings of Judah, who was deposed after having reigned only three months; his elder brother Jehoiakim being raised to the throne instead of him by Pharaoh-Nechoh [a]. So also among the kings of Israel are omitted the names of Zimri, who reigned but seven days; of Tibni, the competitor of Omri, who seemed to have never been in the actual possession of power at all; of Zechariah, who, after Jeroboam II. reigned but six months; and of his successor Shallum, who reigned only one.

[a] 2 Kings xxiii. 30—35.

The next class of rulers alluded to were the foreign monarchs, who governed the children of Israel after the captivity, when they ceased to have princes of their own. The next twenty-three shepherds therefore appointed over the flock must mean, I apprehend, the Babylonian, Persian, and Macedonian kings, to whose dominion they were successively subject, until the recovery of their independence by the Asmonæan family. When they were carried into captivity, and for many years after, Nebuchadnezzar was king of Babylon; who was succeeded by Evilmerodoch, Neriglissar, and Belshazzar. Babylon being then taken by Cyrus the Persian, the following was the order of the new sovereigns; Darius the Mede, Cyrus, Cambyses, Darius Hystaspis, Xerxes, Artaxerxes Longimanus, Darius Nothus, Artaxerxes Mnemon, Ochus, Arogus, and Darius. Here ended the Persian dominion. Then followed the Macedonian, in this order: Alexander, Ptolemy Soter, who after the death of Alexander first seized the government of Judæa, Ptolemy Philadelphus, Ptolemy Euergetes, Ptolemy Philopator, Antiochus the Great, (the Macedonian king of Syria, who wrested the government of Judæa from the Ptolemies[a],) Seleucus Philopator, and Antiochus Epi-

[a] Historians have doubted, whether Antiochus, who seized the province of Judæa when Ptolemy Epiphanes was an infant, ever, in fact, actually resigned it to him afterwards. It does not appear that he did. See Prideaux's Connection, vol. ii. p. 150. But this question affects not the point before us; for the number will be the same, if we substitute Ptolemy Epiphanes for Antiochus,

phanes. If then to the four Babylonian monarchs, the eleven Persian be added, and to these the eight Macedonian, the whole number will amount to twenty-three, precisely the number of the second class referred to.

The third and last class consists of twelve only, which again comprehends princes of their own nation. The first of these was Mattathias, the father of Judas Maccabæus, who rescued his country from the slavery and impiety imposed upon it by Antiochus Epiphanes. Josephus says of him, Παρελθὼν δὲ ἀπὸ τῆς εὐπραγίας εἰς δυναστείαν, καὶ διὰ τὴν ἀπαλλαγὴν τῶν ἀλλοφύλων ἄρξας τῶν σφετέρων ἑκόντων, τελευτᾷ Ἰούδα τῷ πρεσβυτάτῳ τῶν παίδων καταλιπὼν τὴν ἀρχήν. De Bello Judaico, lib. i. cap. 1. *Coming into power by success, and in consequence of the expulsion of foreigners ruling over his own people with their free consent, he died, leaving the government to Judas, the eldest of his surviving sons.* After him came in succession Judas Maccabæus, Jonathan, Simon, John Hyrcanus, Aristobulus, Alexander Jannæus, Alexandra his widow, Aristobulus, Hyrcanus, Antigonus, and Herod.

The reign of Herod was of considerable duration, extending to four and thirty years; at some period of whose reign, probably at an early one, the Book of Enoch seems to have been written. Had the author of it lived to see the end of Herod's successors, he could not have limited the number of

and commence the Syrian rule with Seleucus Philopator, who indisputably governed it.

native princes, after the expulsion of the Macedonians, to twelve; not even if we suppose him to have commenced his computation from Judas Maccabæus, instead of Mattathias. For after the death of Herod the Great, the dominions, over which that monarch ruled, were divided into three parts; Archelaus [a] reigning over Judæa proper, Idumæa, and Samaria; Philip over Auronitis, Trachonitis, Paneas, and Batanæa; and Herod Antipas over Galilee and Peræa. Subsequently also the dominions of Herod the Great were again united, and conferred upon Agrippa; so that, if we even begin to compute from Judas Maccabæus, the number of native princes amounts to fifteen, instead of twelve. But indeed the author of this book could not have thus begun his computation; for, if so, he must have made the number, not twelve, but fourteen; the three sons of Herod, Archelaus, Philip, and Antipas, commencing the government of their respective districts at one and the same time, which circumstance would have instantly carried the amount from eleven to fourteen.

The preceding arguments tend to prove, satisfactorily I confess to my own mind, that this book was written but a few years at most before the beginning of the Christian æra. That it could not

[a] "But when he heard that Archelaus did reign in Judæa in "the room of his father Herod, he was afraid to go thither: not-"withstanding being warned of God in a dream, he turned aside "into the parts of Galilee." Matth. ii. 22; where Herod Antipas ruled. See Luke iii.

have been written *very long* before it, is demonstrated by another allusion which it contains. In chapter liv. 9, "the chiefs of the east among the "Parthians and Medes" are mentioned, who are introduced as hurling kings from their thrones, "springing as lions from their dens, and like fa-"mished wolves into the midst of the flock." Now the Parthians were altogether unknown in history, until the 250th year before Christ, when under the guidance of Arsaces (the family name of all their subsequent kings) they revolted from Antiochus Theus, the then king of Syria. It was not however until the year 230. B.C. that their empire became firmly established, when Arsaces defeated and took prisoner Seleucus Callinicus, the Syrian monarch, and first assumed the title of king of Parthia. By degrees they expelled the Syrian dominion from every province over which it extended east of the Euphrates; so that from about the year 140. B.C. their vast empire reached from the Ganges to the Euphrates, and from the Euphrates to mount Caucasus[a]. But another century elapsed before they came into direct conflict with the power of Rome.

[a] This great extent of dominion took place under Mithridates the Great. "Dum hæc apud Bactros geruntur, interim inter Par-"thos et Medos bellum oritur. Cum varius utriusque populi ca-"sus fuisset, ad postremum victoria penes Parthos fuit. His vi-"ribus auctus Mithridates Mediæ Bacasin præponit, ipse in Hyr-"caniam proficiscitur. Unde reversus bellum cum Elymæorum "rege gessit; quo victo, hanc quoque gentem regno adjecit; "imperiumque Parthorum a monte Caucaso, multis populis in "ditionem redactis, usque ad flumen Euphratem protulit." Justin. lib. xli. cap. 6.

At length however, during the triumvirate of Cæsar, Pompey, and Crassus, the province of Syria was assigned to Crassus; whose insatiable avarice, as well as ambition, prompted him to attempt the overthrow of the Parthian empire. In the year 54. B.C. he crossed the Euphrates, and was at first successful; but in the following year, after having lost his son in battle, he was slain himself, and his whole army destroyed. The Parthians then in their turn invaded Syria; and in the year 41. B.C. made themselves masters of the whole country, the maritime city of Tyre alone excepted[a]. From thence, in the subsequent year, they entered Jerusalem, and raised Antigonus, the last of the Asmonæan race, to the throne, in opposition to Herod, whom they drove out of the country. Nor did the tide of their military renown turn here; for, although they were compelled again to cross the Euphrates in consequence of the death of their accomplished and illustrious general Pacorus[b], still, when in the year 36. B.C. Anthony, if not with the avarice, at least with the ambition of Crassus, renewed the arduous

[a] Ὁ μὲν Πάκορος τὴν Συρίαν ἐχειροῦτο, καὶ πᾶσαν γε αὐτὴν, πλὴν Τύρου, κατεστρέψατο. Dio Cassius, lib. xlviii. §. 26. p. 545. edit. Reimar.

[b] Pacorus was the son of Orodes, the reigning monarch of Parthia. Justin thus feelingly describes the grief of Orodes at the loss of his beloved son: "Multis diebus non alloqui quemquam, "non cibum sumere, non vocem mittere, ita ut etiam mutus fac-"tus videretur. Post multos deinde dies, ubi dolor vocem laxave-"rat, nihil aliud quam Pacorum vocabat; Pacorus illi videri, Pa-"corus audiri videbatur, cum illo loqui, cum illo consistere; in-"terdum quasi amissum flebiliter dolebat." Lib. xlii. cap. 4.

task of subjugating them, they drove him out of the country, which he had invaded, with immense loss, and with complete disgrace. At this time perhaps the credit of the Parthian arms was at the highest[a]; and it is probable that about the same period, or at least not long after, the Book of Enoch was written.

I should likewise add, that the very use of the term ***Parthians*** seems to imply, that the apocryphal Enoch did not live until after the characteristical name of that people became more correctly known, by their frequent incursions into the western parts of Asia. For the author of the first book of Maccabees, who brings down his history to the reign of John Hyrcanus in the year 135. B. C., distinguishes them by the more general name of ***Persians*** in the following passage: "Now in the hun-"dred threescore and twelfth year [of the con-"tracts, *viz.* 140. B. C.] king Demetrius [Nicator] "gathered his forces together, and went into Me-"dia, to get him help to fight against Tryphon.

[a] Dio Cassius, recording the extent of their dominion, observes, that at length they became able to contend with the Romans, and continued to struggle with them as equals in the great contest for empire: *τελευτῶντες δὲ, ἐπὶ τοσοῦτο καὶ τῆς δόξης καὶ τῆς δυνάμεως ἐχώρησαν, ὥστε καὶ τοῖς Ῥωμαίοις τότε ἀντιπολεμῆσαι, καὶ δεῦρο ἀεὶ ἀντίπαλοι νομίζεσθαι.* Lib. xl. §. 14. p. 233. Justin represents them as dividing with the Romans the empire of the whole world. "Parthi," he says, "penes quos, velut divisione "Orbis cum Romanis facta, nunc Orientis imperium est, &c." And subsequently remarks; "A Romanis quoque trinis [binis?] "bellis per maximos duces, florentissimis temporibus lacessiti, "soli ex omnibus gentibus *non pares solum*, verum etiam *victores* "*fuere.*" Lib. xli. cap. 1.

"But when Arsaces, the king of *Persia* and Media, "heard that Demetrius was entered within his borders, he sent one of his princes to take him alive: "who went and smote the host of Demetrius, and "took him, and brought him to Arsaces [a], by "whom he was put in ward." Chap. xiv. 1, 2, 3. Parthia having been originally nothing more than an obscure province of Persia, the people inhabiting that, as well as the other provinces, would at first without distinction be naturally denominated *Persians* by distant and unconnected nations.

Another circumstance likewise seems to prove, that the book was not written at an early period of the Parthian empire; or rather, that it was not written until about the reign of Herod. It is said; "The threshing floor, the path, and the city of my "righteous *people* shall impede *the progress* of "their horses [b]." Now the invasion of Judæa by the Parthians, to which an allusion appears to be here made, did not take place until the year 40. B. C., when they deposed Hyrcanus, and settled Antigonus on the throne, who in the year 37. B. C. was in his turn deposed by the Romans in favour of Herod. Is it not therefore probable, that the Parthian invasion of Judæa at the period mentioned, the only one indeed upon record, must have been in the contemplation of the author when he wrote the preceding passage?

[a] The Arsaces here alluded to was Mithridates, Arsaces being the common name of all the Parthian kings. This occurrence is recorded by Justin, lib. xxxviii. cap. 9. [b] Chap. liv. 10.

If these circumstances alone be not deemed conclusive, they at least strongly corroborate the argument grounded upon the vision of the seventy shepherds or princes.

I should however remark, that Grabe, in his *Spicilegium SS. Patrum*, conjectures, that the Book of Enoch was quoted by Eupolemus; and Fabricius assumes, that it was quoted by Alexander Polyhistor. Now if these critics are correct in their statements, the conclusion will be, that it must have been written at an earlier period than I have supposed; as Alexander Polyhistor lived about ninety years before Christ, and Eupolemus at a still more remote æra. But they appear to have been both mistaken. Grabe produces the following citation in proof of his conjecture; "Validissime autem hoc "confirmatur exinde, quod Alexander Polyhistor, "apud Eusebium, *De Præpar. Evangel.* lib. ix. "cap. 17. pag. 419. testetur, *Eupolemum* de Enocho "scripsisse, Τούτον εὑρηκέναι πρῶτον τὴν ἀστρολογίαν, οὐκ "Αἰγυπτίους—Ἕλληνας δὲ λέγειν τὸν Ἄτλαντα εὑρηκέναι "ἀστρολογίαν· εἶναι δὲ τὸν Ἄτλαντα τὸν αὐτὸν καὶ Ἐνώχ; "*Eum primum invenisse astrologiam, non Ægyp-* "*tios—Et Græcos quidem Atlantem astrologiæ in-* "*ventorem facere, sed Atlantem illum ipsum Eno-* "*chum fuisse* [a]." He then adds a quotation made from the Book of Enoch by G. Syncellus, in which the archangel Uriel is said to have taught Enoch the laws and motions of the heavenly luminaries; and thence concludes, that *Eupolemus* must have derived

[a] P. 345.

his opinion respecting the astronomical knowledge of Enoch from the *same* source. But surely a mere Jewish tradition, that Enoch was the father of astronomy, in which he had been instructed by the angels, must have been alone sufficient for the assertion of Eupolemus, without the necessity of supposing that he derived it from the book in question; or different parts of the book itself may have been composed at different periods.

Fabricius simply states, that Syncellus makes the following quotation from *Alexander Polyhistor;* παραλαβόντας ἀπὸ τοῦ τετάρτου τῶν Ἐγρηγόρων ἄρχοντος Χωραβίηλ, τὸ τοῦ ἡλίου ἀνακυκλευματικὸν μέτρον εἶναι ἐν ζωδίοις δώδεκα, μοίραις τριακοσίαις ἑξήκοντα: *a quarto Egregororum principe Chorabiele edoctos, mensuram periodi solis absolvi per duodecim signa; gradibus trecentis et sexaginta*[a]. But had the learned critic fully consulted the context, he would have found, that the words quoted are those of Georgius Syncellus himself, and not of Alexander Polyhistor. In the preceding page Syncellus had made a long quotation from Alexander Polyhistor, giving an account of the reign of ten kings before the deluge; an account which he deems fabulous, and is endeavouring to refute, as absurd, in the very passage from which Fabricius makes the foregoing extract. He says, Διὸ καὶ περὶ τῶν ἀπείρων ἐτῶν, καὶ τῶν δέκα βασιλέων τῶν πρὸ τοῦ κατακλυσμοῦ, καὶ ὅσα ἄλλα ἄτοπα ἐν αὐτῇ λέλεκται, ἀπαγορεύων μηδὲν εἶναι ἀληθὲς, οὐδὲ τὴν τῶν ἐτῶν εἰς ἀνάλυσιν ἡμέρων (f. τὴν τῶν ἐτῶν εἰς ἡμέρας ἀνάλυσιν) ἢ με-

[a] Codex Pseudepigraphus V. Test. vol. i. p. 198.

ρισμὸν ἀποδέχομαι· οὐδὲ τοὺς ταῦτα ἀλληγορήσαντας, καὶ εἰπόντας τὸν ἐνιαυτὸν ἡμέραν λογίζεσθαι τῶν πρὸ τοῦ κατακλυσμοῦ[a]; *Wherefore renouncing whatsoever absurd and untrue things are read in it respecting an immense period of years, and the ten kings before the deluge, I reject what relates to the solution or partition of years into days, and the theory of those who thus allegorize, and say, that a year before the deluge is to be computed as a day.* Then immediately follows the quotation made by Fabricius; παραλαβόντας, &c. *who have learnt from the fourth chief of the Egregori Chorabiel, that the circular period of the sun is measured by the twelve signs of the zodiac, divided into three hundred and sixty degrees.* This is clearly the language, and expresses the sentiments, not of Alexander Polyhistor, but of Georgius Syncellus; who had previously cited, and is now refuting, the statements of that author.

Upon the whole then we may be assured, that the book was written before the rise of Christianity; most probably at an early period of the reign of Herod. That it could not have been the production of a writer who lived after the inspired authors of the New Testament, or who was even coeval with them, must be manifest from the quotation of St. Jude; a quotation which proves it to have been in his time a work ascribed at least to Enoch himself.

It may perhaps be remarked as a singularity, that a book, composed at less than one hundred, perhaps

[a] G. Syncelli Chronographia, p. 32.

at less than fifty, years before St. Jude's Epistle was written [a], should in so short a space of time have so far imposed upon the public, as to be reputed by any the genuine production of the patriarch Enoch. It by no means however follows, that because the book bore the name of Enoch, it was therefore generally attributed to him, as to its real author. The Book of *Wisdom* bears the name, and the writer of it assumes the character, of Solomon; but who concludes from hence, that it was the actual composition of the inspired monarch himself? If nevertheless at the period under consideration there were indeed any who deemed the Book of Enoch genuine, it was not perhaps so remarkable a circumstance, as it may at first sight appear. For although this book was evidently written by a Jew, its author could not have resided in Palestine; so that it must have been brought from another, and, as I think it may be shewn, from a distant country. Hence its origin might have been, and probably was, involved in obscurity.

In proof that the author could not have resided in Palestine, it is only necessary to take into consideration what is stated in the seventy-first chapter relative to the length of the days at various periods of the year. The internal evidence contained in

[a] This Epistle is generally supposed to have been written about the year seventy. If then we place the composition of the Book of Enoch in the eighth year of Herod, that is, thirty years before Christ, its date will precede that of the Epistle an exact century.

this chapter seems decisive upon the point. For having divided the day and night into *eighteen* parts, the apocryphal Enoch distinctly represents the longest day in the year as consisting of *twelve* out of these eighteen parts [a]. Now the proportion of *twelve* to *eighteen* is precisely the same as *sixteen* to *four* and *twenty*; the present division into hours of the period constituting day and night. If therefore we consider in what latitude a country must be situated to have a day of *sixteen* hours long, we shall immediately perceive that Palestine could not be such a country. It is indeed possible that in order to express an uniformity in the increase of the day after the vernal equinox, so as to lengthen it every month *one* portion regularly, the author might not have been particularly nice with respect to the minor divisions; but he would scarcely have *much* deviated in his result from accurate observation. We may then safely conclude, that the country in which he lived must have been situated not lower than forty-five degrees north latitude, where the longest day is fifteen hours and a half, nor higher perhaps than forty-nine degrees, where the longest day is precisely sixteen hours. This will bring the country, where he wrote, as high up at least as the northern districts of the Caspian and Euxine seas; probably it was situated somewhere between the upper parts of both these seas.

a "At that period the day is lengthened from the night, being "twice *as long as* the night, and becomes twelve parts; but the "night is shortened, and becomes six parts." Ver. 18, 19.

If the latter conjecture be well founded, the author of the Book of Enoch was perhaps one of the tribes which Shalmaneser carried away, and "placed "in Halah and in Habor by the river Goshan, and "in the cities *of the Medes*[a];" and who never returned from captivity. Grotius remarks[b], that some Commentators conceive the *Halah* here mentioned to be *Colchis*, and *Habor* to be *Iberia*, both countries situated in the district to which I have alluded; an opinion which seems corroborated by a passage in Herodotus, who represents the Colchians in his day as using the rite of circumcision. It should likewise be added, that as Media is situated on the southern and south-western coasts of the Caspian sea, a migration of the captive Israelites, who were precluded from returning to their own country, still further northwards, for greater security and independence, seems not improbable. But it is of no importance to fix with accuracy the country in which this book was written; it is sufficient to be assured that its author indisputably resided in a climate remote from Judæa; and this the account given in it respecting the length of day and night, at the dif-

[a] 2 Kings xvii. 6. and 1 Chron. v. 26.

[b] "Alii vero per חלח, *Colchos*, per חבור, *Iberos* Asiæ tum hic, "tum 1. Paral. v. in fine interpretantur; et, qui eo deducti sunt, "putant eos esse, quos *Colchos e Syris ortos et circumcisos fuisse* "narrat Herodotus; *Ponticos* illos scilicet etiam in Act. et Petri "Epistola memoratos." The passage in Herodotus here alluded to is the following; *ἀλλὰ τοῖσι δὴ μᾶλλον, ὅτι μοῦνοι πάντων ἀνθρώπων Κόλχοι, καὶ Αἰγύπτιοι, καὶ Αἰθίοπες περιτάμνονται ἀπ' ἀρχῆς τὰ αἰδοῖα. Φοίνικες δὲ καὶ Σύριοι οἱ ἐν τῇ Παλαιστίνῃ καὶ αὐτοὶ ὁμολογέουσι παρ' Αἰγυπτίων μεμαθηκέναι.* Lib. ii. cap. civ. p. 127. ed. Gale.

ferent seasons of the year, alone fully proves. Composed therefore in the assumed name and character of Enoch, and having been brought into Judæa from a distant country, it could not have been well known, or quoted under any other title than that of the Book of Enoch; and although the generality must from its incongruities have deemed its contents apocryphal, yet might there have been some, who, deceived by its external evidence and pretensions, ignorantly esteemed it to be the genuine production of the patriarch himself.

The fate of apocryphal writings in general has been singular. On one side, from the influence of theological opinion or theological caprice, they have been sometimes injudiciously admitted into the Canon of Scripture; while on the other side, from an over anxiety to preserve that Canon inviolate, they have been not simply rejected, but loaded with every epithet of contempt and obloquy. The feelings perhaps of both parties have on such occasions run away with their judgment. For writings of this description, whatsoever may or may not be their claim to inspiration, at least are of considerable utility, where they indicate the theological opinions of the periods at which they were composed. This I apprehend to be peculiarly the case of the Book of Enoch; which, as having been manifestly written before the doctrines of Christianity were promulgated to the world, must afford us, when it refers to the nature and character of the Messiah, as it repeatedly does so refer, credible proof of what were the Jewish opinions upon those points before the birth of Christ; and consequently before the possible predominance of the Christian creed.

In this book clear and distinct allusions are made to a Being, highly exalted with the Lord of spirits, under the appellations of the Son of man [a], the Elect one [b], the Messiah [c], and the Son of God [d]. Disputes have arisen respecting the nature of the Son of man described in the vision of Daniel; and Unitarians contend, that his existence commenced at the birth of Jesus Christ; affirming, without fear of contradiction, that no Jew of any age ever held the opinion of his preexistence; much less ever regarded him as an object of divine worship. But that the Jewish doctrine before Christ upon this point was totally different from that which the Unitarians assert it to have been, I have shewn in my remarks on the first book of Ezra [e]. The present publication however affords fuller and more decisive testimony upon the same subject.

The apocryphal Enoch evidently copies after Daniel; so much so indeed, that his more minute delineation of the Prophet's vision may be regarded as explanatory of its meaning, according to the received doctrine of the Jews in his own day. In this point of view, at least, his sentiments are of considerable importance; because necessarily uninflu-

[a] Chap. xlvi. 1, 2. xlviii. 2, &c. [b] Chap. xlviii. * 2, &c. [c] Chap. xlviii. 11. li. 4. [d] Chap. civ.* 2. [e] P. 320, 321. 8vo. Oxford, 1820.

enced by Christian prepossessions. Alluding to the Son of man, he says; "*Before* the sun and the "signs were created, *before* the stars of heaven "were formed, his name was invoked in the pre-"sence of the Lord of spirits. ..... All, who dwell "on earth, shall fall down *and worship before him;* "shall bless and glorify him, and sing praises to him "in the name of the Lord of spirits. Therefore the "Elect and the Concealed one *existed* in his pre-"sence *before the world was created, and for ever*[a]." Again, when speaking of the terror which shall afflict the great rulers of the earth in the day of judgment, he expresses himself in the following manner; "They shall be astonished, and shall hum-"ble their countenance; and trouble shall seize "them, when they shall behold the Son of woman "sitting upon the throne of his glory. Then shall "the kings, the princes, and all who possess the "earth, glorify him who has dominion over all "things, him who was concealed; for *from the be-"ginning* the Son of man existed *in secret*, whom "the Most High preserved in the presence of his "power, and revealed to the elect. ...... All the "kings, the princes, the exalted, and those who rule "over the earth, shall fall down on their faces be-"fore him, and *shall worship him*. They shall fix "their hopes on this Son of man, *and shall pray to "him, and petition him for mercy*[b]."

In both these passages the preexistence of the Messiah is asserted in language which admits not the

[a] Chap. xlviii. 3, 4, 5. [b] Chap. lxi. 8, 9, 10, 12, 13.

slightest shade of ambiguity. Nor is it such a preexistence as the philosophical Cabbalists attributed to him, who believed the souls of all men, and consequently that of the Messiah, to have been originally created together, when the world itself was formed; but an existence antecedent to all creation; an existence previous to the formation of the luminaries of heaven; an existence prior to all things visible and invisible, "before every thing *concealed.*" It should likewise be remarked, that the preexistence ascribed to him is a *divine* preexistence; for before all things "his name was invoked in the presence of the Lord "of spirits—the Elect and the Concealed one existed "in his presence—who has dominion over all things, "for from the beginning the Son of man existed "in secret, whom the Most High preserved in the "presence of his power." Hence therefore is it explicitly affirmed, that all the kings of the earth "shall fall down and *worship* before him, shall bless "and glorify him," as a true object of adoration.

Neither is allusion thus only made to the Elect one or the Messiah; but also to another divine Person or Power; both of whom, under the joint denomination of *the Lords*, are stated to have been over the water, that is, as I conceive, over the fluid mass of unformed matter, at the period of creation. "He, "[the Elect one,]" it is stated, "shall call to every "power of the heavens, to all the holy above, "and to the power of God. The Cherubim, the "Seraphim, and the Ophanim, all the angels of "power, and all the angels of the Lords, namely, of "the Elect one, and of the other power, who *was* "upon earth over the water on that day, shall raise "their united voice, &c.[a]" In this passage an obvious reference, I conceive, occurs to the first verse of Genesis, in which it is said, that "the Spirit of "God moved on the face of the waters." As therefore the more full description of the Son of man, here given, may be considered as the Jewish comment of the day upon the vision of Daniel; so also, I apprehend, must the last quoted allusion to the Book of Genesis be considered as a comment of the same nature upon that account of Moses, which describes the commencement of creation. Here then we have not merely the declaration of a *Plurality*, but that of a precise and distinct *Trinity*, of persons, under the supreme appellation of *God and Lords:* the *Lords* are denominated the *Elect one* and *the other* [divine] *Power*, who is represented as engaged in the formation of the world, on that day, that is, on the day of creation. And it should be added, that upon these a particular class of angels is mentioned as appropriately attendant.

This argument, in proof that the Jews before the birth of Christ believed the doctrine of a Trinity, appears to me much more important and conclusive than that which has been indeed frequently, but to my mind, I confess, not satisfactorily, deduced from the philosophical principles of the ancient Cabbala. Cabbalistical theology, I well know, has its *aziluth* or *emanations of Deity;* but these, I am convinced,

[a] Chap. lx. 13, 14.

notwithstanding the persuasions of many Christians upon the subject, were at no period ever contemplated by the Jews themselves as *distinct persons*, but merely as *distinct energies*, in the Godhead. Indeed if the argument has any force at all, it is calculated to prove more than its advocates wish; for it goes to demonstrate, that the Jews believed in *ten*, not in *three*, personal emanations of Deity; for such is the number of the Sephiroth [a]. Imagina-

[a] Those who discover the doctrine of the Christian Trinity in the Sephiroth of the Cabbala, confine the traces of it to the *first three* of them, not considering that all are alike regarded by the Cabbalists as divine emanations; and compose the manifold conception of God, exhibited to us in his works. Before the great Cause of all causes, the most secret of secret beings, created the world; before He created objects cognizable by the intellect, or produced form, He was himself, they say, alone without figure or similitude. But when creation commenced, his existence being only demonstrable by his energies, from the immensity of his own essence sprung forth the first of the divine *Sephiroth* or *Enumerations*, communicating in various degrees an unceasing efflux of Deity to *nine* others, all of which, combined, display to us a tenfold idea of the Godhead. The same union however is supposed to subsist between the *whole ten*, as between the *first three*, or last seven of them; all being considered, as separable indeed in the modifications of action, but as inseparable in nature.

Besides, if the *first three* be detached from the remainder, as purely intellectual emanations, still the great fountain of Deity himself will be forgotten; He, "in whose power it is," as the Zohar remarks, "to increase in them or to diminish his influx, "according to his own good pleasure;" ברשותיה לאוספא בהון ולמחסר נביעו כפום רעותיה. Edit. Mant. vol. II. p. 43. For although the name of the primary source of all divine emanation, the *Or En-Soph*, or *the infinite Light*, as the Cabbalists term him, be sometimes attributed to the *Kether* or *Crown*, the first of the Sephiroth, yet is the *Or En-Soph* himself clearly distinguished from that as from every other Sephirah. The argument therefore

tion is always ready to discover resemblances, where none in reality exist; but sober reasoning can never surely approve the indiscreet attempt of representing Christian truth as arrayed in the meretricious garb of the Jewish Cabbala. That singular, and to those perhaps who penetrate its exterior surface, fascinating system of allegorical subtleties, has no doubt its brighter as well as its darker parts, its true as well as its false allusions; but instead of reducing its wild combinations of opinion to the standard of Scripture, we shall, I am persuaded, be less likely to err, if we refer them to the ancient and predominant philosophy of the east; from which they seem to have originally sprung, and from which they are as inseparable, as the shadow is from its substance.

The passage however under consideration is liable to no objection of this kind. Here there is nothing Cabbalistical; here there is no allegory; but a plain and clear, although slight, allusion to a doctrine, which, had it not formed a part of the popular creed at the time, would scarcely have been intelligible. Three Lords are enumerated; the Lord of spirits, the Lord the Elect one, and the Lord the other Power; an enumeration which evidently implies the acknowledgment of three distinct Persons participating in the name and in the power of the Godhead. Such therefore, from the evidence before us, appears to have been the doctrine of the

of those who reason upon such principles, rests, I apprehend, on no solid foundation; and seems rather calculated to prove a quaternity, than a trinity, of persons in the Godhead: even when *three* only of the Sephiroth are brought into the computation.

Jews respecting the divine nature, antecedently to the rise and promulgation of Christianity.

Upon the whole then, if this singular book be censured, as abounding in some parts with fable and fiction, still should we recollect, that fable and fiction may occasionally prove both amusing and instructive; and can then only be deemed injurious, when pressed into the service of vice and infidelity. Nor should we forget, that much, perhaps most, of what we censure, was grounded upon a national tradition, the antiquity of which alone, independent of other considerations, had rendered it respectable. That the author was uninspired, will be scarcely now questioned; but, although his production was apocryphal, it ought not therefore to be stigmatized as necessarily replete with error; although it be on that account incapable of becoming a rule of faith, it may nevertheless contain much moral as well as religious truth; and may be justly regarded as a correct standard of the doctrine of the times in which it was composed. *Non omnia esse concedenda antiquitati,* is, it is true, a maxim founded upon reason and experience; but, in perusing the present relic of a remote age and country, should the reader discover much to condemn, still, unless he be too fastidious, he will find more to approve; if he sometimes frown, he may oftener smile; nor seldom will he be disposed to admire the vivid imagination of a writer, who transports him far beyond the flaming boundaries of the world,

——— extra
Processit longe flammantia mœnia mundi;

displaying to him every secret of Creation; the splendors of heaven, and the terrors of hell; the mansions of departed souls; and the myriads of the celestial hosts, the Seraphim, Cherubim, and Ophanim, which surround the blazing throne, and magnify the holy name, of the great Lord of spirits, the Almighty Father of men and of angels.

As the arrangement of the chapters and verses in the two MSS. appears to be different, and to have been arbitrarily made, I have uniformly followed that of the Bodleian MS., but have noted the sections, as they appear in the Paris MS., transcribed by Woide, which is more exact than the other in this respect. The Bodleian MS. only marks them in two or three instances.

I have remarked, p. xxxiv, that different parts of the book itself may have been composed at different periods; perhaps it might be also added, that they may have been different tracts, as well as tracts composed by different authors. Thus the first six chapters seem to be Enoch's annunciation of blessings to the righteous, and denunciation of punishment to transgressors. Then commences, in chap. VII. sect. II. his narrative respecting the connexion of the angels with the daughters of men, his elevation to heaven, his vision of the Almighty, his message to the transgressing angels, his vision of heaven, hell, and paradise, and his survey of the world's extremities. These details occupy four sections and thirty chapters. At sect. VI. chap. XXXVII. begins his second vision, which contains, it is said, a hundred and three parables. But of these only three are given. Parable the first extends from chap. XXXVIII. to chap. XLV. (sect. VII.) Parable the second, from chap. XLV. to chap. LVI. (sect. IX.) Parable the third, from chap. LVI. to chap. LXIX. (sect. XII.) But here a singular circumstance occurs. Chapters LXIV. LXV. LXVI. and the first verse of chap. LXVII, are interposed, which contain a vision of the Deluge by Noah, not as foretold by Enoch, but as related in the first person by Noah himself.

The subsequent chapters, LXIX. LXX. (sect. XII.) shortly record another vision of the Almighty. From chap. LXXI. (sect. XIII.) to chap. LXXXII. (sect. XVI.) is contained "the book of the revolutions of the luminaries," explained to Enoch by the angel Uriel. This is clearly a distinct tract, comprising a detail of astronomical observations, which he recounts to his son Mathusala.

The remainder of the book describes dreams and visions which Enoch saw, and which he related to his son Mathusala; and concludes with instructions to his children and exhortations to righteousness.

THE BOOK OF ENOCH.

CHAP. I.

1. THE word of the blessing of Enoch, how he blessed the elect and the righteous, who were to exist in the time of trouble; rejecting[a] all the wicked and ungodly. Enoch, a righteous man, who *was* with God, answered and spoke, while his eyes were open, and *while* he saw a holy vision in the heavens[b]. This the angels shewed me.

2. From them I heard all things, and understood what I saw; that which will not take place in this generation, but in a generation which is to succeed at a distant period, on account of the elect.

3. Upon their account I spoke and conversed with him, who will go forth from his habitation, the Holy and Mighty One, the God of the world:

4. Who will hereafter tread upon Mount Sinai; appear with his hosts; and be manifested in the strength of his power from heaven.

5. All shall be afraid, and the Watchers be terrified.

[a] *to the rejection of.* N. B. The Italic words in the text supply an ellipsis. In the notes they are used to mark the literal sense.

[b] *which* was *in the heavens.*

6. Great fear and trembling shall seize them, even to the ends of the earth. The lofty mountains shall be troubled, and the exalted hills depressed, melting like a honeycomb in the flame. The earth shall be immerged, and all things which are in it perish; while judgment shall come upon all, even upon all the righteous:

7. But to them shall he give peace: he shall preserve the elect, and towards them exercise clemency.

8. Then shall all belong to God; be happy and blessed; and the splendor of the Godhead shall illuminate them.

CHAP. II.

Behold, he comes with ten thousands of his saints, to execute judgment upon them, and destroy the wicked, and reprove all the carnal[a] for every thing which the sinful and ungodly have done, and committed against him[b].

CHAP. III.

1. All who are in the heavens know what is transacted[c] *there.*

2. *They know* that the heavenly luminaries change not their paths; that each rises and sets regularly, every one at its proper period, without transgressing the commands *which they have re-*

[a] *of flesh.* [b] Quoted by St. Jude ver. 14, 15. [c] *the work.*

ceived. They behold the earth, and understand what is there transacted, from the beginning to the end of it.

3. *They see* that every work of God is invariable in the period of its appearance. They behold summer and winter; *perceiving* that the whole earth is full of water; and that the cloud, the dew, and the rain refresh it.

CHAP. IV.

They consider and behold every tree, how it appears to wither, and every leaf to fall off, except of fourteen trees, which are not deciduous; which wait from the old, to the appearance of the new *leaf*, for two or three winters.

CHAP. V.

Again they consider the days of summer, that the sun is upon it at its very beginning; while you seek for a covered and shady spot on account of the burning sun; while the earth is scorched up with fervid heat, and you become incapable of walking either upon the ground or upon the rocks in consequence of that heat.

CHAP. VI.

1. They consider how the trees, when they put forth their green leaves, become covered, and produce fruit; understanding every thing, and knowing that He who lives for ever does all these things for you:

2. *That* the works at the beginning of every existing year, that all his works, are subservient to him, and invariable; yet as God has appointed, so are all things brought to pass.

3. They see, too, how the seas and the rivers together complete their respective operations:

4. *But* you endure not patiently, nor fulfil the commandments of the Lord; but you transgress and calumniate *his* greatness; and malignant are the words in your polluted mouths against his Majesty.

5. Ye withered in heart, no peace shall be to you!

6. Therefore your days shall you curse, and the years of your lives shall perish; perpetual execration shall be multiplied, and you shall not obtain mercy.

7. In those days shall you resign your peace with the eternal maledictions of all the righteous, and sinners shall perpetually execrate you;

8. *Shall execrate* you with the ungodly.

9. The elect shall possess light, joy, and peace; and they shall inherit the earth.

10. But you, ye unholy, shall be accursed.

11. Then shall wisdom be given to the elect, all of whom shall live, and not again transgress by impiety or pride; but shall humble themselves, possessing prudence, and shall not repeat transgression.

12. They shall not be condemned the whole pe-

riod of their lives, nor die in torment and indignation; but the sum of their days[a] shall be completed, and they shall grow old in peace; while the years of their happiness shall be multiplied with joy, and with peace, for ever, the whole duration of their existence.

CHAP. VII. [SECT. II.[b]]

1. [c]It happened after the sons of men had multiplied in those days, that daughters were born to them, elegant and beautiful.

2. And when the angels, the sons of heaven, beheld them, they became enamoured of them, saying to each other; Come, let us select for ourselves wives from the progeny of men, and let us beget children.

3. Then their leader Samyaza said to them; I fear that you may perhaps be indisposed to the performance of this enterprise;

4. And that I alone shall suffer for so grievous a crime.

5. But they answered him and said; We all swear;

6. And bind ourselves by mutual execrations, that we will not change our intention, but execute our projected undertaking.

[a] *the days of their life.*

[b] ምዕ፡ ፪፡ that is ምዕራፍ፡ ፪፡ *Section* II. Paris MS. transcribed by Woide.

[c] The first two extracts made by Syncellus from the Greek commence here, and end with the 15th verse of Chap. X.

7. Then they swore all together, and all bound themselves by mutual execrations. Their whole number was two hundred, who descended upon Ardis, which is the top of mount Armon.

8. That mountain therefore was called[a] Armon, because they had sworn upon it, and bound themselves by mutual execrations.

9. These are the names of their chiefs: Samyaza, who was their leader, Urakabarameel, Akibeel, Tamiel, Ramuel, Danel, Azkeel, Sarakuyal, Asael, Armers, Batraal, Ananc, Zavebe, Samsaveel, Ertael, Turel, Yomyael, Arazyal. These were the prefects of the two hundred angels, and the remainder were all with them.

10. Then they took wives, each choosing for himself; whom they began to approach, and with whom they cohabited; teaching them sorcery, incantations, and the dividing of roots and trees.

11. [b]And the women[c] conceiving brought forth giants;

12. Whose stature was each three hundred cubits. These devoured all *which* the labour of men *produced;* until it became impossible to feed them;

13. When they turned themselves against men, in order to devour them;

[a] *they called.*

[b] This and the following verses of this chapter, viz. 11, 12, 13, 14, 15, seem to belong to the next chapter, and should perhaps be inserted between the 8th and 9th verses of that chapter. Such appears to be their situation in the Greek fragment, quoted by Syncellus.

[c] *They.*

14. And began to injure birds, beasts, reptiles, and fishes, to eat their flesh one after another, and to drink their blood.

15. Then the earth reproved the unrighteous.

CHAP. VIII.

1. Moreover Azazyel taught men to make swords, knives, shields, breastplates, the fabrication of mirrors[a], and the workmanship of bracelets and ornaments, the use of paint, the beautifying of the eyebrows, *the use of* stones of every valuable and select kind, and of all sorts of dyes, so that the world became altered.

2. Impiety increased; fornication multiplied; and they transgressed and corrupted all their ways.

3. Amazarak taught all the sorcerers, and dividers of roots;

4. Armers *taught* the solution of sorcery;

5. Barkayal *taught* the observers of the stars;

6. Akibeel *taught* signs;

7. Tamiel taught astronomy;

8. And Asaradel taught the motion of the moon.

9. And men, being destroyed, cried out; and their voice reached to heaven.

CHAP. IX.

1. Then Michael and Gabriel, Raphael, Suryal, and Uriel, looked down from heaven, and saw the quantity of blood which was shed on earth, and all

[a] *made them see that which was behind them.*

the iniquity which was done upon it, and said one to another; *It is* the voice of their cries;

2. The earth deprived *of her children* has cried even to the gate of heaven.

3. And now to you, O ye holy ones of heaven, the souls of men complain, saying; Obtain justice for us with[a] the Most High. Then they said to their Lord, the King; *Thou art* Lord of lords, God of gods, King of kings. The throne of thy glory is for ever and ever, and for ever and ever is thy name sanctified and glorified. Thou art blessed and glorified.

4. Thou hast made all things; thou possessest power over all things; and all things are open and manifest before thee. Thou beholdest all things, and nothing can be concealed from thee.

5. Thou hast seen what Azazyel has done, how he has taught every species of iniquity upon earth, and has disclosed to the world all the secret things which are done in the heavens.

6. Samyaza also has taught sorcery, to whom thou hast given authority over those who are associated with him. They have gone together to the daughters of men; have lain with them; have become polluted;

7. And have discovered crimes to them.

8. The women likewise have brought forth giants.

9. Thus has the whole earth been filled with blood and with iniquity.

[a] *Bring judgment to us from.*

10. And now behold the souls of those who are dead, cry out,

11. And complain even to the gate of heaven.

12. Their groaning ascends; nor can they escape from the unrighteousness which is committed on earth. Thou knowest all things, before they exist.

13. Thou knowest these things, and what has been done by them; yet thou dost not speak to us.

14. What on account of these things ought we to do to them?

CHAP. X.

1. Then the Most High, the Great and Holy One spoke;

2. And sent Arsayalalyur to the son of Lamech,

3. Saying; Say to him in my name; Conceal thyself.

4. Then explain to him the consummation which is about to take place; for all the earth shall perish; the waters of a deluge shall come over the whole earth, and all things which are in it shall be destroyed.

5. And now teach him how he may escape, and how his seed may remain in all the earth.

6. Again the Lord said to Raphael: Bind Azazyel hand and foot; cast him into darkness; and opening the desert which is in Dudael, cast him in there.

7. Throw upon him hurled and pointed stones; covering him with darkness;

8. There shall he remain for ever; cover his face, that he may not see the light;

9. And in the great day of judgment let him be cast into the fire.

10. Restore the earth, which the angels have corrupted; and announce life to it, that I may revive it.

11. All the sons of men shall not perish in consequence of every secret, by which the Watchers have destroyed, and *which* they have taught, their offspring.

12. All the earth has been corrupted by the effects of the teaching[a] of Azazyel. To him therefore ascribe the whole crime.

13. To Gabriel also the Lord said, Go to the biters, to the reprobates, to the children of fornication; and destroy the children of fornication, the offspring of the Watchers, from among men; bring them forth, and excite[b] them one against another. Let them perish by *mutual* slaughter; for length of days shall not be theirs.

14. They shall all entreat thee, but their fathers shall not obtain *their wishes* respecting them; for they shall hope for eternal life, and that they may live, each of them, five hundred years.

15. To Michael likewise the Lord said; Go and announce *his crime* to Samyaza, and to the others who are with him, who have been associated with women, that they might be polluted with all their

[a] *by the teaching of the work of Azazyel.* [b] *send.*

impurity. And when all their sons shall be slain, when they shall see the perdition of their beloved, bind them for seventy generations underneath the earth, even to the day of judgment, and of consummation, until the judgment, *the effect of* which will last for ever, be completed[a].

16. Then shall they be taken away into the lowest depths of the fire in torments; and in confinement shall they be shut up for ever.

17. Immediately after this shall he, together with them, burn and perish; they shall be bound until the consummation of many generations.

18. Destroy all the souls addicted to dalliance, and the offspring of the Watchers, for they have tyrannized over mankind.

19. Let every oppressor perish from the face of the earth;

20. Let every evil work be destroyed;

21. The plant of righteousness and of rectitude appear, and its produce[b] become a blessing.

22. Righteousness and rectitude shall be for ever planted with delight.

23. And then shall all the saints give thanks, and live until they have begotten a thousand *children*, while the whole period of their youth, and their sabbaths shall be completed in peace. In those days all the earth shall be cultivated in righteousness; it shall be wholly planted with trees, and filled with benediction; every tree of delight shall be planted in it.

[a] Here end the first two extracts made by Syncellus.

[b] *and the work of righteousness and rectitude.*

24. In it shall vines be planted; and the vine which shall be planted in it shall yield fruit to satiety; every seed, which shall be sown in it, shall produce for one measure a thousand; and one measure of olives shall produce ten presses of oil.

25. Purify the earth from all oppression, from all injustice, from all crime, from all impiety, and from all the pollution which is committed upon it. Exterminate them from the earth.

26. Then shall all the children of men be righteous, and all nations shall pay me divine honours, and bless me; all shall adore me.

27. The earth shall be cleansed from all corruption, from every crime, from all punishment, and from all suffering; neither will I again send a deluge upon it from generation to generation for ever.

28. In those days I will open the treasures of blessing which are in heaven, that I may cause them to descend upon earth, and upon all the works and labour of man.

29. Peace and equity shall associate with the sons of men all the days of the world, in every generation of it.

(No CHAP. XI.[a])

CHAP. XII. [SECT. III.[b]]

1. Before all these things Enoch was concealed; nor did any one of the sons of men know where he

[a] The Paris MS. makes the last two verses of the preceding chapter, the xi. chapter. [b] Paris MS.

was concealed, where he had been, and what had happened.

2. He was wholly engaged with the holy ones, and with the Watchers in his days.

3. I, Enoch, was blessing the great Lord and King of peace.

4. And behold the Watchers called me Enoch the scribe.

5. Then *the Lord* said to me; Enoch, scribe of righteousness, go tell the Watchers of heaven, who have deserted the lofty sky, and their holy everlasting station, *who* have been polluted with women,

6. And have done as the sons of men do, by taking to themselves wives, and *who* have been greatly corrupted on the earth;

7. That on the earth they shall never obtain peace and remission of sin. For they shall not rejoice in their offspring; they shall behold the slaughter of their beloved; shall lament for the destruction of their sons; and shall petition for ever; but shall not obtain mercy and peace.

CHAP. XIII.

1. Then Enoch passing on said to Azazyel; Thou shalt not obtain peace. A great sentence is gone forth against thee. He shall bind thee;

2. Neither shall relief, mercy, and supplication be thine, on account of the oppression which thou hast taught;

3. And on account of every act of blasphemy,

tyranny, and sin, which thou hast discovered to the children of men.

4. Then departing *from him* I spoke to them all together;

5. And they all became terrified, and trembled;

6. Beseeching me to write for them a memorial of supplication, that they might obtain forgiveness; and that I might make the memorial of their prayer ascend up before the God of heaven; because they could not themselves thenceforwards address him, nor raise up their eyes to heaven on account of the disgraceful offence for which they were judged.

7. Then I wrote a memorial of their prayer and supplication, for their spirits, for every thing which they had done, and for the subject of their entreaty, that they might obtain remission and rest.

8. Proceeding on, I continued over the waters of Danbadan, which is on the right to the west of Armon, reading the memorial of their prayer, until I fell asleep.

9. And behold a dream came to me, and visions appeared above me. I fell down, and saw a vision of punishment, that I might relate it to the sons of heaven, and reprove them. When I awoke I went to them. All being collected together stood weeping in Oubelseyael, which is situated between Libanos and Seneser, with their faces veiled.

10. I related in their presence all the visions which I had seen, and my dream;

11. And began to utter these words of righteousness, reproving the Watchers of heaven.

CHAP. XIV.

1. This is the book of the words of righteousness, and of the reproof of the Watchers, who belong to the world, according to that which He, who is holy and great, commanded in the vision. I perceived in my dream, that I was now speaking with a tongue of flesh, and with my breath, which the Mighty One has put into the mouth of men, that they might converse with it;

2. And understand with the heart. As he has created and given to men *the power of* comprehending the word of understanding, so has he created and given to me *the power of* reproving the Watchers, the offspring of heaven. I have written your petition; and in my vision it has been shewn me, that what you request will not be granted you as long as the world endures[a].

3. Judgment has been passed upon you: *your request* will not be granted you.

4. From this time forward, never shall you ascend into heaven; He has said, that on the earth He will bind you, as long as the world endures.

5. But before these things you shall behold the destruction of your beloved sons; you shall not possess them, but they shall fall before you by the sword;

[a] *in all the days of the world.*

6. Neither shall you entreat for them, nor for yourselves.

7. But you shall weep and supplicate in silence. The words of the book which I wrote.

8. A vision thus appeared to me.

9. Behold, in *that* vision clouds and a mist invited me[a]; agitated stars[b] and flashes of lightning impelled and pressed me forwards, while winds in the vision assisted my flight, accelerating my progress[c].

10. They elevated me aloft to heaven. I proceeded, until I arrived at a wall built with stones of crystal[d]. A vibrating flame[e] surrounded it, which began to strike me with terror.

11. Into this vibrating flame I entered;

12. And drew nigh to a spacious habitation built also with stones of crystal. Its walls too, as well as pavement, were *formed* with stones of crystal, and crystal likewise was the ground. Its roof had the appearence of agitated[f] stars and flashes of lightning; and among them were cherubim of fire in a stormy sky[g]. A flame burned around its walls; and its portal blazed with fire. When I entered into this dwelling, it was hot as fire and cold as ice. No *trace of* delight or of life was there. Terror overwhelmed me, and a fearful shaking seized me.

[a] *clouds invited me, and a mist invited me.* See remarks.
[b] *the running of the stars.* [c] *hastening me.* [d] በረድ፡ *hail, crystal.* [e] *a tongue of fire.* [f] ምርዋፀ፡ *the course of the.* [g] *and their heaven* (i. e. *whose heaven*) was *water*.

13. Violently agitated and trembling, I fell upon my face. In the vision I looked;

14. And behold there was another habitation more spacious than *the former*, every entrance to which was open before me, erected in *the midst of* a vibrating flame.

15. So greatly did it excel in all points, in glory, in magnificence, and in magnitude, that it is impossible to describe to you either the splendor or the extent of it.

16. Its floor was on fire; above were lightnings and agitated stars, while its roof exhibited a blazing fire.

17. Attentively I surveyed it, and saw that it contained an exalted throne;

18. The appearance of which was like that of frost; while its circumference resembled the orb of the brilliant sun; and *there was* the voice of the cherubim.

19. From underneath this mighty throne rivers of flaming fire issued.

20. To look upon it was impossible.

21. One great in glory sat upon it:

22. Whose robe was brighter than the sun, and whiter than snow.

23. No angel was capable of penetrating to view the face of Him, the Glorious and the Effulgent; nor could any mortal behold Him. A fire was flaming[a] around Him.

[a] *A fire of flaming fire.*

24. A fire also of great extent continued to rise up before Him; so that not one of those who surrounded Him was capable of approaching Him, among the myriads of myriads who were before Him. To Him holy consultation was needless[a]. Yet did not the sanctified, who were near Him, depart far from Him either by night or by day; nor were they removed from Him. I also was so far advanced, with a veil on my face, and trembling. Then the Lord with his *own* mouth called me, saying; Approach hither, Enoch, at my holy word.

25. And He raised me up, making me draw near even to the entrance. My eye was directed to the ground.

CHAP. XV.

1. Then addressing me, He spoke and said[b]; Hear, neither be afraid, O righteous Enoch, thou scribe of righteousness[c]: approach hither, and hear my voice. Go, say to the Watchers of heaven, who have sent thee to pray for them; You ought to pray for men, and not men for you.

2. Wherefore have you forsaken the lofty and holy heaven, which endures for ever, and have lain with women; have defiled yourselves with the daughters of men; have taken to yourselves wives; have acted like the sons of the earth, and have begotten an impious offspring[d]?

[a] *And he required not holy counsel.* [b] *he said with his voice.* [c] *O Enoch, O righteous man, and scribe of righteousness.* [d] *giants.*

3. You being spiritual, holy, and possessing a life[a] which is eternal, have polluted yourselves with women; have begotten in carnal blood; have lusted in the blood of men; and have done as those *who are* flesh and blood do.

4. These however die and perish.

5. Therefore have I given to them wives, that they might cohabit with them; that sons might be born of them; and that this might be transacted upon earth.

6. But you from the beginning were made spiritual, possessing a life which is eternal, and not subject to death for ever[b].

7. Therefore I made not wives for you, because being spiritual, your dwelling is in heaven.

8. [c]Now the giants, who have been born of spirit and of flesh, shall be called upon earth evil spirits, and on earth shall be their habitation. Evil spirits shall proceed from their flesh, because they were created from above; from the holy Watchers was their beginning and primary foundation. Evil spirits shall they be upon earth, and the spirits of the wicked shall they be called. The habitation of the spirits of heaven shall be in heaven; but upon earth shall be the habitation of terrestrial spirits, who are born on earth.

9. The spirits of the giants *shall be like* clouds,

[a] *living a life.* [b] *in all the generations of the world.*
[c] The third extract made by Syncellus begins here, and ends with the first verse of the next chapter.

which shall oppress, corrupt, fall, contend, and bruise upon earth.

10. They shall cause lamentation. No food shall they eat; and they shall be thirsty; they shall be concealed, and shall not[a] rise up against the sons of men, and against women; for they come forth during the days of slaughter and destruction.

CHAP. XVI.

1. And as to the death of the giants, wheresoever their spirits depart from their bodies, let their flesh, that which is perishable, be without judgment. Thus shall they perish, until the day of the great consummation of the great world. A destruction shall take place of[b] the Watchers and the impious.

2. And now to the Watchers, who have sent thee to pray for them, who in the beginning were in heaven,

3. *Say;* In heaven have you been; secret things however have not been manifested to you; yet have you known a reprobated mystery.

4. And this you have related to women in the hardness of your heart, and by that mystery have women and mankind multiplied evils upon the earth.

[a] *and those spirits shall not.* M. De Sacy here remarks, that the sense seems to require an affirmative, instead of a negative, clause.

[a] *It shall be consummated respecting.*

5. Say to them; Never therefore shall you obtain peace.

CHAP. XVII. [SECT. IV.[a]]

1. They raised me up into a certain place[b], where there was the appearance of a burning fire; and when they pleased they assumed the likeness of men.

2. They carried me to a lofty spot, to a mountain, the top of which reached to heaven.

3. And I beheld the receptacles of light and of thunder at the extremities of the place, where it was deepest. There was a bow of fire, and arrows in their quiver, a sword of fire, and every species of lightning.

4. Then they elevated me to a babbling stream[c], and to a fire in the west, which received all the setting of the sun. I came to a river of fire, which flowed like water, and emptied itself into the great sea westwards.

5. I saw every large river, until I arrived at the great darkness. I went to where all of flesh migrate; and I beheld the mountains of the gloom which constitutes winter, and the place from which issues the water in every abyss.

6. I saw also the mouths of all the rivers in the world, and the mouths of the deep.

[a] Paris MS., in which however the title of chap. xvii. is omitted, although the section is noticed. [b] *one place.*
[c] *to water of life, which spoke.*

CHAP. XVIII.

1. I then surveyed the receptacles of all the winds, perceiving that they contributed to adorn[a] the whole creation, and *to preserve* the foundation of the earth.

2. I surveyed the stone *which supports* the corners of the earth.

3. I also beheld the four winds, which bear up the earth, and the firmament of heaven.

4. And I beheld the winds occupying the exalted sky[b],

5. Arising in the midst of heaven and of earth, and constituting the pillars of heaven.

6. I saw the winds which turn the sky, which cause the orb of the sun and of all the stars to set; and over the earth I saw the winds which support the clouds.

7. I saw the path of the angels.

8. I perceived at the extremity of the earth the firmament of heaven above it. Then I passed on towards the south;

6. Where burnt, both by day and night, six mountains formed of glorious stones; three towards the east, and three towards the south.

10. Those which were towards the east were of a variegated stone; one of which was of margarite, and another of antimony. Those towards the south were of a red stone. The middle one reached to

[a] *that in them were the ornaments of.* [b] *the height of heaven.*

heaven like the throne of God; *a throne composed* of alabaster, the top of which was of sapphire. I saw, too, a blazing fire hanging over[a] all the mountains.

11. And there I saw a place on the other side of an extended territory, where waters were collected.

12. I likewise beheld terrestrial fountains, deep in the fiery columns of heaven.

13. And in the columns of heaven I beheld fires, which descended without number, but neither on high, nor into the deep. Over these fountains also I perceived a place which had neither the firmament of heaven above it, nor the solid ground underneath it; neither was there water above it, nor any thing on wing; but the spot was desolate.

14. And there I beheld seven stars, like great blazing mountains, and like spirits entreating me.

15. Then the angel said; This place, until the consummation of heaven and earth, will be the prison of the stars, and the host of heaven.

16. The stars which roll over fire are those which transgressed the commandment of God before their time arrived; for they came not in their proper season. Therefore was He offended with them, and bound them, until the period of the consummation of their crimes in the secret year.

CHAP. XIX.

1. Then Uriel said; Here the angels, who cohabited with women, appointed their leaders;

[a] *which was over.*

2. And being numerous in appearance made men profane, and caused them to err; so that they sacrificed to devils as to gods. For in the great day *there shall be* a judgment, with which they shall be judged, until they are consumed; and their wives also shall be *judged*, who led astray the angels of heaven that they might salute them[a].

3. And I, Enoch, I alone saw the likeness of the end of all things. Nor did any human being see it, as I saw it.

CHAP. XX.

1. These are the names of the angels who watch.

2. Uriel, one of the holy angels, who *presides* over[b] clamor and terror.

3. Raphael, one of the holy angels, who *presides* over the spirits of men.

4. Raguel, one of the holy angels, who inflicts punishment on the world and the luminaries.

5. Michael, one of the holy angels, who, *presiding* over human virtue, commands the nations.

6. Sarakiel, one of the holy angels, who *presides* over the spirits of the children of men that transgress.

7. Gabriel, one of the holy angels, who *presides* over Ikisat[c], over paradise, and over the cherubim.

[a] See remarks. [b] *for* he it is *who* is over. [c] ኢኪሳት፡ *Ikisat*. This appears to be a proper name.

CHAP. XXI.

1. Then I made a circuit to a place in which nothing was completed.

2. And there I beheld neither the tremendous workmanship of an exalted heaven, nor of an established earth, but a desolate spot, prepared, and terrific.

3. There, too, I beheld seven stars of heaven bound in it together, like great mountains, and like a blazing fire. I exclaimed; For what species of crime have they been bound, and why have they been removed to this place? Then Uriel, one of the holy angels who was with me, and who conducted me, answered; Enoch, wherefore dost thou ask; wherefore reason with thyself, and anxiously inquire? These are those of the stars which have transgressed the commandment of the most high God; and are here bound, until the infinite number of the days of their crimes be completed.

4. From thence I afterwards passed on to another terrific place;

5. Where I beheld the operation of a great fire blazing and glittering, in the midst of which there was a division. Columns of fire struggled together to the end of the abyss, and deep was their descent. But neither its measurement nor magnitude was I able to discover; neither could I perceive its origin. Then I exclaimed; How terrible is this place, and how difficult to explore!

6. Uriel, one of the holy angels who was with me, answered and said; Enoch, Why art thou alarmed and amazed at this terrific place, at the sight of this *place of* suffering? This, he said, is the prison of the angels; and here are they kept for ever.

CHAP. XXII. [SECT. V.[a]]

1. From thence I proceeded to another spot, where I saw on the west a great and lofty mountain, a strong rock, and four delightful places.

2. Internally it was deep, capacious, and very smooth; as smooth as if it had been rolled over: it was both deep and dark to behold.

3. Then Raphael, one of the holy angels who were with me, answered and said; These are the delightful places where the spirits, the souls of the dead, will be collected; for them were they formed; and here will be collected all the souls of the sons of men.

4. These places, in which they dwell, shall they occupy until the day of judgment, and until their appointed period.

5. Their appointed period will be long, even until the great judgment. And I saw the spirits of the sons of men who were dead; and their voices reached to heaven, while they were accusing[b].

6. Then I inquired of Raphael, an angel who was with me, and said; Whose spirit is that, the voice of which reaches *to heaven,* and accuses?

[a] Paris MS. [b] *blaming* or *reproving*.

7. He answered, saying; This is the spirit of Abel, who was slain by Cain his brother; and who will accuse that brother[a], until his seed be destroyed from the face of the earth;

8. Until his seed perish from the seed of the human race.

9. At that time therefore I inquired respecting him, and respecting the general judgment, saying; Why is one separated from another? He answered; Three *separations* have been made between the spirits of the dead, and thus have the spirits of the righteous been separated.

10. Namely, *by* a chasm, *by* water, and *by* light above it.

11. And in the same way likewise are sinners separated when they die, and are buried in the earth; judgment not overtaking them in their lifetime.

12. Here their souls are separated. Moreover abundant is their suffering until the time of the great judgment, the castigation, and the torment of those who eternally execrate, whose souls are punished and bound there for ever.

13. And thus has it been from the beginning of the world. Thus has there existed a separation between the souls of those who utter complaints, and of those who watch for their destruction, to slaughter them in the day of sinners.

[a] *and he will accuse him.*

14. A receptacle of this sort has been formed[a] for the souls of unrighteous men, and of sinners; of those who have completed crime, and associated with the impious, whom they resemble. Their souls shall not be annihilated in the day of judgment, neither shall they arise from this place. Then I blessed God,

15. And said; Blessed be my Lord, the Lord of glory and of righteousness, who reigns over all for ever and for ever.

CHAP. XXIII.

1. From thence I went to another place, towards the west, unto the extremities of the earth;

2. Where I beheld a fire blazing and running along without cessation, which intermitted its course neither by day nor by night; but continued always the same.

3. I inquired, saying; What is this, which never ceases?

4. Then Raguel, one of the holy angels who were with me, answered,

5. And said; This blazing fire, which thou beholdest running towards the west, is *that of* all the luminaries of heaven.

CHAP. XXIV.

1. I went from thence to another place, and saw a mountain of fire flashing both by day and night.

[a] *Thus has it been made.*

I proceeded towards it; and perceived seven splendid mountains, which were all different from each other.

2. Their stones were brilliant and beautiful; all were brilliant and splendid to behold; and beautiful was their surface. These *mountains* were towards the east, and strengthened by being placed one upon another; and three were towards the south, strengthened in a similar manner. There were likewise deep valleys, which did not approach each other. And the seventh mountain was in the midst of them. In length they all resembled the seat of a throne, and odoriferous trees surrounded them.

3. Among these there was a tree of an unceasing smell; nor of those which were in Eden was there one of all the fragrant trees which smelt like this. Its leaf, its flower, and its bark never withered, and its fruit was beautiful.

4. Its fruit resembled the cluster of the palm. I exclaimed; Behold! this tree is goodly in aspect, pleasing in its leaf, and the sight of its fruit is delightful to the eye. Then Michael, one of the holy and glorious angels who were with me, and *one* who presided over them, answered,

5. And said; Enoch, Why dost thou inquire respecting the odour of this tree?

6. *Why* art thou inquisitive to know it?

7. Then I, Enoch, replied to him, and said; Concerning every thing I am desirous of instruction, but particularly concerning this tree.

8. He answered me, saying; That mountain which thou beholdest, the extent of whose head resembles the seat of the Lord, will be the seat on which shall sit the holy and great Lord of glory, the everlasting King, when He shall come and descend to visit the earth with goodness.

9. And that tree of an agreeable smell, not one of carnal *odour*[a], there shall be no power to touch, until the period of the great judgment. When all shall be punished and consumed for ever, this shall be bestowed on the righteous and humble. The fruit of this *tree* shall be given to the elect. For towards the north life shall be planted in the holy place, towards the habitation of the everlasting King.

10. Then shall they greatly rejoice and exult in the Holy One. The sweet odour shall enter into their bones; and they shall live a long life on the earth, as thy forefathers have lived; neither in their days shall sorrow, distress, trouble, and punishment afflict them.

11. And I blessed the Lord of glory, the everlasting King, because He has prepared *this tree* for the saints, formed it, and declared that He would give it to them.

CHAP. XXV.

1. From thence I proceeded to the middle of the earth, and beheld a happy and fertile spot, which contained branches continually sprouting from the trees which were planted in it. There I saw a holy

[a] *of flesh.*

mountain, and underneath it water on the eastern side, which flowed towards the south. I saw also on the east another mountain as high as that; and between them there were deep, but not wide valleys.

2. Water ran towards the mountain to the west of this; and underneath there was likewise another mountain.

3. There was a valley, but not a wide one, below it; and in the midst of them were other deep and dry valleys towards the extremity of the three. All these valleys, which were deep, but not wide, consisted of a strong rock, with a tree which was planted in them. And I wondered at the rock and at the valleys, being extremely surprised.

CHAP. XXVI.

1. Then I said; What means this blessed land, all these lofty trees, and the accursed valley between them?

2. Then Uriel, one of the holy angels who were with me, replied; This valley is the accursed of the accursed for ever. Here shall be collected all who utter with their mouths unbecoming language against God, and speak harsh things of his glory. Here shall they be collected. Here shall be their territory.

3. In the latter days an example of judgment shall be made of them in righteousness before the saints; while those who have received mercy shall

for ever, all their days, bless God, the everlasting King.

4. And at the period of judgment shall they bless Him for his mercy, as He has distributed it to them. Then I blessed God, addressing myself to Him, and making mention, as was meet, of his greatness.

CHAP. XXVII.

1. From thence I proceeded towards the east, to the middle of the mountain in the desert, the level surface only of which I perceived.

2. It was full of trees of the seed alluded to; and water leaped down upon it.

3. There appeared a cataract composed as of many cataracts both towards the west and towards the east. Upon one side were trees; upon the other water and dew.

CHAP. XXVIII.

1. Then I went to another place from the desert, towards the east of that mountain *which* I had approached.

2. There I beheld choice trees, particularly *those which produce* the sweet smelling drugs, frankincense and myrrh[a]; and trees unlike to each other.

3. And over it, above them, was the elevation of the eastern mountain at no great distance.

[a] *trees of judgment, particularly furniture of the sweet smell of frankincense and myrrh.*

CHAP. XXIX.

1. I likewise saw another place with valleys of water which never wasted.

2. *Where* I perceived a goodly tree, which in smell resembled Zasakinon [a].

3. And towards the sides of these valleys I perceived cinnamon of a sweet odour. Over them I advanced towards the east.

CHAP. XXX.

1. Then I beheld another mountain containing trees, from which water flowed like Neketro [b]. Its name was Sarira [c], and Kalboneba [d]. And upon this mountain I beheld another mountain, upon which were trees of Alva [e].

2. These trees were full, like almond trees, and strong; and when they produced fruit, it was superior to all perfume.

CHAP. XXXI.

1. After these things, surveying the entrances of the north, above the mountains, I perceived seven mountains replete with pure nard, odoriferous trees, cinnamon and papyrus.

2. From thence I passed on above the summits of those mountains to some distance eastwards, and

[a] ዘሰኪኖን፡ [b] ኔቄጥሮ፡ [c] ሰሪራ፡ [d] ከልበኔበ፡
[e] ዘአልዋ፡

went over the Erythræan sea. And when I was advanced far beyond it, I passed along above the angel Zateel, and arrived at the garden of righteousness. In this garden I beheld, among other trees, some which were numerous and large, and which flourished there.

3. Their fragrance was agreeable and powerful [a], and their appearance both varied and elegant. The tree of knowledge also was there, of which if any one eats, he becomes endowed with great wisdom.

4. It was like a species of the tamarind tree, bearing fruit which resembled grapes extremely fine; and its fragrance extended to a considerable distance. I exclaimed; How beautiful is this tree, and how delightful is its appearance!

5. Then holy Raphael, an angel who was with me, answered and said; This is the tree of knowledge, of which thy ancient father and thy aged mother ate, who were before thee; and who, obtaining knowledge, their eyes being opened, and knowing themselves to be naked, were expelled from the garden.

CHAP. XXXII.

1. From thence I went on towards the extremities of the earth; where I saw large beasts different from each other, and birds various in their countenances and forms, as well as with notes of different sounds.

[a] *good and great.*

2. To the east of these beasts I perceived the extremities of the earth, where heaven ceased. The gates of heaven stood open, and I beheld the celestial stars come forth. I numbered them as they proceeded out of the gate, and wrote them all down, as they came out one by one according to their number. *I wrote down* their names altogether, their times and their seasons, as the angel Uriel, who was with me, pointed them out to me.

3. He shewed them all to me, and wrote down *an account of* them.

4. He also wrote down for me their names, their regulations, and their operations.

CHAP. XXXIII.

1. From thence I advanced on towards the north, to the extremities of the earth.

2. And there I saw a great and glorious wonder at the extremities of the whole earth.

3. I saw there heavenly gates opening into heaven; three of them distinctly separated. The northern winds proceeded from them, blowing cold, hail, frost, snow, dew, and rain.

4. From one of the gates they blew mildly; but when they blew from the two *other gates*, it was with violence and force. They blew over the earth strongly.

CHAP. XXXIV.

1. From thence I went to the extremities of the world westwards;

2. Where I perceived three gates open, as I had seen in the north[a]; the gates and passages through them being of equal magnitude.

CHAP. XXXV.

1. Then I proceeded to the extremities of the earth southwards; where I saw three gates open to the south, from which issued dew, rain, and wind.

2. From thence I went to the extremities of heaven eastwards; where I saw three heavenly gates open to the east, which had smaller gates within them. Through each of these small gates the stars of heaven passed on, and proceeded towards the west by a path which was seen by them, and that at every period *of their appearance.*

3. When I beheld *them,* I blessed; every time, *in which they appeared,* I blessed the Lord of glory, who had made those great and splendid signs, that they might display the magnificence of his works to angels and to the souls of men; and that these might glorify all his works and operations; might see the effect of his power; might glorify the great labour of his hands; and bless him for ever.

CHAP. XXXVII.[b] [SECT. VI.[c]]

1. The vision which he saw, the second vision of wisdom, which Enoch saw, the son of Jared, the son of Malaleel, the son of Canan, the son of Enos, the

[a] *east.* An error evident from the context. [b] Chap. xxxvi. does not occur in the MS. [c] Paris MS. and Bodleian MS.

son of Seth, the son of Adam. This is the commencement of the word of wisdom, which I received to declare and tell to those who dwell upon earth. Hear from the beginning, and understand to the end, the holy things which I utter in the presence of the Lord of spirits. Those who were before *us* thought it good to speak;

2. And let not us, who come after, obstruct the beginning of wisdom. Until the present period never has there been given before the Lord of spirits that which I have received, wisdom according to the capacity of my intellect[a], and according to the pleasure of the Lord of spirits; that which I have received from him[b], a portion of life eternal.

3. *What I received from him* was in a hundred and three parables, which I declared to the inhabitants of the world.

CHAP. XXXVIII.

1. Parable the first. When the congregation of the righteous shall be manifested; and sinners be judged for their crimes, and be troubled in the sight of the world;

2. When righteousness shall be manifested in the presence of the righteous themselves, who will be elected for their *good* works *duly* weighed by the Lord of spirits; and when the light of the righteous and the elect, who dwell on earth, shall be

[a] *according as I have thought.*

[b] *which has been given to me by him.*

manifested; where will the habitation of sinners be, and where the place of rest for those who have rejected the Lord of spirits? It would have been better for them, had they been never born.

3. When, too, the secrets of the righteous shall be revealed, then shall sinners be judged; and impious men shall be afflicted in the presence of the righteous and the elect.

4. From that period those who possess the earth shall cease to be[a] powerful and exalted. Neither shall they be capable of beholding the countenances of the holy; for the light of the countenances of the holy, the righteous, and the elect, has been seen by the Lord of spirits.

5. Yet shall not the mighty kings of that period be destroyed; but be delivered into the hands of the righteous and the holy.

6. Nor thenceforwards shall any obtain commiseration from the Lord of spirits, because their lives *in this world* will have been completed.

CHAP. XXXIX.

1. In those days shall the elect and holy race descend from the upper heavens, and their seed shall then be with the sons of men. Enoch received books of indignation and wrath, and books of hurry and agitation.

2. Never shall they obtain mercy, saith the Lord of spirits.

[a] *shall not be.*

3. A cloud then snatched me up, and the wind raised me above the surface of the earth, placing me at the extremity of the heavens.

4. There I saw another vision; I *saw* the habitation and dormitory of the saints. There my eyes beheld their habitation with the angels, and their dormitory with the holy ones. They were entreating, supplicating, and praying for the sons of men; while righteousness like water flowed before them, and mercy like dew *was scattered* over the earth. And thus *shall it be* with them for ever and for ever.

5. At that time my eyes beheld the dwelling[a] of the elect, of truth, faith, and righteousness.

6. Countless shall be the number of the holy and the elect, in the presence of God[b] for ever and for ever.

7. Their residence I beheld under the wings of the Lord of spirits. All the holy and the elect sung before him, in appearance like a blaze of fire; their mouths being full of blessings, and their lips glorifying the name of the Lord of spirits. And righteousness incessantly *dwelt* before him.

8. There was I desirous of remaining, and my soul longed for that habitation. There was my antecedent inheritance; for thus had I prevailed[c] before the Lord of spirits.

9. At that time I glorified and extolled the name

[a] *place.* [b] *in his presence.* [c] *There was my portion before; for thus had it been prevailed respecting me.*

of the Lord of spirits with blessing and with praise; for He has established it with blessing and with praise, according to his own good pleasure [a].

10. That place long did my eyes contemplate. I blessed and said; Blessed be He, blessed from the beginning for ever. In the beginning, before the world was created, and without end is his knowledge [b].

11. What is this world? Of every existing generation those shall bless thee who do not sleep *in the dust*, but stand before thy glory, blessing, glorifying, exalting thee, and saying; The holy, holy, Lord of spirits, fills the whole world of spirits.

12. There my eyes beheld all who, without sleeping, stand before Him and bless Him, saying; Blessed be thou, and blessed be the name of God for ever and for ever. Then my countenance became changed, until I was incapable of seeing.

CHAP. XL.

1. After this I beheld thousands of thousands, and myriads of myriads, and an infinite number of people, standing before the Lord of spirits.

2. On the four wings likewise of the Lord of spirits, on the four sides, I perceived others, besides those who were standing *before Him*. Their names, too, I know; because the angel, who proceeded with

[a] *according to the will of the Lord of spirits.*
[b] *without end He knows.*

me, declared them to me, discovering to me every secret thing.

3. Then I heard the voices of those upon the four sides magnifying the Lord of glory.

4. The first voice blessed the Lord of spirits for ever and for ever.

5. The second voice I heard blessing the elect One, and the elect who suffer [a] on account of the Lord of spirits.

6. The third voice I heard petitioning and praying for those who dwell upon earth, and supplicate the name of the Lord of spirits.

7. The fourth voice I heard expelling the impious angels [b], and prohibiting them from entering into the presence of the Lord of spirits, to prefer accusations against the inhabitants of the earth.

8. After this I besought the angel of peace, who proceeded with me, to explain all that was concealed. I said to him; Who are those *whom* I have seen on the four sides, and whose words I have heard and written down? He replied; The first is the merciful, the patient, the holy Michael.

9. The second is he who *presides* over every suffering and every affliction [c] of the sons of men, the holy Raphael. The third, who *presides* over all that is powerful, is Gabriel. And the fourth, who *presides* over repentance, and the hope of those who will inherit eternal life, is Phanuel. These are the

[a] *are crucified* or *tormented.* [b] *the Satans.* [c] *wound.*

four angels of the most high God, and their four voices, which at that time I heard.

CHAP. XLI.

1. After this I beheld the secrets of the heavens and of paradise [a], according to its divisions; and of human action [b], as they weigh it there in balances. I saw the habitations of the elect, and the habitations of the holy. And there my eyes beheld all the sinners, who denied the Lord of glory, and whom they were expelling from thence, and dragging away, as they stood *there;* no punishment proceeding against them from the Lord of spirits.

2. There, too, my eyes beheld the secrets of the lightning and the thunder; and the secrets of the winds, how they are distributed as they blow over the earth: the secrets of the winds, of the dew, and of the clouds. There I perceived the place from which they issued forth, and became saturated with the dust of the earth.

3. There I saw the receptacles of wood [c], out of which the winds became separated, the receptacle of hail, the receptacle of snow, the receptacle of the clouds, and the cloud itself, *which* continued over the earth before *the creation of* the world.

4. I beheld also the receptacles of the moon, whence the moons [d] came, whither they proceeded,

[a] መንግሥት፡ *the kingdom* or *paradise*, *κατ' ἐξοχήν*. See Ludolf's Lexicon. [b] *the work* or *labour of man.* [c] ዐፀዋን፡ *of woods.* [d] *they.*

their glorious return, and how one became more splendid than another. *I marked* their rich progress, their unchangeable progress, their disunited and undiminished progress; their observance of a mutual fidelity by a stable oath[a]; their proceeding forth before the sun, and their adherence to the path *allotted* them[b], in obedience to the command of the Lord of spirits. Potent is his name for ever and for ever.

5. After this *I perceived, that* the path both concealed and manifest of the moon, as well as the progress of its path, was there completed by day and by night; while each, one with another, looked towards the Lord of spirits, magnifying and praising without cessation, since praise to them is rest; for in the splendid sun there is a frequent conversion to blessing and to malediction.

6. The course of the moon's path to the righteous is light, but to sinners it is darkness; in the name of the Lord of spirits, who created *a division* between light and darkness, and, separating the spirits of men, strengthened the spirits of the righteous in the name of his own righteousness.

7. Nor does the angel prevent *this,* neither is he endowed with the power of preventing it; for the Judge beholds them all, and judges them all in his own presence.

CHAP. XLII.

1. Wisdom found not a place *on earth* where she could inhabit; her dwelling therefore is in heaven.

[a] *by an oath to which they adhered.* [b] *to their path.*

2. Wisdom went forth to dwell among the sons of men, but she obtained not an habitation. Wisdom returned to her place, and seated herself in the midst of the angels. But iniquity went forth after her return, who unwillingly found *an habitation*, and resided among them, as rain in the desert, and as dew in a thirsty land.

CHAP. XLIII.

1. I beheld another splendor, and the stars of heaven. I observed that He called them all by their respective names, and that they heard. In a righteous balance I saw that He weighed out with their light the amplitude of their places, and the day of their appearance[a], and their conversion. Splendor produced splendor; and their conversion *was* into the number of the angels, and of the faithful.

2. Then I inquired of the angel, who proceeded with me, and explained to me secret things, What *their names* were. He answered; A similitude of these has the Lord of spirits shewn thee. They are the names of the righteous who dwell upon earth, and who believe in the name of the Lord of spirits for ever and for ever.

CHAP. XLIV.

Another thing also I saw respecting splendor; that it rises out of the stars, and becomes splendor; being incapable of forsaking them.

[a] *of their existing.*

CHAP. XLV. [SECT. VII.[a]]

1. Parable the second, respecting those who deny[b] the name of the habitation of the holy ones, and of the Lord of spirits.

2. Heaven they shall not ascend, nor shall they come on the earth. This shall be the portion of sinners, who deny the name of the Lord of spirits, and who are thus reserved for the day of punishment and of affliction.

3. In that day shall the Elect one sit upon a throne of glory; and shall choose their conditions and countless habitations, (while their spirits within them shall be strengthened, when they behold my Elect one,) *shall choose them* for those who have fled for protection to my holy and glorious name.

4. In that day I will cause my Elect one to dwell in the midst of them; will change *the face of* heaven; will bless it, and illuminate it for ever.

5. I will also change *the face of* the earth; will bless it; and cause those whom I have elected to dwell upon it. But those who have committed sin and iniquity shall not inhabit it[c]; for I have marked their proceedings[d]. My righteous ones will I satisfy with peace, placing them before me; but

[a] In the Paris MS. it is section viii. In the Bodleian MS. section vii. [b] In the Bodleian MS. there seems here an evident omission. It reads እ፡ ይክሕዱ፡ This omission is supplied in the Paris MS., where it is ዲበ፡ እለ፡ ይክሕዱ፡ I have followed the latter. [c] *tread upon it.* [d] *for I have seen them.*

the condemnation of sinners shall draw near, that I may destroy them from the face of the earth.

CHAP. XLVI.

1. There I beheld the Ancient of days[a], whose head was like white wool, and with him another, whose countenance resembled that of man. His countenance was full of grace, like *that of* one of the holy angels. Then I inquired of one of the angels[b], who went with me, and who shewed me every secret thing, concerning this Son of man; who He was; whence He was; and why He accompanied the Ancient of days.

2. He answered and said to me; This is the Son of man, to whom righteousness belongs; with whom righteousness has dwelt; and who will reveal all the treasures of that which is concealed; for the Lord of spirits has chosen Him; and his portion has surpassed[c] all before the Lord of spirits in everlasting uprightness.

3. This Son of man, whom thou beholdest, shall raise up kings and the mighty from their couches, and the powerful from their thrones; shall loosen the bridles of the powerful, and break in pieces the teeth of sinners.

4. He shall hurl kings from their thrones and

[a] ርእስ፡ መዋዕል፡ *the Chief* or *Head of days*, Daniel vii. 9.
[b] The words, *Then I inquired of one of the angels*, are omitted in the Bodleian MS. They occur in the Paris MS. [c] *conquered*.

their dominions; because they will not exalt and praise Him, nor humble themselves *before Him*, by whom[a] their kingdoms were granted to them. The countenance likewise of the mighty shall He cast down, filling them with confusion. Darkness shall be their habitation, and worms shall be their bed; nor from *that* their bed shall they hope to be again raised, because they exalted not the name of the Lord of spirits.

5. They shall condemn the stars of heaven, shall lift up their hands against the Most High, shall tread upon and inhabit the earth, exhibiting all their works of iniquity, even their works of iniquity. Their strength shall be in their riches, and their faith in the gods whom they have formed with their own hands. They shall deny the name of the Lord of spirits, and shall expel Him from the temples, in which they assemble;

6. And *with Him* the faithful, who suffer in the name of the Lord of spirits.

CHAP. XLVII.

1. In that day the prayer of the holy and the righteous, and the blood of the righteous, shall ascend from the earth into the presence of the Lord of spirits.

2. In that day shall the holy ones assemble, who dwell above the heavens, and with united voice petition, supplicate, praise, laud, and bless the name

[a] *from whence.*

of the Lord of spirits, on account of the blood of the righteous which has been shed; that the prayer of the righteous may not be intermitted before the Lord of spirits; that for them He would execute judgment; and that his patience may not endure for ever.

3. At that time I beheld the Ancient of days, while He sat upon the throne of his glory, *while* the book of the living was opened in his presence, and *while* all the powers which were above the heavens stood around and before Him.

4. Then were the hearts of the saints full of joy, because the consummation[a] of righteousness was arrived, the supplication of the saints heard, and the blood of the righteous appreciated by the Lord of spirits.

CHAP. XLVIII.

1. In that place I beheld a fountain of righteousness, which never failed, encircled by many springs of wisdom. Of these all the thirsty drank, and were filled with wisdom, having their habitation with the righteous, the elect, and the holy.

2. In that hour was this Son of man invoked before[b] the Lord of spirits, and his name in the presence of the Ancient of days.

3. Before the sun and the signs were created, before the stars of heaven were formed, his name was invoked in the presence of the Lord of spirits. A support shall He be for the righteous and the holy

[a] *the number.* [b] ብኀበ፡ *ad, apud.*

to lean upon, without falling; and he shall be the light of nations.

4. He shall be the hope of those whose hearts are troubled. All, who dwell on earth, shall fall down and worship before him; shall bless and glorify Him, and sing praises to the name of the Lord of spirits.

5. Therefore the Elect and the Concealed one existed in His presence, before the world was created, and for ever.

6. In His presence *he existed*, and has revealed to the saints and to the righteous the wisdom of the Lord of spirits; for he has preserved the lot of the righteous, because they have hated and rejected this world of iniquity, and have detested all its works and ways, in the name of the Lord of spirits.

7. For in His name shall they be preserved; and His will shall be their life. In those days shall the kings of the earth and the mighty men, who have gained the world by their achievements[a], become humble in countenance.

8. For in the day of their anxiety and trouble their souls shall not be saved; and *they shall be* in subjection to[b] those whom I have chosen.

9. I will cast them like hay into the fire, and like lead into the water. Thus shall they burn in the presence of the righteous, and sink in the presence of the holy; nor shall a tenth part of them be found.

[a] *by the work of their own hands.* [b] *in the hands of.*

10. But in the day of their trouble, the world shall obtain tranquillity[a].

11. In His presence shall they fall, and not be raised up again; nor shall there be any one to take them out of His hands, and to lift them up: for they have denied the Lord of spirits, and His Messiah. The name of the Lord of spirits shall be blessed.

CHAP. XLVIII[b].

1. Wisdom is poured forth like water, and glory fails not before Him for ever and ever; for potent is He in all the secrets of righteousness.

2. But iniquity passes away like a shadow, and possesses not a fixed station: for the Elect one stands before the Lord of spirits; and His glory is for ever and ever; and His power from generation to generation.

3. With Him dwells the spirit of intellectual wisdom, the spirit of instruction and of power, and the spirit of those who sleep in righteousness; He shall judge secret things.

4. Nor shall any be able to utter a single word before Him; for the Elect one is in the presence of the Lord of spirits, according to his own pleasure.

CHAP. XLIX.

1. In those days the saints and the chosen shall undergo a change. The light of day shall rest upon

[a] *rest shall be on earth.* [b] Chap. xlviii. occurs twice.

them; and the splendor and glory of the saints shall be changed.

2. In the day of trouble evil shall be heaped up upon sinners; but the righteous shall triumph in the name of the Lord of spirits.

3. Others shall be made to see, that they must repent, and forsake the works of their hands; and that glory awaits them not in the presence of the Lord of spirits; yet that by his name they may be saved. The Lord of spirits will have compassion on them; for great is his mercy; and righteousness is in his judgment, and in the presence of his glory; nor in his judgment shall iniquity stand. He who repents not before Him shall perish.

4. Henceforward I will not have mercy on them, saith the Lord of spirits.

CHAP. L.

1. In those days shall the earth deliver up from her womb, and hell deliver up from hers, that which it has received; and destruction shall restore that which it owes.

2. He shall select the righteous and holy from among them; for the day of their salvation has approached.

3. And in those days shall the Elect one sit upon his throne, while every secret of intellectual wisdom shall proceed from his mouth; for the Lord of spirits has gifted and glorified him.

4. In those days the mountains shall skip like

rams, and the hills shall leap like young sheep[a] satiated with milk; and all *the righteous* shall become angels in heaven.

5. Their countenance shall be bright with joy; for in those days shall the Elect one be exalted. The earth shall rejoice; the righteous shall inhabit it, and the elect possess it[b].

CHAP. LI.

1. After that period, in the place where I had seen every secret sight, I was snatched up in a whirlwind, and carried off westwards.

2. There my eyes beheld the secrets of heaven, and all which existed on earth; a mountain of iron, a mountain of copper[c], a mountain of silver, a mountain of gold, a mountain of fluid metal[d], and a mountain of lead.

3. And I inquired of the angel who went with me, saying; What are these things, which in secret I behold?

4. He said; All these things which thou beholdest shall be for the dominion of the Messiah, that he may command, and be powerful upon earth.

5. And that angel of peace answered me, saying; Wait but a short time, and thou shalt understand[e], and every secret thing shall be revealed to thee, which the Lord of spirits has decreed. Those moun-

[a] Psalm cxiv. 4. [b] *go and walk upon it.* [c] ፀሪቅ: *nummus minutissimus. Obolus.* Lud. Lex. [d] ነጠብጠብ: *gutta, stilla.* [e] *see.*

tains which thou hast seen, the mountain of iron, the mountain of copper, the mountain of silver, the mountain of gold, the mountain of fluid metal, and the mountain of lead, all these in the presence of the Elect one shall be like a honeycomb before the fire, and like water descending from above upon these mountains; and shall become debilitated before his feet.

6. In those days men[a] shall not be saved by gold and by silver.

7. Nor shall they have it in their power to secure themselves, and to fly.

8. There shall be neither iron for war, nor a coat of mail for the breast.

9. Copper shall be useless; useless also that which neither rusts nor consumes away; and lead shall not be coveted.

10. All these things shall be rejected, and perish from off the earth, when the Elect one shall appear in the presence of the Lord of spirits.

CHAP. LII.

1. There my eyes beheld a deep valley; and wide was its entrance.

2. All who dwell on land, on the sea, and in islands, shall bring to it gifts, presents, and offerings; yet that deep valley shall not be full. Their hands shall commit iniquity. Whatsoever they produce by labour, the sinners shall devour with crime. But

[a] *they*.

they shall perish from the face of the Lord of spirits, and from the face of his earth. They shall stand up, and shall not fail for ever and ever.

3. I beheld the angels of punishment, who were dwelling *there*, and preparing every instrument of Satan.

4. Then I inquired of the angel of peace, who proceeded with me, for whom those instruments were preparing.

5. He said; These they are preparing for the kings and powerful ones of the earth, that thus[a] they may perish.

6. After which the righteous and chosen house of his congregation shall appear, thenceforward unchangeable, in the name of the Lord of spirits.

7. Nor shall those mountains exist in his presence, as the earth and the hills, as the fountains of water *exist*. And the righteous shall be relieved from the vexation of sinners.

CHAP. LIII.

1. Then I looked and turned myself to another part of the earth, where I beheld a deep valley burning with fire.

2. To this valley they brought monarchs and the mighty.

3. And there my eyes beheld the instruments which they were making, fetters of iron without weight[b].

[a] *by this.* [b] *in which there was not weight.*

4. Then I inquired of the angel of peace, who proceeded with me, saying; For whom are these fetters and instruments prepared?

5. He replied; These are prepared for the host of Azazeel, that they may be delivered over and adjudged to the lowest condemnation; and that their angels may be overwhelmed with hurled stones, as the Lord of spirits has commanded.

6. Michael and Gabriel, Raphael and Phanuel shall be strengthened in that day, and shall then cast them into a furnace of blazing fire, that the Lord of spirits may be avenged of them for their crimes; because they became ministers of Satan, and seduced those who dwell upon earth.

7. In those days shall punishment go forth from the Lord of spirits; and the receptacles of water which are above the heavens shall be opened, and the fountains likewise, which are under the heavens and under the earth.

8. All the waters, which are in the heavens and above them, shall be mixed together.

9. The water which is above heaven shall be the agent[a];

10. And the water which is under the earth shall be the recipient[b]: and all shall be destroyed who dwell upon earth, and who dwell under the extremities of heaven.

11. By these means shall they understand the

[a] *male.* [b] *female.*

iniquity which they have committed on earth; and by these means shall they perish.

CHAP. LIV.

1. Afterwards the Ancient of days repented, and said; In vain have I destroyed all the inhabitants of the earth.

2. And He sware by his great name, *saying;* Henceforwards I will not act thus towards all those who dwell upon earth.

3. But I will place a sign in the heavens[a]; and it shall be a faithful witness[b] between me and them for ever, as long as the days of heaven and earth last upon the earth.

4. Afterwards, according to this my decree, when I shall be disposed to seize them beforehand, by the instrumentality of angels, in the day of affliction and trouble, my wrath and my punishment shall remain upon them, my punishment and my wrath, saith God the Lord of spirits.

5. O ye kings, O ye mighty, who inhabit the world, you shall behold my Elect one, sitting upon the throne of my glory. And He shall judge Azazeel, all his associates, and all his hosts, in the name of the Lord of spirits.

6. There likewise I beheld hosts of angels who were moving in punishment, confined in a net-work

[a] Genesis ix. 13. "I do set my bow in the cloud, and it shall "be for a token of a covenant between me and the earth."

[b] *faith,* or *fidelity.*

of iron and brass. Then I inquired of the angel of peace, who proceeded with me, To whom those under confinement were going?

7. He said; To each of their elect and their beloved, that they may be cast into the fountains and deep recesses of the valley.

8. And that valley shall be filled with their elect and beloved; the days of whose life shall be consumed, but the days of their error shall be innumerable.

9. Then shall princes[a] combine together, and conspire. The chiefs of the east, among the Parthians and Medes, shall remove kings, in whom a spirit of perturbation shall enter. They shall hurl them from their thrones, springing as lions from their dens, and like famished wolves into the midst of the flock.

10. They shall go up, and tread upon the land of their elect. The land of their elect shall be before them. The threshing floor, the path, and the city of my righteous *people* shall impede *the progress of* their horses. They shall rise up to destroy each other; their right hand shall be strengthened; nor shall a man acknowledge his friend or his brother;

11. Nor the son his father and his mother; until the number of the dead bodies shall be *completed*, by their death and punishment. Neither shall this take place without cause.

[a] መላእክት፡ *princes*, or *angels*.

12. In those days shall the mouth of hell be opened, into which they shall be immerged; hell shall destroy and swallow up sinners from the face of the elect.

CHAP. LV.

1. After this I beheld another army of chariots, with men riding in them.

2. And they came upon the wind from the east, from the west, and from the south [a].

3. The sound of the noise of their chariots was heard.

4. And when that agitation took place, the saints out of heaven perceived it; the pillar of the earth shook from its foundation; and the sound was heard from the extremities of the earth unto the extremities of heaven at the same time.

5. Then they all fell down, and worshipped the Lord of spirits.

6. This is the end of the second parable.

CHAP. LVI. [SECT. IX.[b]]

1. I now began to utter the third parable, concerning the saints and the elect.

2. Blessed are ye, O saints and elect, for glorious is your lot.

3. The saints shall exist in the light of the sun, and the elect in the light of everlasting life, the days of whose life shall never terminate; nor shall the days of the saints be numbered, who seek for

[a] *from the midst of the day.* [b] Paris MS.

light, and obtain righteousness with the Lord of spirits.

4. Peace be to the saints with the Lord of the world.

5. Henceforward shall the saints be told to seek in heaven the secrets of righteousness, the portion of faith; for like the sun has it arisen upon the earth, while darkness has passed away. There shall be light interminable[a]; nor shall they enter upon the enumeration of time; for darkness shall be previously destroyed, and light shall increase before the Lord of spirits; before the Lord of spirits shall the light of uprightness increase for ever.

CHAP. LVII.

1. In those days my eyes beheld the secrets of the lightnings and the splendors, and the judgment belonging to them.

2. They lighten for a blessing and for a curse, according to the will of the Lord of spirits.

3. And there I saw the secrets of the thunder, when it rattles[b] above in heaven, and its sound is heard.

4. The habitations also of the earth were shewn to me. The sound of the thunder is for peace and for blessing, as well as for a curse, according to the word of the Lord of spirits.

5. Afterwards every secret of the splendors and

[a] *which cannot be numbered.*

[b] *it is grinding,* as in a mortar.

of the lightnings was seen by me. For blessing and for fertility they lighten.

CHAP. LVIII.[a] [SECT. X.[b]]

1. In the five hundredth year, and in the seventh month, on the fourteenth *day* of the month, of the lifetime of Enoch, in that parable, I saw that the heaven of heavens shook; that it shook violently; and that the powers of the Most High, and the angels, thousands of thousands, and myriads of myriads, were agitated with great agitation. And when I looked, the Ancient of days was sitting on the throne of his glory, while the angels and saints were standing around him. A great trembling came upon me, and terror seized me. My loins were bowed down and loosened; my reins were dissolved; and I fell upon my face. The holy Michael, another holy angel, one of the holy ones, was sent, who raised me up.

2. And when he raised me, my spirit returned; for I was incapable of enduring this vision of violence, its agitation, and the concussion of heaven.

3. Then holy Michael said to me; Wherefore art thou disturbed at this vision?

4. Hitherto has existed the day of mercy; and He has been merciful and long-suffering towards all who dwell upon the earth.

[a] There is no chap. lviii. in the MS. I have therefore divided chap. lix. into two parts, denominating this first part chap. lviii. [b] Paris MS.

5. But when the time shall come, then *shall* the power, the punishment, and the judgment *take place*, which the Lord of spirits has prepared for those who prostrate themselves to the judgment of righteousness, for those who abjure that judgment, and for those who take *his* name in vain.

6. That day has been prepared for the elect *as a day of* covenant; and for sinners *as a day of* inquisition.

7. In that day shall be distributed *for food* two monsters; a female monster, whose name is Leviathan, dwelling in the depths of the sea, above the springs of waters;

8. And a male *monster*, whose name is Behemoth; which possesses, *moving* on his breast, the invisible wilderness.

9. His name was Dendayen [a] in the east of the garden, where the elect and the righteous will dwell; where he received *it* from my ancestor, who was man, from Adam the first of men, whom the Lord of spirits made.

10. Then I asked of another angel to shew me the power of those monsters, how they became separated on the same day, one *being* in the depths of the sea, and one in the dry desert.

11. And he said; Thou, son of man, art here desirous of understanding secret things.

12.[b] And the angel of peace, who was with me,

[a] ዴንዳይን፡

[b] These last three verses, viz. 12, 13, 14, are placed in both MSS. at the end of chap. lix; but they

said; These two monsters are by the power of God prepared to become food, that the punishment of God may not be in vain.

13. Then shall children be slain with their mothers, and sons with their fathers.

14. And when the punishment of the Lord of spirits shall continue, upon them shall it continue, that the punishment of the Lord of spirits may not take place in vain. After that, judgment shall exist with mercy and longsuffering.

CHAP. LIX.

1. Then another angel, who proceeded with me, spoke to me;

2. And shewed me the first and last secrets in heaven above, and in the depths of the earth:

3. In the extremities of heaven, and in the foundations of it, and in the receptacle of the winds.

4. *He shewed me* how their spirits were divided; how they were balanced; and how both the springs and the winds were numbered according to the force of their spirit.

5. *He shewed me* the power of the moon's light, that its power is a just one; as well as the divisions of the stars, according to their respective names;

6. *That* every division is divided; that the lightning flashes;

so evidently belong to this account of the Leviathan and Behemoth, that I have ventured to insert them here.

7. That its troops[a] immediately obey; and that a cessation takes place during thunder in the continuance of its sound. Nor are the thunder and the lightning separated; neither do both of them move with one spirit; yet are they not separated.

8. For when the lightning lightens, the thunder sounds, and the spirit at a proper period pauses, making an equal division between them; for the receptacle, upon which their periods depend, is *loose* as sand[b]. Each of them at a proper season is restrained with a bridle; and turned by the power of the spirit, which thus propels *them* according to the spacious extent of the earth.

9. The spirit likewise of the sea is potent and strong; and as a strong power causes it to ebb[c], so is it driven forwards, and scattered against the mountains of the earth. The spirit of the frost has its angel; in the spirit of hail there is a good angel; the spirit of snow ceases in its strength, and a solitary spirit is in it, which ascends from it like vapour, and is called refrigeration.

10. The spirit also of mist dwells with them in their receptacle; but it has a receptacle to itself; for its progress is in splendor,

11. In light, and in darkness, in winter and in summer. Its receptacle is bright, and an angel is *in it.*

12. The spirit of dew *has* its abode in the extre-

[a] *Their host.* [b] *the receptacle of their times* is *what sand is.*
[c] *turns it back with a bridle.*

mities of heaven, in connection with the receptacle of rain; and its progress is in winter and in summer. The cloud produced by it, and the cloud of the mist, become united; one gives to the other; and when the spirit of rain is in motion from its receptacle, angels come, and opening its receptacle, bring it forth.

13. When likewise it is sprinkled over all the earth, it forms an union with every kind of water on the ground; for the waters remain on the ground, because *they afford* nourishment to the earth from the Most High, who is in heaven.

14. Upon this account therefore there is a regulation in the quantity of rain [a], which the angels receive.

15. These things I saw; all of them, even paradise [b].

CHAP. LX.

1. In those days I beheld long ropes given to those angels; who took to their wings, and fled, advancing towards the north.

2. And I inquired of the angel, saying; Wherefore have they taken those long ropes, and gone forth? He said; They are gone forth to measure.

3. The angel, who proceeded with me, said; These are the measures of the righteous; and cords shall the righteous bring, that they may trust in [c] the name of the Lord of spirits for ever and ever.

[a] *a measure in the rain.*

[b] *even to the garden of the righteous.* [c] *lean upon.*

4. The elect shall begin to dwell with the elect.

5. And these are the measures which shall be given to faith, and *which* shall strengthen the word of righteousness.

6. These measures shall reveal all the secrets in the depth of the earth.

7. And *it shall be*, that those who have been destroyed in the desert, and who have been devoured by the fish of the sea, and by wild beasts, shall return, and trust in[a] the day of the Elect one; for none shall perish in the presence of the Lord of spirits, nor shall any be capable of perishing.

8. Then they received the commandment, all *who were* in the heavens above; to whom a combined power, voice, and splendor, like fire, were given.

9. And first, with *their* voice, they blessed Him, they exalted Him, they glorified Him with wisdom, and ascribed to Him wisdom with the word, and with the breath of life.

10. Then the Lord of spirits seated upon the throne of his glory the Elect one;

11. Who shall judge all the works of the holy, in heaven above, and in a balance shall He weigh their actions. And when He shall lift up his countenance to judge their secret ways in the word of the name of the Lord of spirits, and their progress in the path of the righteous judgment of God most high;

12. They shall all speak with united voice; and

[a] *lean upon.*

bless, glorify, exalt, and praise, in the name of the Lord of spirits.

13. He shall call to every power of the heavens, to all the holy above, and to the power of God. The Cherubim, the Seraphim, and the Ophanin, all the angels of power, and all the angels of the Lords, namely, of the Elect one, and of the other Power, who *was* upon earth over the water on that day,

14. Shall raise their united voice; shall bless, glorify, praise, and exalt with the spirit of faith, with the spirit of wisdom and patience, with the spirit of mercy, with the spirit of judgment and peace, and with the spirit of benevolence; all shall say with united voice; Blessed is He; and the name of the Lord of spirits shall be blessed for ever and for ever; all, who sleep not, shall bless it in heaven above.

15. All the holy in heaven shall bless it; all the elect who dwell in the garden of life; and every spirit of light, who is capable of blessing, glorifying, exalting, and praising thy holy name; and every mortal man[a], more than the powers *of heaven*, shall glorify and bless thy name for ever and ever.

16. For great is the mercy of the Lord of spirits; long-suffering is He; and all his works, all his power, great as are the things which He has done, has He revealed to the saints and to the elect, in the name of the Lord of spirits.

[a] *all of flesh.*

CHAP. LXI.

1. Thus the Lord commanded the kings, the princes, the exalted, and those who dwell on earth, saying; Open your eyes, and lift up your horns, if you are capable of comprehending the Elect one.

2. The Lord of spirits sat upon the throne of his glory.

3. And the spirit of righteousness was poured out over him.

4. The word of his mouth shall destroy all the sinners and all the ungodly, who shall perish at his presence.

5. In that day shall all the kings, the princes, the exalted, and those who possess the earth, stand up, behold, and perceive, that He is sitting on the throne of his glory; that before Him the saints shall be judged in righteousness;

6. And that nothing, which shall be spoken before Him, shall be *spoken* in vain.

7. Trouble shall come upon them, as upon a woman in travail, whose labour is severe, when her child comes to the mouth of the womb, and she finds it difficult to bring forth.

8. One portion of them shall look upon another. They shall be astonished, and shall humble their countenance;

9. And trouble shall seize them, when they shall behold this Son of woman sitting upon the throne of his glory.

10. Then shall the kings, the princes, and all who possess the earth, glorify Him who has dominion over all things, Him who was concealed; for from the beginning the Son of man existed in secret [a], whom the Most High preserved in the presence of his power, and revealed to the elect.

11. He shall sow the congregation of the saints, and of the elect; and all the elect shall stand before Him in that day.

12. All the kings, the princes, the exalted, and those who rule over the earth, shall fall down on their faces before Him, and shall worship Him.

13. They shall fix their hopes on this Son of man, shall pray to Him, and petition Him for mercy.

14. Then shall the Lord of spirits hasten to expel them from his presence. Their faces shall be full of confusion, and their faces shall darkness cover [b]. The angels shall take them to punishment, that vengeance may be inflicted on those who have oppressed his children and his elect. And they shall become an example to the saints and to his elect. Through them shall these be made joyful; for the anger of the Lord of spirits shall rest upon them.

15. Then the sword of the Lord of spirits shall be drunk with their blood [c]; but the saints and elect shall be safe in that day; nor the face of the sinners and the ungodly shall they thenceforwards behold.

16. The Lord of spirits shall remain over them:

[a] *was concealed.* [b] *be added to their faces.* [c] *be drunk from them.*

17. And with this Son of man shall they dwell, eat, lie down, and rise up, for ever and ever.

18. The saints and the elect have arisen from the earth, have left off to depress their countenances, and have been clothed with the garment of life. That garment of life is with the Lord of spirits, in whose presence your garment shall not wax old, nor shall your glory diminish.

CHAP. LXII.

1. In those days the kings who possess the earth shall be punished by the angels of his wrath[a], wheresoever they shall be delivered up, that he may give rest for a short period; and that they may fall down and worship before the Lord of spirits, confessing their sins before him.

2. They shall bless and glorify the Lord of spirits, saying; Blessed is the Lord of spirits, the Lord of kings, the Lord of princes, the Lord of the rich, the Lord of glory, and the Lord of wisdom.

3. He shall enlighten every secret thing.

4. Thy power is from generation to generation; and thy glory for ever and ever.

5. Deep are all thy secrets, and numberless; and thy righteousness cannot be computed.

6. Now we know, that we should glorify and bless the Lord of kings, Him who is King over all things.

7. They shall also say; Who has granted us rest

[a] *punishment.*

to glorify, laud, bless, and confess in the presence of his glory?

8. And now small is the rest we desire; but we do not find *it;* we reject, and do not possess *it.* Light has passed away from before us; and darkness *has covered* our thrones for ever.

9. For we have not confessed before Him; we have not glorified the name of the Lord of kings; we have not glorified the Lord in all his works; but we have trusted in the sceptre of our dominion and of our glory.

10. In the day of our suffering and of our trouble He will not save us, neither shall we find rest. We confess that our Lord is faithful in all his works, in all his judgments, and in his righteousness.

11. In his judgments He pays no respect to persons; and we must depart from his presence, on account of our *evil* deeds.

12. All our sins are truly without number.

13. Then shall they say to themselves; Our souls are satiated with the instruments of crime;

14. But that prevents us not from descending to the flaming womb of hell.

15. Afterwards, their countenances shall be filled with darkness and confusion before the Son of man; from whose presence they shall be expelled, and before whom the sword shall remain to expel them.

16. Thus saith the Lord of spirits; This is the decree and the judgment against the princes, the

kings, the exalted, and those who possess the earth, in the presence of the Lord of spirits.

CHAP. LXIII.

1. I saw also other countenances in that secret place. I heard the voice of an angel, saying; These are the angels who have descended from heaven to earth, and have revealed secrets to the sons of men, and have seduced the sons of men to the commission of sin.

CHAP. LXIV. [SECT. XI.[a]]

1. In those days Noah saw that the earth became inclined, and that destruction approached.

2. Then he lifted up his feet, and went to the ends of the earth, to the dwelling of his great grandfather Enoch.

3. And Noah cried with a bitter voice; Hear me; hear me; hear me: three times. And he said; Tell me what is transacting upon earth; for the earth labours, and is violently shaken. Surely I shall perish with it.

4. After this there was a great perturbation on earth, and a voice was heard from heaven. I fell down on my face, when my great grandfather Enoch came and stood by me.

5. He said to me; Why hast thou cried out to me with a bitter cry and lamentation?

[a] Chapters lxiv. lxv. lxvi. and the first verse of lxvii. evidently contain a vision of Noah, and not of Enoch.

6. A commandment has gone forth from the Lord against those who dwell on the earth, that they may be destroyed[a]; for they know every secret of the angels, every oppressive and secret power of the devils[b], and every power of those who commit sorcery, as well as of those who make molten *images* in the whole earth.

7. *They know* how silver is produced from the dust of the earth, and how on the earth the *metallic* drop exists; for lead and tin are not produced from earth, as the primary fountain of their production.

8. There is an angel standing upon it, and that angel struggles to prevail.

9. Afterwards my great grandfather Enoch seized me with his hand, raising me up, and saying to me; Go, for I have asked the Lord of spirits respecting this perturbation of the earth; who replied; On account of their impiety have their innumerable judgments been consummated before Me. Respecting the moons have they inquired, and they have known that the earth will perish with those who dwell upon it, and that to these there will be *no place of* refuge for ever.

10. They have discovered secrets, and *they are* those who have been judged; but not thou, my son. The Lord of spirits knows that thou art pure and good, *free* from the reproach of *discovering* secrets.

11. He, the holy One, will establish thy name in the midst of the saints, and will preserve thee from

[a] *their end may be.* [b] *the Satans.*

those who dwell upon the earth. He will establish thy seed in righteousness, with dominion and great glory[a]; and from thy seed shall spring forth[b] righteous and holy men without number for ever.

CHAP. LXV.

1. After this he shewed me the angels of punishment, who were prepared to come, and to open all the mighty waters[c] under the earth:

2. That they may be for judgment, and for the destruction of all those who remain and dwell upon the earth.

3. And the Lord of spirits commanded the angels who went forth, not to take up the men and preserve *them.*

4. For those angels *presided* over all the mighty waters. Then I went out from the presence of Enoch.

CHAP. LXVI.

1. In those days the word of God came to me[d], and said; Noah, behold, thy lot[e] has ascended up to Me, a lot void of crime[f], a lot beloved[g] and upright.

2. Now then shall the angels labour at the trees; but when they proceed to this, I will put my hand upon it, and preserve it.

3. The seed of life shall arise[h] from it, and a

[a] *for kings, and for great glory.* [b] *shall go forth a spring of.* [c] *the power of water.* [d] *was with me.* [e] *portion.* [f] *fault.* [g] *of love.* [h] *be.*

change shall take place[a], that the dry land may not be left empty. I will establish thy seed before Me for ever and ever, and the seed of those who dwell with thee on the surface of the earth. It shall be blessed and multiplied in the presence of the earth, in the name of the Lord.

4. And they shall confine those angels who disclosed impiety. In that burning valley *it is, that they shall be confined,* which at first my great grandfather Enoch shewed me in the west, where there were mountains of gold and silver, of iron, of fluid metal, and of tin.

5. I beheld that valley in which there was great perturbation, and *where* the waters were troubled.

6. And when all this was effected, from the fluid mass of fire, and the perturbation which prevailed[b] in that place, there arose a strong smell of sulphur, which became mixed with the waters; and the valley of the angels, who had been guilty of seduction, burned underneath its soil.

7. Through that valley also rivers of fire were flowing[c], to which those angels shall be condemned, who seduced the inhabitants of the earth.

8. And in those days shall these waters be to kings, to princes, to the exalted, and to the inhabitants of the earth, for the healing of the soul and body, and for the judgment of the spirit.

9. Their spirits shall be full of revelry[d], that they may be judged in their bodies; because they

[a] *shall enter.* [b] *troubled them.* [c] *went.* [d] *sport.*

have denied the Lord of spirits, and *although* they perceive their condemnation day by day, they believe not in his name.

10. And as the inflammation of their bodies shall be great, so shall their spirits undergo a change for ever.

11. For no word which is uttered before the Lord of spirits shall be in vain.

12. Judgment has come upon them, because they trusted in their carnal revelry[a], and denied the Lord of spirits.

13. In those days shall the waters of that valley[b] be changed; for when the angels shall be judged, then shall the heat of those springs of water experience an alteration.

14. And when the angels shall ascend, the water of the springs shall *again* undergo a change, and be frozen. Then I heard holy Michael answering and saying; This judgment, with which the angels shall be judged, shall bear testimony against the kings, the princes, and those who possess the earth.

15. For these waters of judgment shall be for their healing, and for the death of their bodies. But they shall not perceive and believe that the waters will be changed, and become a fire, which shall blaze for ever.

CHAP. LXVII.

1. After this he gave me the characteristical

[a] *sport of their bodies.* [b] *its waters.*

marks[a] of all the secret things in thc book of my great grandfather Enoch, and in the parables which had been given to him; inserting them for me among the words of the book of parables.

2. At that time holy Michael answered and said to Raphael; The power of the spirit hurries me away, and impels me on[b]. The severity of the judgment, of the secret judgment of the angels, who is capable *of beholding*; the endurance of that severe judgment which has taken place and been made permanent; without being melted at the sight of it[c]? Again holy Michael answered and said to holy Raphael; Who is there whose heart is not softened by it, and whose reins are not troubled at this thing?

3. Judgment has gone forth against them by those who have thus dragged them away; and that was, when they stood in the presence of the Lord of spirits.

4. In like manner also holy Rakael said to Raphael; They shall not be before the eye of the Lord; since the Lord of spirits has been offended with them; for like Lords[d] have they conducted themselves. Therefore will He bring upon them a secret judgment for ever and ever.

5. For neither shall angel nor man receive a por-

[a] *the signs.* [b] *irritates* or *excites me.* [c] *and not be melted in the presence of it.* [d] በአምሳለ፡ እግዚእ፡ *instar Domini. In the similitude of,* or, *as the Lord.*

tion of it; but they alone shall receive their own judgment for ever and ever.

CHAP. LXVIII.

1. After this judgment they shall be astonished and irritated; for it shall be exhibited to the inhabitants of the earth.

2. Behold the names of those angels. These are their names. The first of them is Samyaza; the second, Arstikapha; the third, Armen; the fourth, Kakabael; the fifth, Turel; the sixth, Rumyel; the seventh, Danyal; the eighth, Kael; the ninth, Barakel; the tenth, Azazel; the eleventh, Armers; the twelfth, Bataryal; the thirteenth, Basasael; the fourteenth, Ananel; the fifteenth, Turyal; the sixteenth, Simapiseel; the seventeenth, Yetarel; the eighteenth, Tumael; the nineteenth, Tarel; the twentieth, Rumel; the twenty-first, Azazel.

3. These are the chiefs of their angels, and the names of the leaders of their hundreds, and the leaders of their fifties, and the leaders of their tens.

4. The name of the first is Yekun: he it was who seduced all the sons of the holy angels; and causing them to descend on earth, led astray the offspring of men.

5. The name of the second is Kesabel, who pointed out evil counsel to the sons of the holy angels, and induced them to corrupt their bodies by generating mankind.

6. The name of the third is Gadrel: he dis-

covered every stroke of death to the children of men.

7. He seduced Eve; and discovered to the children of men the instruments of death, the coat of mail, the shield, and the sword for slaughter; every instrument of death to the children of men.

8. From his hand were *these things* derived to them who dwell upon earth, from that period for ever.

9. The name of the fourth is Penemue: he discovered to the children of men bitterness and sweetness;

10. And pointed out to them every secret of their wisdom.

11. He taught men to understand writing, and *the use of* ink and paper.

12. Therefore numerous have been those who have gone astray from every period of the world, even to this day.

13. For men were not born for this, thus with pen and with ink to confirm their faith;

14. Since they were not created, except that, like the angels, they might remain righteous and pure.

15. Nor would death, which destroys every thing, have affected them;

16. But by this their knowledge they perish, and by this also *its* power consumes[a] *them*.

17. The name of the fifth is Kasyade: he dis-

[a] *eats, feeds upon, devours.*

covered to the children of men every wicked stroke of spirits and of demons:

18. The stroke of the embryo in the womb, to diminish *it;* the stroke of the spirit *by* the bite of the serpent, and the stroke which is *given* in the midday *by* the offspring of the serpent, the name of which is Tabaet[a].

19. This is the number of the Kesbel[b]; the principal part of the oath which the Most High, dwelling in glory, revealed to the holy ones.

20. Its name is Beka[c]. He spoke to holy Michael to discover to them the secret name, that they might understand that secret name, and thus remember the oath; and that those who pointed out every secret thing to the children of men might tremble at that name and oath.

21. This is the power of that oath; for powerful it is, and strong.

22. And He established this oath of Akae[d] by the instrumentality[e] of the holy Michael.

23. These are the secrets of this oath, and by it were they confirmed.

24. Heaven was suspended *by it* before the world was made, for ever.

25. By it has the earth been founded upon the flood; while from the concealed parts of the hills the agitated waters proceed forth from the creation to the end of the world.

[a] ተበዐት: *male.* [b] ክስ-በእል: [c] ቤቃ: [d] አከዐ:
[e] *by the hands.*

26. By this oath the sea has been formed, and the foundation of it.

27. During the period of *its* fury He has established the sand against it, which continues unchanged for ever; and by this oath the abyss has been made strong; nor is it removeable from its station for ever and ever.

28. By this oath the sun and moon complete their progress, never swerving from the command *given* to them for ever and ever.

29. By this oath the stars complete their progress;

30. And when their names are called, they return an answer, for ever and ever.

31. Thus *in* the heavens *take place* the blowings of the winds: all of them have breathings [a], and *effect* a complete combination of breathings.

32. There the treasures of thunder are kept, and the splendor of the lightning.

33. There are kept the treasures of hail and of frost, the treasures of snow, the treasures of rain and of dew.

34. All these confess and laud before the Lord of spirits.

35. They glorify with all their power of praise; and He sustains them in all that *act of* thanksgiving, while they laud, glorify, and exalt the name of the Lord of spirits for ever and ever.

36. And with them He establishes this oath, by

[a] or *spirits*.

which they and their paths are preserved; nor does their progress perish.

37. Great was their joy.

38. They blessed, glorified, and exalted, because the name of the Son of man was revealed to them.

39. He sat upon the throne of his glory; and the principal part of the judgment was assigned to Him, the Son of man. Sinners shall disappear and perish from the face of the earth, while those who seduced them shall be bound with chains for ever.

40. According to their ranks of corruption shall they be imprisoned, and all their works shall disappear from the face of the earth; nor thenceforward shall there be any to corrupt; for the Son of man has been seen, sitting on the throne of his glory.

41. Every thing wicked shall disappear, and depart from before his face; and the word of the Son of man shall become powerful in the presence of the Lord of spirits.

42. This is the third parable of Enoch.

CHAP. LXIX. [SECT. XII.[a]]

1. After this the name of the Son of man, living with the Lord of spirits[b], was exalted by the inhabitants of the earth.

2. It was exalted in the chariots of the Spirit; and the name went forth in the midst of them.

[a] Paris MS. [b] *the name of Him living with Him, of this Son of man, living with the Lord of spirits.*

3. From that time I was not drawn in the midst of them; but He seated me between two spirits, between the north and the west, where the angels received their ropes, to measure out a place[a] for the elect and the righteous.

4. There I beheld the fathers of the first men, and the saints, who dwell in that place for ever.

CHAP. LXX.

1. Afterwards my spirit was concealed, ascending into the heavens. I beheld the sons of the holy angels treading on flaming fire, whose garments and robes were white, and whose countenances were transparent as crystal.

2. I saw two rivers of fire glittering like the hyacinth.

3. Then I fell on my face before the Lord of spirits.

4. And Michael, one of the archangels, took me by my right hand, raised me up, and brought me out *to* where *was* every secret *of* mercy and secret *of* righteousness.

5. He shewed me all the hidden things of the extremities of heaven, all the receptacles of the stars, and the splendors of all, from whence they went forth before the face of the holy.

6. And he concealed the spirit of Enoch in the heaven of heavens.

[a] *to measure me a place.*

7. There I beheld, in the midst of that light, a building raised with stones of ice[a];

8. And in the midst of these stones vibrations[b] of living fire. My spirit saw around the circle of[c] this flaming habitation, on one of its extremities, *that there were* rivers full of living fire, which encompassed it.

9. Then the Seraphim, the Cherubim, and Ophanin surrounded *it:* these are those who never sleep, but watch the throne of his glory.

10. And I beheld angels innumerable, thousands of thousands, and myriads of myriads, who surrounded that habitation.

11. Michael, Raphael, Gabriel, Phanuel, and the holy angels who were in the heavens above, went in and out of it. Michael, Raphael, and Gabriel went out of that habitation, and holy angels innumerable.

12. With them *was* the Ancient of days, whose head *was* white as wool, and pure, and his robe *was* indescribable.

13. Then I fell upon my face, while all my flesh was dissolved, and my spirit became changed.

14. I cried out with a loud voice, with a powerful spirit, blessing, glorifying, and exalting.

15. And those blessings, which proceeded from my mouth, became acceptable in the presence of the Ancient of days.

16. The Ancient of days came with Michael and

[a] *that in it* there was *that which was built with stones of ice.*
[b] *tongues.* [c] *around that which encompassed.*

Gabriel, Raphael and Phanuel, with thousands of thousands, and myriads of myriads, which could not be numbered.

17. Then that angel came to me, and with his voice saluted me, saying; Thou art the offspring of man, who art born for righteousness, and righteousness has rested on thee.

18. The righteousness of the Ancient of days shall not forsake thee.

19. He said; On thee shall He confer peace[a] in the name of the existing world; for from thence has peace gone forth since the world was created.

20. And thus shall it happen to thee for ever and ever.

21. All who shall exist, and who shall walk in thy path of righteousness, shall not forsake thee for ever.

22. With thee shall be their habitations, with thee their lot; nor from thee shall they be separated for ever and ever.

23. And thus shall length of days be with the offspring of man.

24. Peace shall be to the righteous; and the path of integrity shall the righteous pursue[b], in the name of the Lord of spirits, for ever and ever.

CHAP. LXXI. [SECT. XIII.[c]]

1. The book of the revolutions of the luminaries of heaven, according to their respective classes, their

[a] *He shall call to thee peace.* [b] *his upright path* shall be *to the righteous.* [c] Paris MS.

respective powers, their respective periods, their respective names, the places where they commence their progress[a], and their respective months, which Uriel, the holy angel who was with me, explained to me; he who conducts them. The whole account of them, according to every year of the world for ever, until a new work shall be effected, which will be eternal.

2. This is the first law of the luminaries. The sun *and* the light arrive at the gates of heaven, which are on the east, and on the west of it at the western gates of heaven.

3. I beheld the gates whence the sun goes forth; and the gates where the sun sets;

4. In which gates also the moon rises and sets; and *I beheld* the conductors of the stars, among those who precede them; six *gates were* at the rising, and six at the setting of the sun.

5. All these respectively, one after another, are on a level; and numerous windows are on the right and on the left sides of those gates.

6. First proceeds forth that great luminary, which is called the sun; the orb of which is as the orb of heaven, the whole of it being replete with splendid and flaming fire.

7. Its chariot, where it ascends, the wind blows.

8. The sun sets in heaven, and, returning by the north, to proceed towards the east, is conducted so

[a] *the places of their nativity.*

as to enter by that gate, and illuminate the face of heaven.

9. In the same manner it goes forth in the first month by a great gate.

10. It goes forth through the fourth of those six gates, which are at the rising of the sun.

11. And in the fourth gate, through which the sun with the moon proceeds, in the first part of it, there are twelve open windows; from which issues out a flame, when they are opened at their proper periods.

12. When the sun rises in heaven, it goes forth through this fourth gate thirty days, and by the fourth gate in the west of heaven on a level with it descends.

13. During that period the day is lengthened from the day, and the night curtailed from the night for thirty days. And then the day is longer by two parts than the night.

14. The day is precisely ten parts, and the night is eight.

15. The sun goes forth through this fourth gate, and sets in it, and turns to the fifth gate during thirty days; after which it proceeds from, and sets in, the fifth gate.

16. Then the day becomes lengthened by a second portion, so that it is eleven parts; while the night becomes shortened, and is only seven parts.

17. The sun *now* returns to the east, entering

[a] *And he.*

into the sixth gate, and rising and setting in the sixth gate thirty-one days, on account of its signs.

18. At that period the day is longer than the night, being twice *as long as* the night; and becomes twelve parts;

19. But the night is shortened, and becomes six parts. Then the sun rises up, that the day may be shortened, and the night lengthened.

20. And the sun returns towards the east, entering into the sixth gate, where it rises and sets for thirty days.

21. When that period is completed, the day becomes shortened precisely one part, so that it is eleven parts, while the night is seven parts.

22. Then the sun goes from the west, from that sixth gate, and proceeds eastwards, rising in the fifth gate for thirty days, and setting again westwards in the fifth gate of the west.

23. At that period the day becomes shortened two parts; and is ten parts, while the night is eight parts.

24. Then the sun goes from the fifth gate, as it sets in the fifth gate of the west; and rises in the fourth gate for thirty-one days, on account of its signs, setting in the west.

25. At that period the day is made equal with the night; and, being equal with it, the night becomes nine parts, and the day nine parts.

26. Then the sun goes from that gate, as it sets in the west; and returning to the east proceeds by

the third gate for thirty days, setting in the west at the third gate.

27. At that period the night is lengthened from the day during thirty mornings, and the day is curtailed from the day during thirty days; the night being ten parts precisely, and the day eight parts.

28. The sun now goes from the third gate, as it sets in the third gate in the west; but returning to the east, it proceeds by the second gate of the east for thirty days.

29. In like manner also it sets in the second gate in the west of heaven.

30. At that period the night is eleven parts, and the day seven parts.

31. Then the sun goes at that time from the second gate, as it sets in the second gate in the west; but returns to the east, *proceeding* by the first gate, for thirty-one days.

32. And sets in the west in the first[a] gate.

33. At that period the night is lengthened as much again as the day.

34. It is twelve[b] parts precisely, while the day is six parts.

35. The sun has *thus* completed its beginnings, and a second time goes round from these beginnings.

36. Into that gate it enters for thirty days, and sets in the west, in the opposite part *of heaven.*

[a] *second*. A manifest error. The Paris MS. is correct. [b] *eleven*. A mistake of the transcriber. In the Paris MS. it is *twelve*.

37. At that period the night is contracted in its length a fourth part, that is, one portion, and becomes eleven parts.

38. The day is seven parts.

39. Then the sun returns, and enters into the second gate of the east.

40. It returns by these beginnings thirty days, rising and setting.

41. At that period the night is contracted in its length. It becomes ten [a] parts, and the day eight parts. Then the sun goes from that second gate, and sets in the west; but returns to the east, and rises in the east, in the third gate, thirty-one days, setting in the west of heaven.

42. At that period the night becomes shortened. It is nine parts. And the night is equal with the day. The year is precisely three hundred and sixty-four days.

43. The lengthening of the day and night, and the contraction of the day and night, are made to differ from each other by the progress of the sun.

44. By means of this progress the day is daily lengthened, and the night nightly shortened [b].

45. This is the law and progress of the sun, and its turning when it turns back, turning during sixty days [c], and going forth. This is the great everlasting luminary, that which He names the sun for ever and ever.

[a] *seven.* Another error. [b] *approaches.* [c] that is, it is sixty days in the same gates.

46. This also is that which goes forth a great luminary, and which is named after its peculiar kind, as God commanded.

47. And thus it goes in and out, neither slackening nor resting; but running on in its chariot by day and by night. It shines with a seventh portion of light from the moon; but the dimensions of both are equal.

CHAP. LXXII. [SECT. XIV.[a]]

1. After this law I beheld another law of an inferior luminary, the name of which is the moon, and the orb of which is as the orb of heaven.

2. Its chariot, *which* it secretly ascends, the wind blows; and light is given to it by measure.

3. Every month at its exit and entrance it becomes changed; and its periods are as the periods of the sun. And when in like manner its light is to exist, its light is a seventh portion from the light of the sun.

4. Thus it rises, and at its commencement towards the east goes forth for thirty days.

5. At that time it appears, and becomes to you the beginning of the month. Thirty days *it is* with the sun in the gate from which the sun goes forth.

6. Half of it is in extent seven portions, one *half;* and the whole of its orb is void of light, except a seventh portion out of the fourteen portions of its light. And in a day it receives a seventh por-

[a] Paris MS.

tion, or half *that portion*, of its light. Its light is by sevens, by one portion, and by the half *of a portion*. It sets with the sun.

7. And when the sun rises, the moon rises with it; receiving a half portion of light.

8. On that night, when it commences its period[a], previously to the day of the month, the moon sets with the sun.

9. And on that night it is dark *in* its fourteen portions, that is, *in each* half; but it rises on that day with one seventh portion precisely, and in its progress declines from the rising of the sun.

10. During the remainder of its period[b] its light increases to fourteen portions.

CHAP. LXXIII.

1. Then I saw another progress and regulation which He effected in the law of the moon[c]. The progress of the moons, and every thing *relating to them*, Uriel shewed me, the holy angel who conducted them all.

2. Their stations I wrote down as he shewed them to me.

3. I wrote down their months, as they occur, and the appearance of their light, until it is completed in fifteen days.

4. In each of its two seven portions it completes all its light at rising and at setting.

[a] *at the beginning of its morning*, or *day*. [b] *of its day*.
[c] *in that law*.

5. On stated months it changes *its* settings; and on stated months it makes its progress *through* each *gate*. In two *gates* the moon sets with the sun, *viz.* in those two gates which are in the midst, in the third and fourth gate. *From the third gate* it goes forth for seven days, and makes its circuit.

6. Again it returns to the gate whence the sun goes forth, and in that completes the whole of its light. Then it declines from the sun, and enters in eight days into the sixth gate, *and returns in seven days to the third gate*, from which the sun goes forth.

7. When the sun proceeds from the fourth gate, the *moon* goes forth for seven days, until it passes from the fifth *gate*.

8. Again it returns in seven days to the fourth gate, and completing all its light, declines, and passes on by the first gate in eight days;

9. And returns in seven days to the fourth gate, from which the sun goes forth.

10. Thus I beheld their stations, as according to the fixed order of the months the sun rises and sets.

11. At those times there is an excess of thirty days belonging to the sun in five years; all the days belonging to each year of the five years, when completed, amount to three hundred and sixty-four days; and to the sun and stars belong six days; six days in each of the five years; *thus* thirty days belong to them;

12. So that the moon has thirty days less than the sun and stars.

13. The moon brings on all the years exactly, that their stations may come neither too forwards nor too backwards a single day; but that the years may be changed with correct precision in three hundred and sixty-four days. In three years the days are one thousand and ninety-two; in five years they are one thousand eight hundred and twenty; and in eight years two thousand nine hundred and twelve days.

14. To the moon alone belong in three years one thousand and sixty-two days; in five years it has fifty days less *than the sun*, for an addition being made to the *one thousand and* sixty-two days, in five years there are one thousand seven hundred and seventy days; and the days of the moon in eight years are two thousand eight hundred and thirty-two days.

15. For its days in eight years are less *than those of the sun by* eighty days, which eighty days are its diminution in eight years.

16. The year then becomes truly complete according to the station of the moons, and the station of the sun; which rise in the *different* gates; which rise and set in them for thirty days.

CHAP. LXXIV.

1. *These are* the leaders of the chiefs of the thousands, *those* which *preside* over all creation,

and over all the stars; with the four *days* which are added and never separated from the place allotted them, according to the complete computation of the year.

2. And these serve four days, which are not computed in the computation of the year.

3. Respecting them, men greatly err; for these luminaries truly serve, in the mansion of the world, one *day* in the first gate, one in the third gate, one in the fourth, and one in the sixth gate.

4. And the harmony of the world becomes complete every three hundred and sixty-fourth state of it. For the signs,

5. The seasons,

6. The years,

7. And the days, Uriel shewed me; the angel whom the Lord of glory appointed over all the luminaries

8. Of heaven in heaven, and in the world; that they might rule in the face of the sky, and, appearing over the earth, become

9. Conductors of the days and nights; the sun, the moon, the stars, and all the ministers of heaven, which make their circuit with all the chariots of heaven.

10. Thus Uriel shewed me twelve gates open for the circuit of the chariots of the sun in heaven, from which the rays of the sun shoot forth.

11. From these proceed heat over the earth, when they are opened in their stated seasons. They are

for the winds, and the spirit of the dew, when in their seasons they are opened; opened in heaven at *its* extremities.

12. Twelve gates I beheld in heaven, at the extremities of the earth, through which the sun, moon, and stars, and all the works of heaven, proceed at their rising and setting.

13. Many windows also are open on the right and on the left.

14. One window at a *certain* season grows extremely hot. So also are there gates from which the stars go forth as they are commanded, and in which they set according to their number.

15. I saw likewise the chariots of heaven, running in the world above to those gates in which the stars turn, which never set. One of these is greater than all, which goes round the whole world.

CHAP. LXXV. [SECT. XV.[a]]

1. And at the extremities of the earth I beheld twelve gates open for all the winds, from which they proceed and blow over the earth.

2. Three of them are open in the front of heaven, three in the west, three on the right side of heaven, and three on the left. The first three are those which are towards the east, three are towards the north, three behind those which are upon the left, towards the south, and three on the west.

3. From four of them proceed winds of blessing,

[a] Paris MS.

and of health; and from eight proceed winds of punishment; when they are sent to destroy the earth, and the heaven above it, all its inhabitants, and all which are in the waters, or on dry land.

4. The first of these winds proceeds from the gate termed the eastern, through the first gate on the east, which inclines southwards. From this goes forth destruction, drought, heat, and perdition.

5. From the second gate, the middle one, proceeds equity. There issue from it rain, fruitfulness, health, and dew; and from the third gate northwards proceed cold and drought.

6. After these proceed the south winds through three principal gates; through their first gate, which inclines eastwards, proceeds a hot wind.

7. But from the middle gate proceed grateful odour, dew, rain, health, and life.

8. From the third gate, which is westwards, proceed dew, rain, blight, and destruction.

9. After these are the winds to the north, which is called the sea. *They proceed* from three gates. The first [a] gate *is that* which is on the east, inclining southwards; from this proceed dew, rain, blight, and destruction. From the middle direct gate proceed rain, dew, life, and health. And from the third gate, which is westwards, inclining towards the south [b], proceed mist, frost, snow, rain, dew, and blight.

[a] *seventh.* Perhaps the seventh which had been enumerated.
[b] *the north.* An error in both MSS.

10. After these *in the* fourth *quarter* are the winds to the west. From the first gate, inclining northwards, proceed dew, rain, frost, cold, snow, and chill; from the middle gate proceed rain, health, and blessing;

11. And from the last gate, which is southwards, proceed drought, destruction, scorching, and perdition.

12. The *account of the* twelve gates of the four quarters of heaven is ended.

13. All their laws, all their *infliction* of punishment, and the health *produced* by them, have I explained to thee, my son Mathusala.

CHAP. LXXVI.

1. The first wind is called the eastern, because it is the first.

2. The second is called the south, because the Most High there descends, and frequently there descends *He who* is blessed for ever.

3. The western wind has the name of diminution, because there all the luminaries of heaven are diminished, and descend.

4. The fourth wind, which is named the north, is divided into three parts; one of which is for the habitation of man; another for seas of water, with valleys, woods, rivers, shady places, and snow; and the third part *contains* paradise.

5. Seven high mountains I beheld, higher than all the mountains of the earth, from which frost

proceeds; while days, seasons, and years, depart and pass away.

6. Seven rivers I beheld upon earth, greater than all rivers, one of which takes its course from the west; into a great sea its water flows.

7. Two come from the north to the sea, their waters flowing into the Erythræan sea, on the east. And with respect to the remainder, four take their course in the cavity of the north, *two* to their sea, the Erythræan sea, and two are poured into a great sea, where also it is said *there is* a desert.

8. Seven great islands I saw in the sea and on the earth. Seven in the great sea.

CHAP. LXXVII.

1. The names of the sun are these: one Aryares[a], the other Tomas[b].

2. The moon has four names. The first is Asonya[c]; the second, Ebla[d]; the third, Benase[e]; and the fourth, Erae[f].

3. These are the two great luminaries, whose orbs are as the orbs of heaven; and the dimensions of both are equal.

4. In the orb of the sun *there is* a seventh portion of light, which is added to it from the moon. By measure it is put in, until a seventh portion of *the light of* the sun is departed. They set, enter

[a] ኦርያሬስ፡ [b] ቶማስ፡ [c] አሶንያ፡ [d] ዕቡላ፡
[e] ቡናሴ፡ [f] ኤሩዕ፡

into the western gate, circuit by the north, and through the eastern gate go forth over the face of heaven.

5. When the moon rises, it appears in heaven; and the half of a seventh portion of light is all *which is* in it.

6. In fourteen *days* the whole of its light is completed.

7. *By* three quintuples light is put into it, until *in* fifteen *days* its light is completed, according to the signs of the year; it has three quintuples.

8. The moon has the half of a seventh portion.

9. During its diminution on the first day its light decreases a fourteenth part; on the second day it decreases a thirteenth part; on the third day a twelfth part; on the fourth day an eleventh part; on the fifth day a tenth part; on the sixth day a ninth part; on the seventh day it decreases an eighth part; on the eighth day it decreases a seventh part; on the ninth day it decreases a sixth part; on the tenth day it decreases a fifth part; on the eleventh day it decreases a fourth part; on the twelfth day it decreases a third part; on the thirteenth day it decreases a second part; on the fourteenth day it decreases a half of its seventh part; and on the fifteenth day the whole remainder of its light is consumed.

10. On stated months the moon has twenty-nine days.

11. It also has a period of twenty-eight days.

12. Uriel likewise shewed me another regulation, when light is poured into the moon, how it is poured into it from the sun.

13. All the time that the moon is in progress with its light, it is poured *into it* in the presence of the sun, until *its* light is in fourteen days completed in heaven.

14. And when it is wholly extinguished, its light is consumed in heaven; and on the first day it is called the new moon, for on that day light is received into it.

15. It becomes precisely completed on the day that the sun descends into the west, while the moon ascends at night from the east.

16. The moon then shines all the night, until the sun rises before it; when the moon disappears in turn before the sun.

17. Where light comes to the moon, there again it decreases, until all its light is extinguished, and the days of the moon pass away.

18. Then its orb remains solitary without light.

19. During three months it effects in thirty days *each month* its period; and during three *more* months it effects it in twenty-nine days each. *These are the times* in which it effects its decrease in its first period, and in the first gate, *namely*, in one hundred and seventy-seven days.

20. And at the time of its going forth during three months it appears thirty days each, and during three *more* months it appears twenty-nine days each.

21. In the night it appears for each twenty *days* as *the face of* a man, and in the day as heaven; for it is nothing else except its light.

CHAP. LXXVIII.

1. And now, my son Mathusala, I have shewn thee every thing; and *the account of* every ordinance of the stars of heaven is finished.

2. He shewed me every ordinance respecting these, which *takes place* at all times and in all seasons under every influence, in all years, at the arrival and under the rule of each, during every month and every week. *He shewed me* also the decrease of the moon, which is effected in the sixth gate; for in that sixth gate is its light consumed.

3. From this is the beginning of the month; and its decrease is effected in the sixth gate in its period, until a hundred and seventy-seven days are completed; according to the mode of computation by weeks[a], twenty-five *weeks* and two days.

4. *Its period* is less than that of the sun, according to the ordinance of the stars, by five days in one half year[b] precisely,

5. When that *their* visible situation is completed. Such is the appearance and likeness of every luminary, which Uriel, the great angel who conducts them, shewed to me.

[a] *according to the ordinance of the week.* [b] *in one time.*

CHAP. LXXIX.

1. In those days Uriel answered and said to me; Behold, I have shewed thee all things, O Enoch;

2. And all things have I revealed to thee. Thou seest the sun, the moon, and those which conduct the stars of heaven, which cause all their operations, seasons, and arrivals to return.

3. In the days of sinners the years shall be shortened.

4. Their seed shall be backward in their prolific soil; and every thing done on earth shall be subverted, and disappear in its season. The rain shall be restrained, and heaven shall stand still.

5. In those days the fruits of the earth shall be late, and not flourish in their season; and in their season the fruits of the trees shall be withholden.

6. The moon shall change its laws, and not be seen at its proper period. But in those days shall heaven be seen; and barrenness shall take place in the borders of the great chariots in the west. *Heaven* shall shine more than *when illuminated by* the orders of light; while many chiefs among the stars of authority shall err, perverting their ways and works.

7. Those shall not appear in their season, who command them, and all the classes of the stars shall be shut up against sinners.

8. The thoughts of those who dwell on earth

shall transgress within them; and they shall be perverted in all their ways.

9. They shall transgress, and think themselves gods; while evil shall be multiplied among them.

10. And punishment shall come upon them, so that all of them shall be destroyed.

CHAP. LXXX.

1. He said; O Enoch, look on the book which heaven has gradually dropped down [a]; and, reading that which is written in it, understand every part of it.

2. Then I looked on all which was written, and understood all, reading the book and every thing written in it, all the works of man;

3. And of all the children of flesh upon earth, during the generations of the world.

4. Immediately after I blessed the Lord, the King of glory, who has thus for ever formed the whole workmanship of the world.

5. And I glorified the Lord, on account of his long-suffering and blessing towards the children of the world.

6. At that time I said; Blessed is the man, who shall die righteous and good, against whom no catalogue of crime has been written, and with whom iniquity is not found.

7. Then those three holy ones caused me to ap-

[a] *has distilled.*

proach, and placed me on the earth, before the door of my house.

8. And they said unto me; Explain every thing to Mathusala thy son; and inform all thy children, that no flesh shall be justified before the Lord; for He is their Creator.

9. During one year we will leave thee with thy children, until thou shalt again recover thy strength, that thou mayest instruct thy family, write these things, and explain them to all thy children. But in another year they shall take thee from the midst of them, and thy heart shall be strengthened; for the elect shall point out righteousness to the elect; the righteous with the righteous shall rejoice, congratulating each other; but sinners with sinners shall die,

10. And the perverted with the perverted shall be drowned.

11. Those likewise who act righteously shall die on account of the works of man, and shall be gathered together on account of the works of the wicked.

12. In those days they finished conversing with me.

13. And I returned to my fellow men, blessing the Lord of worlds.

CHAP. LXXXI.

1. Now, my son Mathusala, all these things I speak unto thee, and write for thee. To thee I

have revealed all, and have given thee books of every thing.

2. Preserve, my son Mathusala, the books written by thy father[a]; that thou mayest transmit them to future generations.

3. Wisdom have I given to thee, to thy children, and thy posterity, that they may transmit to their children, for generations for ever, this wisdom in their thoughts; and that those who comprehend *it* may not slumber, but hear with their ears; that they may learn this wisdom, and be deemed worthy of eating *this* wholesome food.

4. Blessed are all the righteous; blessed all who walk in *the paths of* righteousness; in whom no crime *is found*, as in sinners, when all their days are numbered.

5. With respect to the progress of the sun in heaven, it enters and goes out of *each* gate for thirty days, with the leaders of the thousand classes of the stars; with four which are added, and appertain to the four quarters of the year, which conduct them, and accompany them at four periods.

6. Respecting these, men greatly err, and do not compute them in the computation of every age; for they greatly err respecting them; nor do men know accurately that they are in the computation of the year. But indeed these are marked down[b] for ever;

[a] *the books of the hand of thy father.*

[b] ልኩዓን፡ from ለከዐ፡ *to impress, express,* or *to seal.*

one in the first gate, one in the third, one in the fourth, and one in the sixth:

7. So that the year is completed in three hundred and sixty-four days.

8. Truly has been stated[a], and accurately has been computed that which is marked down; for the luminaries, the months, the fixed periods, the years, and the days, Uriel has explained to me, and communicated to me[b]; whom the Lord of all creation, on my account, commanded (according to the might of heaven, and the power which it possesses both by night and by day) to explain *the laws of* light to man, of the sun, moon, and stars, and of all the powers of heaven, which are turned with their respective orbs.

9. This is the ordinance of the stars, which set in their places, in their seasons, in their periods, in their days, and in their months.

10. These are the names of those who conduct them, who watch and enter in their seasons, according to their ordinance in their periods, in their months, in *the times of* their influence, and in their stations.

11. Four conductors of them first enter, who separate the four quarters of the year. After these, twelve conductors of their classes, who separate the months and the year *into* three hundred and sixty-four *days*, with the leaders of a thousand, who dis-

[a] *have they related.* [b] *has breathed into me.*

tinguish between the days, as well as between the four additional ones; which, *as* conductors, divide the four quarters of the year.

12. These leaders of a thousand are in the midst of the conductors, and the conductors are added each behind his station, and their conductors make the separation. These are the names of the conductors, who separate the four quarters of the year, who are appointed *over them;* Melkel, Helammelak,

13. Meliyal, and Narel[a].

14. And the names of those who conduct them are Adnarel, Jyasusal, and Jyelumeal[b].

15. These are the three who follow after the conductors of the classes *of stars;* each following after the three conductors of the classes, which themselves follow after those conductors of the stations, who divide the four quarters of the year.

16. In the first part of the year rises and rules Melkyas[c], who is named Tamani[d], and Zahay[e].

17. All the days of his influence, *during* which he rules, are ninety-one days.

18. And these are the signs of the days which are seen upon earth. In the days of his influence *there is* perspiration, heat, and trouble. All the trees become fruitful; the leaf of every tree comes forth; the corn is reaped; the rose and every species

[a] ምልክል: ህልአምሜለክ: ሜልኢየለ: ናሬል: [b] አድናርኤል: ሊየሱሳል: ኢይሉሜአል: [c] ምልክያስ: [d] ተመዓኒ: [e] ፀሐይ: *the sun.*

of flowers blossoms in the field; and the trees of winter are dried up.

19. These are the names of the conductors who are under them, Barkel, Zelsabel[a]; and another additional conductor of a thousand is named Heloyalef[b], the days of whose influence have been completed. The other conductor next after them *is* Helemmelek[c], whose name they call the splendid Zahay[d].

20. All the days of his light are ninety-one days.

21. These are the signs of the days upon earth, heat and drought; while the trees bring forth their fruits, warmed and concocted, and give their fruits to dry.

22. The flocks follow and yean. All the fruits of the earth are collected, with every thing in the fields, and the vines are trodden. This takes place during the time of his influence.

23. These are their names and orders, and *the names* of the conductors who are under them, of those who are chiefs of a thousand, Gedaeyal, Keel, Heel[e].

24. And the name of the additional leader of a thousand is Asphael[f].

25. The days of his influence have been completed.

[a] በርክኤል፡ ዜልሱብል፡ [b] ሄሎያሌፍ፡ [c] ህልእመሜሌክ፡ [d] ፀሐየ፡ *the sun.* [e] ጌደኤያል፡ ኬኤል፡ ሄኤል፡ [f] አስፋኤል፡

CHAP. LXXXII. [SECT. XVI.[a]]

1. And now I have shewn thee, my son Mathusala, every sight which I saw prior to thy birth[b]. I will relate another vision, which I saw before I was married; they resemble each other.

2. The first was when I was learning a book; and the other before I was married to thy mother. I saw a potent vision;

3. And on account of these things besought the Lord.

4. I was lying down in the house of my grandfather Malalel, *when* I saw in a vision heaven purifying, and snatched away.

5. And falling to the earth, I saw likewise the earth absorbed by a great abyss; and mountains suspended over mountains.

6. Hills were sinking upon hills, lofty trees were gliding[c] off from their trunks, and were in the act of being projected, and of sinking into the abyss.

7. *Being alarmed* at these things, my voice faltered[d]. I cried out and said; The earth is destroyed. Then my grandfather Malalel raised me up, and said to me; Why dost thou thus cry out, my son? and wherefore dost thou thus lament?

8. I related to him the whole vision which I had seen. He said to me; Confirmed is that which thou hast seen, my son;

[a] Paris MS. [b] *before thee.* [c] *cutting.* [d] *the word fell down in my mouth.*

9. And potent the vision of thy dream respecting every secret sin of the earth. Its substance shall sink into the abyss, and a great destruction take place.

10. Now, my son, rise up; and beseech the Lord of glory, (for thou art faithful,) that a remnant may be left upon earth, and that He would not wholly destroy it. My son, all this *calamity* upon earth comes down from heaven[a]; upon earth shall there be a great destruction.

11. Then I arose, prayed, and entreated; and wrote down my prayer for the generations of the world, explaining every thing to my son Mathusala.

12. When I went out below, and looking up to heaven beheld the sun proceeding from the east, the moon descending to the west, a few *scattered* stars, and every thing which God[b] has known from the beginning, I blessed the Lord of judgment, and magnified Him; because He has sent forth the sun from the chambers[c] of the east; that, ascending and rising in the face of heaven, it might spring up, and pursue the path which has been pointed out to it.

CHAP. LXXXIII.

1. I lifted up my hands in righteousness, and blessed the holy and the great One. I spoke with the breath of my mouth, and with a tongue of flesh, which God has formed for all the sons of mortal

[a] *all this upon earth is from heaven.* [b] *he.* [c] *windows.*

men, that with it they may speak; giving them breath, a mouth, and a tongue to converse with.

2. Blessed art Thou, O Lord, the King, great and powerful in thy greatness, Lord of all the creatures of heaven, King of kings, God of the whole world, whose reign, whose kingdom, and whose majesty endure for ever and ever.

3. From generation to generation shall thy dominion *exist*. All the heavens are thy throne for ever, and all the earth thy footstool for ever and for ever.

4. For Thou hast made *them*, and over all Thou reignest. No act whatsoever exceeds thy power. With thee wisdom is unchangeable; nor from thy throne and from thy presence is it ever averted. Thou knowest all things, seest and hearest them; nor is any thing concealed from thee; for Thou perceivest all things.

5. The angels of thy heavens have transgressed; and on mortal flesh shall thy wrath remain[a], until the day of the great judgment.

6. Now then, O God, Lord and mighty King, I entreat thee, and beseech thee to grant my prayer, that a posterity may be left to me on earth, and that the whole human race may not perish;

7. That the earth may not be left destitute, and destruction take place for ever.

8. O my Lord, let the race perish from off the earth which has offended thee, but a righteous

[a] *be.*

and upright race establish for a posterity[a] for ever. Hide not thy face, O Lord, from the prayer of thy servant.

CHAP. LXXXIV. [SECT. XVII.[b]]

1. After this I saw another dream, and explained it all to thee, my son. Enoch arose and said to his son Mathusala; To thee, my son, will I speak. Hear my word; and incline thine ear to the visionary dream of thy father. Before I married thy mother Edna, I saw a vision on my bed;

2. And behold, a cow sprung forth from the earth;

3. And this cow was white.

4. Afterwards a female heifer sprung forth; and with it another heifer[c]: one of them was black, and one was red[d].

5. The black heifer then struck the red one, and pursued it over the earth.

6. From that period I could see nothing more of the red heifer; but the black one increased in bulk, and a female heifer came with him.

7. After this I saw that many cows proceeded forth, resembling him, and following after him.

8. The first female young one also went out in the presence of the first cow; and sought the red heifer; but found him not.

[a] *the plant of a seed.* [b] Paris MS. [c] The sense seems to require that the passage should be, "*two other heifers.*"
[d] Cain and Abel.

9. And she lamented with a great lamentation, while she was seeking him.

10. Then I looked until that first *cow* came to her, from which time she became silent, and ceased to lament.

11. Afterwards she calved another white cow.

12. And again calved many cows and black heifers.

13. In my sleep also I perceived a white bull, which in like manner grew, and became a large white bull.

14. After him many white cows came forth, resembling him.

15. And they began to calve many *other* white cows, which resembled them and followed each other.

CHAP. LXXXV.

1. Again I looked attentively[a], while sleeping, and surveyed heaven above.

2. And behold a single star fell from heaven.

3. Which being raised up, ate and fed among those cows.

4. After that, I perceived *other* large and black cows; and behold all of them changed their stalls and pastures, while their young began to lament one with another. Again I looked in *my* vision, and surveyed heaven; when behold I saw many stars which descended, and projected themselves from heaven to where the first star was,

[a] *with my eyes.*

5. Into the midst of those young ones; while the cows were with them, feeding in the midst of them.

6. I looked at and observed them; when behold, they all protruded their parts of shame like horses, and began to ascend the young cows, all of whom became pregnant, and brought forth elephants, camels, and asses.

7. At these all the cows were alarmed and terrified; when they began biting[a] with their teeth, swallowing, and striking with their horns.

8. They began also to devour the cows; and behold all the children of the earth trembled, shook with terror at them, and suddenly fled away.

CHAP. LXXXVI.

1. Again I perceived them, when they began to strike and to swallow each other; and the earth cried out. Then I raised my eyes a second time towards heaven, and saw in a vision, that, behold, there came forth from heaven as it were the likeness of white men. One came forth from thence, and three with him.

2. Those three, who came forth last, seized me by my hand; and raising me up from the generations of the earth, elevated me to a high station.

3. Then they shewed me a lofty tower on the earth, while every hill became diminished. And they said; Remain here, until thou perceivest what

[a] ኦኀዘ፡ ይኔዝሩ፡ *biting*. See chap. x. 13. note.

shall come upon those elephants, camels, and asses, upon the stars, and upon all the cows.

CHAP. LXXXVII.

1. Then I looked at that one of the four *white men*, who came forth first.

2. He seized the first star which fell down from heaven.

3. And, binding it hand and foot, he cast it into a valley; a valley narrow, deep, stupendous, and gloomy.

4. Then one of them drew his sword, and gave it to the elephants, camels, and asses, who began to strike each other. And the whole earth shook on account of them.

5. And when I looked in the vision, behold, one of those four angels, who came forth, hurled from heaven, collected together, and took all the great stars, whose parts of shame resembled those of horses; and binding them all hand and foot, cast them into the cavities of the earth.

CHAP. LXXXVIII.

1. Then one of those four went to the white cows, and taught them a mystery. While the cow was trembling, it was born, and became a man[a], and fabricated for himself a large ship. In this he dwelt, and three cows[b] dwelt with him in that ship, which covered them.

[a] Noah. [b] Shem, Ham, and Japhet.

2. Again I lifted up my eyes towards heaven, and saw a lofty roof. Above it were seven cataracts, which poured forth on a certain village much water.

3. Again I looked, and behold there were fountains open on the earth in that large village.

4. The water began to boil up, and rose over the earth; so that the village was not seen, while its whole soil was covered with water.

5. Much water was over it, darkness, and clouds. Then I surveyed the height of this water; and it was elevated above the village.

6. It flowed over the village, and stood higher than the earth.

7. Then all the cows which were collected there, while I looked on them, were drowned, swallowed up, and destroyed in the water.

8. But the ship floated above it. All the cows, the elephants, the camels, and the asses, were drowned on the earth, and all cattle. Nor could I perceive them. Neither were they able to get out, but perished, and sunk into the deep.

9. Again I looked in the vision until those cataracts from that lofty roof were removed, and the fountains of the earth became equalized, while other depths were opened;

10. Into which the water began to descend, until the dry ground appeared.

11. The ship remained on the earth; the darkness receded; and it became light.

12. Then the white cow, which became a man,

went out of the ship, and the three cows with him.

13. One of the three cows was white, resembling that cow; one of them was red as blood; and one of them was black. And the white cow left them.

14. Then began wild beasts and birds to bring forth.

15. Of all these the different kinds assembled together, lions, tigers, wolves, dogs, wild boars, foxes, rabbits, and the hanzar[a],

16. The siset, the avest[b], kites, the phonkas[c], and ravens.

17. Then a white cow[d] was born in the midst of them.

18. And they began to bite each other; when the white cow, which was born in the midst of them, brought forth a wild ass and a white cow at the same time, and *after that* many wild asses. Then the white cow[e], which was born, brought forth a black wild sow and a white sheep[f].

19. That wild sow also brought forth many swine;

20. And that sheep brought forth twelve sheep[g].

21. When those twelve sheep grew up, they delivered one of them[h] to the asses[i].

22. Again those asses delivered that sheep to the wolves[k];

[a] ሐንዘር፡ [b] ሲሴት፡ አመስት፡ [c] ፎንቃስ፡ [d] Abraham. [e] Isaac. [f] Esau and Jacob. [g] The twelve Patriarchs. [h] Joseph. [i] The Midianites. [k] The Egyptians.

23. And he grew up in the midst of them.

24. Then the Lord brought the eleven *other* sheep, that they might dwell and feed with him in the midst of the wolves.

25. They multiplied, and there was abundance of pasture for them.

26. But the wolves began to frighten and oppress them, while they destroyed their young ones.

27. And they left their young in torrents of deep water.

28. Now the sheep began to cry out on account of their young, and fled for refuge to their Lord. One[a] however, which was saved, escaped, and went away to the wild asses.

29. I beheld the sheep moaning, crying, and petitioning their Lord,

30. With all their might, until the Lord of the sheep descended at their voice from *his* lofty habitation; went to them; and inspected them.

31. He called to that sheep which had secretly stolen away from the wolves, and told him to make the wolves understand that they were not to touch the sheep.

32. Then that sheep went to the wolves with the word of the Lord, when another met him[b], and proceeded with him.

33. Both of them together entered the dwelling of the wolves; and conversing with them made

[a] Moses. [b] Aaron.

them understand, that from thenceforwards they were not to touch the sheep.

34. Afterwards I perceived the wolves greatly prevailing over the sheep with their whole force. The sheep cried out; and their Lord came to them.

35. He began to strike the wolves, who commenced a grievous lamentation; but the sheep were silent, nor from that time did they cry out.

36. I then looked at them, until they departed from the wolves. The eyes of the wolves were blind, who went out and followed them with all their might. But the Lord of the sheep proceeded with them, and conducted them.

37. All his sheep followed him.

38. His countenance *was* terrific and splendid, and glorious was his aspect. Yet the wolves began to follow the sheep, until they overtook them in a certain lake of water [a].

39. Then that lake became divided; the water standing up on both sides before their face.

40. And while their Lord was conducting them, He placed Himself between them and the wolves.

41. The wolves however perceived not the sheep, but went into the midst of the lake, following them, and running after them into the lake of water.

42. But when they saw the Lord of the sheep, they turned to fly from before his face.

43. Then the water of the lake returned, and that suddenly, according to its nature. It became full,

[a] The Red sea.

and was raised up, until it covered the wolves. And I saw that all of them which had followed the sheep perished, and were drowned.

44. But the sheep passed over this water, proceeding to a wilderness, which was without both water and grass. And they began to open their eyes and to see.

45. Then I beheld the Lord of the sheep inspecting them, and giving them water and grass.

46. The sheep *already mentioned* was proceeding *with them*, and conducting them.

47. And when he had ascended the top of a lofty rock, the Lord of the sheep sent him to them.

48. Afterwards I perceived their Lord standing before them, with an aspect terrific and severe.

49. And when they all beheld him, they were frightened at his countenance.

50. All of them were alarmed, and trembled. They cried out after that sheep; and to the other sheep who had been with him, and who was in the midst of them, *saying*; We are not able to stand before our Lord, or to look upon him.

51. Then that sheep who conducted them went away, and ascended the top of the rock;

52. When the *rest of the* sheep began to grow blind, and to wander from the path which he had shewn them; but he knew it not.

53. Their Lord however was moved with great indignation against them; and when that sheep had learned *what had happened*,

54. He descended from the top of the rock, and coming to them, found that there were many,

55. Which had become blind;

56. And had wandered from his path. As soon as they beheld him, they feared, and trembled at his presence;

57. And became desirous of returning to their fold.

58. Then that sheep, taking with him other sheep, went to those which had wandered,

59. And afterwards began to kill them. They were terrified at his countenance. Then he caused those which had wandered to return; who went back to their fold.

60. I likewise saw there in the vision, that this sheep became a man, built an house for the Lord of the sheep, and made them all stand in that house.

61. I perceived also that the sheep which proceeded to meet this sheep, their conductor, died. I saw, too, that all the great sheep perished, while smaller ones rose up in their place, entered into a pasture, and approached a river of water[a].

62. Then that sheep, their conductor, who became a man, was separated from them, and died.

63. All the sheep sought after him, and cried for him with bitter lamentation.

64. I saw likewise that they ceased to cry after that sheep, and passed over the river of water.

65. And that there arose other sheep, all of

[a] The river Jordan.

whom conducted them[a], instead of those who were dead, and who had *previously* conducted them.

66. Then I saw that the sheep entered into a goodly place, and a territory delectable and glorious.

67. I saw also that they became satiated; that their house was in the midst of a delectable territory; and that sometimes their eyes were opened, and that sometimes they were blind; until another sheep[b] arose and conducted them. He brought them all back; and their eyes were opened.

68. Then dogs, foxes, and wild boars began to devour them, until *again* another sheep[c] arose, the master of the flock, one of themselves, a ram, to conduct them. This ram began to butt on every side those dogs, foxes, and wild boars, until they all perished.

69. But the *former* sheep opened his eyes, and saw the ram in the midst of them, who had laid aside his glory.

70. And he began to strike the sheep, treading upon them, and behaving himself without dignity.

71. Then their Lord sent the *former* sheep *again* to a still different[d] sheep[e], and raised him up to be a ram, and to conduct them instead of that sheep who had laid aside his glory.

72. Going therefore to him, and conversing with him alone, he raised up that ram, and made him a

[a] The Judges of Israel. [b] Samuel. [c] Saul. [d] *another.* [e] David.

prince and leader of the flock. All the time that the dogs[a] troubled the sheep,

73. The first ram paid respect to this latter ram.

74. Then the latter ram arose, and fled away from before his face. And I saw that those dogs caused the first ram to fall.

75. But the latter ram arose, and conducted the smaller sheep.

76. That ram likewise begat many sheep, and died.

77. Then there was a smaller sheep[b], a ram, instead of him, which became a prince and leader, conducting the flock.

78. And the sheep increased in size, and multiplied.

79. And all the dogs, foxes, and wild boars feared, and fled away from him.

80. That ram also struck and killed all the wild beasts, so that they could not again prevail in the midst of the sheep, nor at any time ever snatch them away.

81. And that house was made large and wide; a lofty tower being built upon it by the sheep, for the Lord of the sheep.

82. The house was low, but the tower was elevated and very high.

83. Then the Lord of the sheep stood upon that tower, and caused a full table to approach before him.

[a] The Philistines. [b] Solomon.

84. Again I saw that those sheep wandered, and went various ways, forsaking that their house;

85. And that their Lord called to some among them, whom he sent[a] to them.

86. But these the sheep began to kill. And when one of them was saved from slaughter[b], he leaped, and cried out against those who were desirous of killing him.

87. But the Lord of the sheep delivered him from their hands, and made him ascend to him, and remain with him.

88. He sent also many others to them, to testify, and with lamentations to exclaim, against them.

89. Again I saw, when some of them forsook the house of their Lord, and his tower; wandering on all sides, and growing blind.

90. I saw that the Lord of the sheep made a great slaughter among them in their pasture, until they cried out to him in consequence of that slaughter. Then he departed from the place *of his habitation*, and left them in the power of lions, tigers, wolves, and the zeebt[c], and in the power of foxes, and of every beast.

91. And the wild beasts began to tear them.

92. I saw, too, that he forsook the house of their fathers, and their tower; giving them all into the power of lions to tear and devour them; into the power of every beast.

[a] The prophets. [b] Elijah. [c] ጽዑብት፡

93. Then I began to cry out with all my might, imploring the Lord of the sheep, and shewing him how the sheep were devoured by all the beasts of prey.

94. But he looked on in silence, rejoicing that they were devoured, swallowed up, and carried off; and leaving them in the power of every beast for food. He called also seventy shepherds, and resigned to them *the care of* the sheep, that they might overlook them;

95. Saying to them and to their associates; Every one of you henceforwards overlook the sheep, and whatsoever I command you, do; and I will deliver *them* to you numbered[a].

96. I will tell you which of them shall be slain; these destroy. And he delivered the sheep to them.

97. Then he called to another, and said; Understand, and watch every thing which the shepherds shall do to these sheep; for many more of them shall perish than I have commanded.

98. Of every excess and slaughter, which the shepherds shall commit, *there shall be* an account; as, how many may have perished by my command, and how many they may have destroyed of their own heads.

99. Of all the destruction *brought about by* each of the shepherds there shall be an account; and according to the number I will cause a recital to be made before me, how many they have destroyed of

[a] *with number.*

their own heads, and how many they have delivered up to destruction, that I may have this testimony against them; that I may know all their proceedings; and that, delivering *the sheep* to them, I may see what they will do; whether they will act as I have commanded them, or not.

100. *Of this* however they shall be ignorant; neither shalt thou make any explanation to them, neither shalt thou reprove them; but there shall be an account of all the destruction *done* by them in their respective seasons. Then they began to kill, and destroy more than it was commanded them.

101. And they left the sheep in the power of lions, so that very many of them were devoured and swallowed up by lions and tigers; and wild boars preyed upon them. That tower they burnt, and overthrew that house.

102. Then I grieved extremely on account of the tower, and because the house of the sheep was overthrown.

103. Neither was I afterwards able to perceive, whether they *again* entered that house.

104. The shepherds likewise, and their associates, delivered them to all the wild beasts, that they might devour them. Each of them in his season, according to his number, was delivered up; each of them, one with another, was described in a book, how many of them, one with another, were destroyed, in a book.

105. More however than was ordered, every *shepherd* killed and destroyed.

106. Then I began to weep, and was greatly indignant, on account of the sheep.

107. In like manner also I saw in the vision him who wrote, how he wrote down one, destroyed by the shepherds, every day. He ascended, remained, and exhibited each of his books to the Lord of the sheep, *containing* all which they had done, and all which each of them had made away with;

108. And all which they had delivered up to destruction.

109. He took the book up in his hands, read it, sealed it, and deposited it.

110. After this, I saw shepherds overlooking for twelve hours.

111. And behold three of the sheep [a] departed, arrived, went in; and began building all which was fallen down of that house.

112. But the wild boars[b] hindered them, although they prevailed not.

113. Again they began to build as before, and raised up that tower, which was called a lofty tower.

114. And again they began to place before the tower a table, with every impure and unclean kind of bread upon it.

115. Moreover also all the sheep were blind, and could not see; as were the shepherds likewise.

[a] Zerubbabel, Joshua, and Nehemiah. [b] The Samaritans.

116. Thus were they delivered up to the shepherds for a great destruction, who trod them under foot, and devoured them.

117. Yet was their Lord silent, until all the sheep in the field were destroyed. The shepherds and the sheep were all mixed together; but they did not save them from the power of the beasts.

118. Then he who wrote the book ascended, exhibited it, and read it at the residence of the Lord of the sheep. He petitioned him for them, and prayed, pointing out every act of the shepherds, and testifying before him against them all. Then taking the book, he deposited it with him, and departed.

CHAP. LXXXIX.

1. And I observed during the time, that thus thirty-seven[a] shepherds were overlooking, all of whom finished in their respective periods as the first. Others then received them into their hands, that they might overlook them in their respective periods, every shepherd in his own period.

2. Afterwards I saw in the vision, that all the birds of heaven arrived; eagles, the avest[b], kites and ravens. The eagle instructed them all.

3. They began to devour the sheep, to peck out their eyes, and to eat up their bodies.

4. The sheep then cried out; for their bodies were devoured by the birds.

[a] An apparent error for *thirty-five*. See verse 7. The kings of Judah and Israel; see Preliminary Dissertation. [b] አውስት፡

5. I also cried out, and groaned in my sleep against that shepherd which overlooked the flock.

6. And I looked, while the sheep were eaten up by the dogs, by the eagles, and by the kites. They neither left them their body, nor their skin, nor their muscles, until their bones alone remained; until their bones fell upon the ground. And the sheep became diminished.

7. I observed likewise during the time, that twenty-three shepherds[a] were overlooking; who completed in their respective periods fifty-eight periods.

8. Then were small lambs born of those white sheep; who began to open their eyes and to see, crying out to the sheep.

9. The sheep however cried not out to them, neither did they hear what they uttered to them; but were deaf, blind, and obdurate in the greatest degree.

10. I saw in the vision that ravens flew down upon those lambs;

11. That they seized one of them; and that tearing the sheep in pieces, they devoured them.

12. I saw also, that horns grew upon those lambs; and that the ravens lighted down upon their horns.

[a] The kings of Babylon, &c. during and after the captivity. See Prelim. Dissert. The numbers thirty-*five* and twenty-three make fifty-eight; and not thirty-*seven*, as erroneously put in the first verse.

13. I saw, too, that a large horn sprouted out on an animal[a] among the sheep, and that their eyes were opened.

14. He looked at them. Their eyes were wide open; and he cried out to them.

15. Then the dabelat[b] saw him; all of whom ran to him.

16. And besides this, all the eagles, the avest, the ravens and the kites, were still carrying off the sheep, flying down upon them, and devouring them. The sheep were silent, but the dabelat lamented and cried out.

17. Then the ravens contended, and struggled with them.

18. They wished among them to break his horn; but they prevailed not over him.

19. I looked on them, until the shepherds, the eagles, the avest, and the kites came.

20. Who cried out to the ravens to break the horn of the dabela[c]; to contend with him; and to kill him. But he struggled with them, and cried out, that help might come to him.

21. Then I perceived that the man came who had written down the names of the shepherds, and who ascended up before the Lord of the sheep.

22. He brought assistance, and caused every one to see him descending to the help of the dabela.

23. I perceived likewise that the Lord of the

[a] በ: on *one*. [b] ደቤላት: [c] ደቤላ:

sheep came to them in wrath, while all those who saw him fled away; all fell down in his tabernacle before his face; while all the eagles, the avest, ravens, and kites assembled, and brought with them all the sheep of the field.

24. All came together, and strove to break the horn of the dabela.

25. Then I saw, that the man, who wrote the book at the word of the Lord, opened the book of destruction, of that destruction which the last twelve shepherds[a] wrought; and pointed out before the Lord of the sheep, that they destroyed more than those who preceded them.

26. I saw also that the Lord of the sheep came to them, and taking in his hand the sceptre of his wrath seized the earth, which became rent asunder; while all the beasts and birds of heaven fell from the sheep, and sunk into the earth, which closed over them.

27. I saw, too, that a large sword was given to the sheep, who went forth against all the beasts of the field to slay them.

28. But all the beasts and birds of heaven fled away from before their face.

29. And I saw a throne erected in a delectable land;

30. Upon this sat the Lord of the sheep, who received all the sealed books;

[a] The native princes of Judah after its delivery from the Syrian yoke.

31. Which were opened before him.

32. Then the Lord called the first seven white ones, and commanded them to bring before Him the first of the first stars, which preceded the stars whose parts of shame resembled those of horses; the first star, which fell down first; and they brought them all before Him.

33. And He spoke to the man who wrote in his presence, who was one of the seven white ones, saying; Take those seventy shepherds, to whom I delivered up the sheep, and *who* receiving them killed more of them than I commanded. Behold, I saw them all bound, and all standing before Him. First came on the trial of the stars, which, being judged, and found guilty, went to the place of punishment. They thrust them into *a place*, deep, and full of flaming fire, and full of pillars of fire. Then the seventy shepherds were judged, and being found guilty, were thrust into the flaming abyss.

34. At that time likewise I perceived, that one abyss was thus opened in the midst of the earth, which was full of fire.

35. And to this were brought the blind sheep; which being judged, and found guilty, were all thrust into that abyss of fire on the earth, and burnt.

36. The abyss was on the right of that house.

37. And I saw the sheep burning, and their bones consuming.

38. I stood beholding Him immerge that ancient

house, while they brought out its pillars, every plant in it, and the ivory infolding it. They brought it out, and deposited it in a place on the right side of the earth.

39. I also saw, that the Lord of the sheep produced a new house, great, and loftier than the former, which He bounded by the former circular spot. All its pillars were new, and its ivory new, as well as more abundant than the former ancient *ivory*, which he had brought out.

40. And while all the sheep which were left were in the midst of it, all the beasts of the earth, and all the birds of heaven, fell down and worshipped them, petitioning them, and obeying them in every thing.

41. Then those three, who were clothed in white, and who, holding me by my hand, had before caused me to ascend, while the hand of him *who* spoke held me; raised me up, and placed me in the midst of the sheep, before the judgment took place.

42. The sheep were all white, with wool long and pure. Then all who had perished, and had been destroyed, every beast of the field, and every bird of heaven, assembled in that house; while the Lord of the sheep rejoiced with great joy, because all were good, and had come back again to his dwelling.

43. And I saw that they laid down the sword which had been given to the sheep, and returned it to his house, sealing it up in the presence of the Lord.

44. All the sheep would have been inclosed in that house, had it been capable of containing them[a]; and the eyes of all were open, gazing on the good One; nor was there one among them who did not behold Him.

45. I likewise perceived that the house was large, wide, and extremely full. I saw, too, that a white cow was born, whose horns were great; and that all the beasts of the field, and all the birds of heaven, were alarmed at him, and entreated him at all times.

46. Then I saw that the nature of all of them was changed, and that they became white cows;

47. And that the first, *who* was in the midst of them, spoke[b], when that word became a large beast, upon the head of which were great and black horns;

48. While the Lord of the sheep rejoiced over them, and over all the cows.

49. I lay down in the midst of them: I awoke; and saw the whole. This is the vision which I saw, lying down and waking. Then I blessed the Lord of righteousness, and gave glory to Him.

50. Afterwards I wept abundantly, nor did my tears cease, so that I became incapable of enduring it. While I was looking on, they flowed[c] on account of what I saw; for all was come and gone by; every individual circumstance respecting the conduct of mankind was seen by me.

[a] *were inclosed in that house, and it did not contain them.*
[b] *became a word.* [c] *descended.*

51. In that night I remembered my former dream; and therefore wept and was troubled, because I had seen that vision.

CHAP. XC. [SECT. XVIII.[a]]

1. And now, my son Mathusala, call to me all thy brethren, and assemble for me all the children of thy mother; for a voice calls me, and the spirit is poured out upon me, that I may shew you every thing which shall happen to you for ever.

2. Then Mathusala went, called to him all his brethren, and assembled his kindred.

3. And conversing with all his children in truth,

4. *Enoch* said; Hear, my children, every word of your father, and listen in uprightness to the voice of my mouth; for I would gain your attention, while I address you. My beloved; be attached to integrity, and walk in it.

5. Approach not integrity with a double heart; nor be associated with double-minded men: but walk, my children, in righteousness, which will conduct you in good paths; and be truth your companion.

6. For I know, that oppression will exist and prevail on earth; that on earth great punishment shall in the end take place; and that there shall be a consummation of all iniquity, which shall be cut off from its root, and every fabric *raised by* it shall pass away. Iniquity however shall again be renew-

[a] Paris MS.

ed, and consummated on earth. Every act of crime, and every act of oppression and impiety, shall be a second time embraced.

7. When therefore iniquity, sin, blasphemy, tyranny, and every *evil* work, shall increase, and *when* transgression, impiety, and uncleanness also shall increase, *then* upon them all shall great punishment be inflicted from heaven.

8. The holy Lord shall go forth in wrath, and upon them all shall great punishment from heaven be inflicted[a].

9. The holy Lord shall go forth in wrath, and with punishment, that he may execute judgment upon the earth.

10. In those days oppression shall be cut off from its roots, and iniquity with fraud shall be eradicated, perishing from under heaven.

11. Every place of strength[b] shall be surrendered with its inhabitants; with fire shall it be burnt. They shall be brought from every part of the earth, and be cast into a judgment of fire. They shall perish in wrath, and by a judgment overpowering them[c] for ever.

12. Righteousness shall be raised up from slumber; and wisdom shall be raised up, and conferred upon them.

[a] This verse is wanting in the Paris MS. as transcribed by Woide. It seems in the Bodleian MS. to be a mere lapse of the transcriber, who wrote the same words twice over.

[b] *tower, palace,* or *temple.* [c] *powerful judgment.*

13. Then shall the roots of iniquity be cut off; sinners perish by the sword; and blasphemers be annihilated every where[a].

14. Those who meditate oppression, and those who blaspheme, by the sword shall perish[b].

15. And now, my children, I will describe and point out to you the path of righteousness and the path of oppression.

16. I will again point them out to you, that you may know what is to come.

17. Hear now, my children, and walk in the path of righteousness, but shun that of oppression; for all who walk in the path of iniquity shall perish for ever.

CHAP. XCI. [SECT. XIX.[c]]

1. That which was written by Enoch. He wrote all this instruction of wisdom for every man of dignity, and every judge of the earth; for all my children who shall dwell upon earth, and for subsequent generations, conducting themselves uprightly and peaceably.

[a] *cut off.* [b] Between the 14th and 15th verses of this chapter six others are inserted both in the Bodleian and Paris MSS., which I have transposed so as to constitute the 13th, 14th, 15th, 16th, 17th, and 18th verses of the ninety-second chapter. This transposition seemed absolutely necessary to make sense of that chapter; in which, after the enumeration of seven weeks, or periods, the account of the eighth, ninth, and tenth weeks, contained in the verses transposed, seemed necessary to complete the narrative. Here they are clearly unconnected and misplaced.

[c] Paris MS.

2. Let not your spirit be grieved on account of the times; for the holy, the great One, has prescribed a period[a] to all.

3. Let the righteous man arise from slumber; let him arise, and proceed in the path of righteousness, in all its paths; and let him advance[b] in goodness and in eternal clemency. Mercy shall be shewed to the righteous man; upon him shall be conferred integrity and power for ever. In goodness and in righteousness shall he exist, and shall walk in everlasting light; but sin shall perish in eternal darkness, nor be seen from this time forward for evermore.

CHAP. XCII.

1. After this, Enoch began to speak from a book.

2. And Enoch said; Concerning the children of righteousness, concerning the elect of the world, and concerning the plant of righteousness and integrity.

3. *Concerning* these things will I speak, and *these things* will I explain to you, my children: I *who* am Enoch. In consequence of that which has been shewn to me, from my heavenly vision and from the voice of the holy angels have I acquired knowledge; and from the tablet of heaven have I acquired understanding.

4. Enoch then began to speak from a book, and said; I have been born the seventh in the first

[a] *has given days.* [b] *his goings* be.

week, while judgment and righteousness wait with patience.

5. But after me, in the second week, great wickedness shall arise, and fraud shall spring forth.

6. In that week[a] the end of the first shall take place, in which mankind shall be safe.

7. But when *the first* is completed[b], iniquity shall grow up; and he shall execute the decree upon sinners[c].

8. Afterwards, in the third week, during its completion, a man[d] of the plant of righteous judgment shall be selected; and after him the plant of righteousness shall come for ever.

9. Subsequently, in the fourth week, during its completion, the visions of the holy and the righteous shall be seen, the order of generation after generation *shall take place*, and an habitation shall be made for them[e]. Then in the fifth week, during its completion, the house of glory and of dominion[f] shall be erected for ever.

10. After that, in the sixth week, all those who are in it shall be darkened, the hearts of all of them shall be forgetful of wisdom, and in it shall a man[g] ascend.

11. During its completion also the house of dominion shall be burnt with fire, and all the race of the elect root shall be dispersed[h].

[a] *in it.* [b] *after it has been completed.* [c] The deluge.
[d] Abraham. [e] The Law. [f] Temple of Solomon.
[g] Elijah. [h] Babylonian captivity.

12. Afterwards, in the seventh week, a perverse generation shall arise; abundant shall be its deeds, and all its deeds perverse. During its completion, the righteous, selected from the plant of everlasting righteousness, shall be rewarded; and to them shall be given sevenfold instruction respecting every part of his creation.

13. Afterwards there shall be another week, the eighth of righteousness, to which shall be given a sword to execute judgment and justice upon all oppressors.

14. Sinners shall be delivered up into the hands of the righteous, who during its completion shall acquire habitations by their righteousness; and the house of the great King shall be built up for ever. After that, in the ninth week, shall the judgment of righteousness be revealed to the whole world.

15. Every work of the ungodly shall disappear from the whole earth; the world shall be marked for destruction; and all men shall be on the look-out for the path of integrity.

16. And after this, on the seventh day of the tenth week, there shall be an everlasting judgment, which shall be executed upon the Watchers; and a spacious eternal heaven shall spring forth in the midst of the angels.

17. The former heaven shall depart and pass away; a new heaven shall appear; and all the celestial powers shine with sevenfold splendor for ever. Afterwards likewise shall there be many weeks,

which shall eternally exist in goodness and in righteousness.

18. Neither shall sin be named there for ever and for ever[a].

19. Who is there of all the children of men, capable of hearing the voice of the Holy One without emotion?

20. Who is there capable of thinking his thoughts? Who capable of contemplating all the workmanship of heaven? Who of comprehending the deeds of heaven?

21. He may behold its animation, but not its spirit. He may be capable of conversing *respecting it*, but not of ascending *to it*. He may see all the boundaries of these things, and meditate upon them; but he can make nothing like them.

22. Who of all men is able to understand the breadth and length of the earth?

23. By whom have been seen the dimensions of all these things? Is it every man who is capable of comprehending the extent of heaven; what its elevation is, and by what it is supported?

24. How many are the numbers of the stars; and where all the luminaries remain at rest?

[a] The preceding six verses, viz. 13th, 14th, 15th, 16th, 17th, and 18th, are taken from between the 14th and 15th verses of the ninetieth chapter, where they are to be found in the MSS. But the sense in this place seemed so manifestly to require them here, that I have ventured to transpose them.

CHAP. XCIII.

1. And now let me exhort you, my children, to love righteousness, and to walk in it; for the paths of righteousness are worthy of acceptation; but the paths of iniquity shall suddenly fail, and be diminished.

2. To men of note in their generation the paths of oppression and death are revealed; but they keep far from them, and do not follow them.

3. Now, too, let me exhort you *who are* righteous, not to walk in the paths of evil and oppression, nor in the paths of death. Approach them not, that you may not perish; but covet,

4. And choose for yourselves righteousness, and a good life.

5. Walk in the paths of peace, that you may live, and be found worthy. Retain my words in your inmost thoughts, and obliterate them not from your hearts; for I know that sinners counsel men to commit crime craftily. They are not found in every place, nor does every counsel possess a little of them.

6. Wo to those who build up iniquity and oppression, and who lay the foundation of fraud; for suddenly shall they be subverted, and never obtain peace.

7. Wo to those who build up their houses with crime; for from their very foundations shall their

houses[a] be demolished, and by the sword shall they *themselves* fall. Those, too, who acquire gold and silver, shall justly and suddenly perish. Wo to you who are rich, for in your riches have you trusted; but from your riches you shall be removed; because you have not remembered the Most High in the days of your prosperity: [you shall be removed, because you have not remembered the Most High in the days of your prosperity[b].]

8. You have committed blasphemy and iniquity; and are destined to the day of the effusion of blood, to the day of darkness, and to the day of the great judgment.

9. This I declare and point out to you, that He who created you will destroy you.

10. When you fall, He will not shew you mercy; but your Creator will rejoice in your destruction.

11. Let those then, who shall be righteous among you in those days, detest sinners, and the ungodly.

CHAP. XCIV.

1. O that my eyes were clouds of water, that I might weep over you, and pour forth my tears like rain[c], and rest from the sorrow of my heart!

2. Who has permitted you to hate and to transgress? Judgment shall overtake you, ye sinners.

3. The righteous shall not fear the wicked; be-

[a] *they*. [b] These lines are evidently a repetition of the preceding, from an error in the transcription, They do not occur in the Paris MS. [c] *a cloud of water*.

cause God will again bring them into your power, that you may avenge yourselves of them according to your pleasure.

4. Wo to you who shall be so bound by execrations, that you cannot be released from them; the remedy being far removed from you on account of your sins. Wo to you who recompense your neighbour with evil; for you shall be recompensed according to your works.

5. Wo to you, ye false witnesses, you who aggravate iniquity; for you shall suddenly perish.

6. Wo to you, ye sinners; for you reject the righteous; for you receive or reject *at pleasure* those who *commit* iniquity; and their yoke shall prevail over you.

CHAP. XCV.

1. Wait in hope, ye righteous; for suddenly shall sinners perish from before you, and you shall exercise dominion over them, according to your will.

2. In the day of the sufferings of sinners your offspring shall be elevated, and lifted up like eagles. Your nest shall be more exalted than that of the avest; you shall ascend, and enter into the cavities of the earth, and into the clefts of the rocks for ever, like hares, from the sight of the ungodly;

3. Who shall groan over you, and weep like sirens.

4. You shall not fear those who trouble you; for restoration shall be yours; a splendid light shall

shine around you, and the voice of tranquillity shall be heard from heaven. Wo to you, sinners; for your wealth makes you resemble saints, but your hearts reproach you, *knowing* that you are sinners. This word shall testify against you, for the remembrance of crime.

5. Wo to you who feed upon the glory of the corn, and drink the strength of the deepest spring[a], and in *the pride of* your power tread down the humble.

6. Wo to you who drink water at pleasure[b]; for suddenly shall you be recompensed, consumed, and withered, because you have forsaken the fountain of life.

7. Wo to you who act iniquitously, fraudulently, and blasphemously; there shall be a remembrance against you for evil.

8. Wo to you, ye powerful, who with power strike down righteousness; for the day of your destruction shall come; *while* at that very time many and good days shall be the portion of the righteous[c], *even* at the period of your judgment.

CHAP. XCVI.

1. The righteous are confident that sinners will be disgraced, and perish in the day of iniquity.

2. You shall yourselves be conscious of it; for the Most High will remember your destruction,

[a] *of the root of the spring.* [b] *at all times.* [c] *shall come to the righteous.*

and the angels shall rejoice over it. What will you do, ye sinners, and where will you fly in the day of judgment, when you shall hear the words of the prayer of the righteous?

3. You are not like them who in this respect witness against you; you are associates of sinners.

4. In those days shall the prayers of the righteous come up before the Lord. When the day of your judgment shall arrive; and every circumstance of your iniquity be related before the great and the holy One;

5. Your faces shall be covered with shame; while every deed, strengthened by crime, shall be rejected.

6. Wo unto you, sinners, who in the midst of the sea, and on dry land, are those against whom an evil record exists. Wo to you who squander silver and gold, not obtained in righteousness, and say; We are rich, possess wealth, and have acquired every thing which we can desire.

7. Now then will we do whatsoever we are disposed to do; for we have amassed silver; our barns are full, and the husbandmen of our families are like overflowing water [a].

8. Like water shall your falsehood pass away; for your wealth will not be permanent, but shall suddenly ascend from you, because you have obtained it all iniquitously; to extreme malediction shall you be delivered up.

[a] *like much water.*

9. And now I swear to you, ye crafty, as well as simple ones; that you, often contemplating the earth, you *who are* men, clothe yourselves more elegantly[a] than married women, and both together more so than unmarried ones, every where *arraying yourselves* in majesty, in magnificence, in authority, and in silver: but gold, purple, honour, and wealth, like water, flow away.

10. Erudition therefore and wisdom are not theirs. Thus[b] shall they perish, together with their riches, with all their glory, and with their honours;

11. While with disgrace, with slaughter, and in extreme penury, shall their spirits be thrust into a furnace of fire.

12. I have sworn to you, ye sinners, that neither mountain nor hill has been or shall be subservient[c] to woman.

13. Neither in this way has crime been sent down to us[d] upon earth, but men of their own heads have invented it; and greatly shall those who give it efficiency be execrated.

14. Barrenness shall not be *previously* inflicted on woman; but on account of the work of her hands shall she die childless.

15. I have sworn to you, ye sinners, by the holy

[a] *put elegance upon you more.* The transcriber of the Bodleian MS. has here written by mistake አነ፡ *ego* for ሠነ፡ *pulchritudo.* The Paris MS. reads correctly. [b] *And in it.* [c] *a servant.* Perhaps in furnishing them with treasures for ornaments. [d] *has our crime been sent down.*

and the great One, that all your evil deeds are disclosed in the heavens; and that none of your oppressive acts are concealed and secret.

16. Think not in your minds, neither say in your hearts, that every crime is not manifested and seen. In heaven it is daily written down before the Most High. Henceforwards shall it be manifested; for every act of oppression which you commit shall be daily recorded, until the period of your condemnation.

17. Wo to you, ye simple ones, for you shall perish in your simplicity. To the wise you will not listen, and that which is good you shall not obtain[a].

18. Now therefore know that you are destined to the day of destruction; nor hope that sinners shall live; but in process of time you shall die[b]; for you are not marked[c] for redemption;

19. But are destined to the day of the great judgment, to the day of distress, and the extreme ignominy of your souls.

20. Wo to you, ye obdurate in heart, who commit crime, and feed on blood. Whence *is it that* you feed on good things, drink, and are satiated? Is it not because our Lord, the Most High, has abundantly supplied every good thing upon earth? To you there shall not be peace.

21. Wo to you who love the deeds of iniquity. Why do you hope for that which is good? Know

[a] *shall not find you.* [b] *you shall go on, and die.* [c] *pointed out.*

that you shall be given up into the hands of the righteous; who shall cut off your necks, slay you, and shew you no compassion.

22. Wo to you who rejoice in the trouble of the righteous; for a grave shall not be dug for you.

23. Wo to you who frustrate the word of the righteous; for to you there shall be no hope of life.

24. Wo to you who write down the word of falsehood, and the word of the wicked; for their falsehood they record, that they may hear and not forget folly.

25. To them there shall be no peace; but they shall surely die suddenly.

CHAP. XCVII.

1. Wo to them who act impiously, who laud and honour the word of falsehood. You have been lost in perdition; and have never led a virtuous life.

2. Wo to you who change the words of integrity. They transgress against the everlasting decree;

3. And cause the heads of those who are not sinners to be trodden down upon the earth.

4. In those days you, O ye righteous, shall have been deemed worthy of having your prayers rise up in remembrance; and shall have deposited them in testimony before the angels, that they might record the sins of sinners in the presence of the Most High.

5. In those days the nations shall be overthrown;

but the families of the nations shall rise again in the day of perdition.

6. In those days they who become pregnant shall go forth, carry off their children, and forsake them. Their offspring shall slip from them, and while suckling them shall they forsake them; they shall never return to them, and never instruct their beloved.

7. Again I swear to you, ye sinners, that crime has been prepared for the day of blood, which never ceases.

8. They shall worship stones, and engrave golden, silver, and wooden images. They shall worship impure spirits, demons, and every idol, in temples; but no help shall be obtained for them [a]. Their hearts shall become impious through their folly, and their eyes be blinded with mental superstition [b]. In their visionary dreams shall they be impious and superstitious [c], lying in all their actions, and worshipping a stone. Altogether shall they perish.

9. But in those days blessed shall they be, to whom the word of wisdom is delivered; who point out and pursue the path of the Most High; who walk in the way of righteousness, and who act not impiously with the impious.

10. They shall be saved.

11. Wo to you who expand the crime of your neighbour; for in hell shall you be slain.

[a] *shall be found from them.* [b] *with the fear of their heart.*
[c] *and fear.*

12. Wo to you who lay the foundation of sin and deceit, and who are bitter on earth; for on it shall you be consumed.

13. Wo to you who build your houses by the labour of others, every part of which is constructed with brick [a], and with the stone of crime; I tell you, that you shall not obtain peace.

14. Wo to you who despise the extent of the everlasting inheritance of your fathers, while your souls follow after idols; for to you there shall be no tranquillity.

15. Wo to them who commit iniquity, and give aid to blasphemy, who slay their neighbour until the day of the great judgment; for your glory shall fall; malevolence shall He put into your hearts, and the spirit of his wrath shall stir *you* up, that every one of you may perish by the sword.

16. Then shall all the righteous and the holy remember your crimes.

CHAP. XCVIII.

1. In those days shall fathers be struck down with their children in the presence of each other [b]; and brethren with their brethren shall fall dead; until a river shall flow from their blood.

2. For a man shall not restrain his hand from his children, nor from his children's children; his mercy will be to kill them [c].

[a] *every structure of which* is *brick.* [b] *in one place.* [c] *he has been merciful, that he may kill.*

3. Nor shall the sinner restrain his hand from his honoured brother. From the dawn of day to the setting sun shall the slaughter continue[a]. The horse shall wade up to his breast, and the chariot shall sink to its axle[b], in the blood of sinners.

CHAP. XCIX.

1. In those days the angels shall descend into places of concealment, and gather together in one spot all who have assisted in crime.

2. In that day shall the Most High rise up to execute the great judgment upon all sinners, and to commit the guardianship of all the righteous and holy to the holy angels, that they may protect them as the apple of an eye, until every evil and every crime be annihilated.

3. Whether *or not* the righteous sleep securely[c], wise men shall then truly perceive.

4. And the sons of the earth shall understand every word of that book, knowing that their riches cannot save them in the ruin of their crimes.

5. Wo to you, ye sinners, when you shall be afflicted on account of the righteous in the day of the great trouble; shall be burnt in the fire; and be recompensed according to your deeds.

6. Wo to you, ye perverted in heart, who are watchful to obtain an accurate knowledge of evil, and to discover terrors. No one shall assist you.

[a] *they shall be slain.* [b] *its upper part.* [c] *a deep sleep.*

7. Wo to you, ye sinners; for with the words of your mouths, and with the work of your hands, have you acted impiously; in the flame of a blazing fire shall you be burnt.

8. And now know ye, that the angels shall inquire into your conduct in heaven; of the sun, the moon, and the stars, *shall they inquire* respecting your sins; for upon earth you exercise jurisdiction over the righteous.

9. Every cloud shall bear witness against you, the snow, the dew, and the rain; for all of them shall be withholden from you, that they may not descend upon you, nor become subservient to your crimes.

10. Now then bring gifts of salutation to the rain; that, not being withholden, it may descend upon you; and to the dew, if it has received from you gold and silver. But when the frost, snow, cold, every snowy wind, and every suffering belonging to them, fall upon you, in those days you will be utterly incapable of standing before them.

CHAP. C.

1. Attentively consider heaven, all ye progeny of heaven, and all ye works of the Most High; fear Him, nor conduct yourselves criminally before Him.

2. If He shut up the windows of heaven, restraining the rain and dew, that it may not descend upon earth on your account, what will you do?

3. And if He send his wrath upon you, and upon all your deeds, you are not they who can supplicate Him; you who utter[a] against his righteousness, language proud and powerful[b]. To you there shall be no peace.

4. Do you not see the commanders[c] of ships, how their vessels are tossed about by the waves, torn to pieces by the winds, and exposed to the greatest peril?

5. That they therefore fear, because their whole property is embarked with them on the ocean; and that they forebode evil[d] in their hearts, because it may swallow them up, and they may perish in it?

6. Is not the whole sea, all its waters, and all its commotion, the work of Him, the Most High; of Him who has sealed up all its exertions, and girded it on every side with sand?

7. *Is it not* at his rebuke dried up, and alarmed; while all its fish with every thing *contained* in it die? And will not you, ye sinners, who are on earth, fear Him? Is not He the maker of heaven and earth, and of all things which are in them?

8. And who has given erudition and wisdom to all that move *progressive* upon the earth, and over the sea?

9. Are not the commanders of ships terrified at the ocean? And shall not sinners be terrified at the Most High.

[a] *for you utter.* [b] *great and powerful things.* [c] *kings.*
[d] *think not good.*

CHAP. CII.[a]

1. In those days, when He shall cast the calamity of fire upon you, whither will you fly, and where will you be safe?

2. And when He sends forth his word against you, are you not spared, and terrified?

3. All the luminaries are agitated with great fear; and all the earth is spared, while it trembles, and suffers anxiety.

4. All the angels fulfil the commands *received* by them, and are desirous of being concealed from the presence of the great Glory; while the children of the earth are alarmed and troubled.

5. But you, ye sinners, are for ever accursed; to you there shall be no peace.

6. Fear not, ye souls of the righteous; but wait with patient hope for the day of your death in righteousnesss. Grieve not, because your souls descend in great trouble, with groaning, lamentation, and sorrow, to the receptacle of the dead. In your lifetime your bodies have not received a recompense in proportion to your goodness[b], but in the period of your existence have sinners existed; in the period of execration and of punishment.

7. And when you die, sinners say concerning you; As we die, the righteous die. What profit have they in their works? Behold, like us, they ex-

[a] There is no chap. ci. in the MSS.

[b] *your flesh has not found according to your goodness.*

pire in sorrow and in darkness. What advantage have they over us? Henceforward are we equal. What will be within their grasp, and what before their eyes[a] for ever? For behold they are dead; and never will they again[b] perceive the light. I say unto you, ye sinners; You have been satiated with meat and drink, with human plunder and rapine, with sin, with the acquisition of wealth, and with the sight of good days. Have you not marked the righteous, how their end is in peace? for no oppression is found in them even to the day of their death. They perish, and are as if they were not, while their souls descend in trouble to the receptacle of the dead.

CHAP. CIII.

1. But now I swear to you, ye righteous, by the greatness of his splendor and his glory; by his illustrious kingdom and by his Majesty, to you I swear, that I comprehend this mystery; that I have read the tablet of heaven, have seen the writing of the holy Ones, and have discovered what is written and impressed on it concerning you.

2. *I have seen* that all goodness, joy, and glory has been prepared for you, and been written down for the spirits of them who die eminently righteous and good[c]. To you it shall be given in return for

[a] *What will they obtain, and what behold.* [b] *henceforward for ever.* [c] *in righteousness and in much goodness.*

your troubles; and your portion *of happiness* shall far exceed the portion of the living.

3. The spirits of you who die in righteousness shall exist and rejoice. Their spirits shall exult; and their remembrance shall be before the face of the mighty One from generation to generation. Nor shall they now fear disgrace.

4. Wo to you, sinners, when you die in your sins; and they, who are like you, say respecting you, Blessed are these sinners. They have lived out their whole period[a]; and now they die in happiness[b] and in wealth. Distress and slaughter they knew not[c] while alive; in honour they die; nor ever in their lifetime did judgment overtake them.

5. *But* has it not been shewn to them, that, *when* to the receptacle of the dead their souls shall be made to descend, their evil deeds shall become their greatest torment? Into darkness, into the snare, and into the flame, which shall burn to the great judgment, shall their spirits enter; and the great judgment shall take effect for ever and for ever[d].

6. Wo to you; for to you there shall be no peace. Neither can you say to the righteous, and to the good who are alive, In the days of our trouble have we been afflicted; every *species of* trouble have we seen, and many evil things have suffered[e].

7. Our spirits have been consumed, lessened, and diminished.

[a] *They have seen all their days* [b] *in goodness.* [c] *they saw not.* [d] *shall be for every generation, even for ever.* [e] *found.*

8. We have perished; nor has there been a possibility of help for us in word or in deed: we have found none, but have been tormented and destroyed.

9. We have not expected to live[a] day after day.

10. We hoped indeed to have been the head;

11. But we have become the tail. We have been afflicted, when we have exerted ourselves; but we have been devoured by sinners[b] and the ungodly; their yoke has been heavy upon us.

12. Those have exercised dominion over us who detest and who goad us; and to those who hate us have we humbled our neck; but they have shewn no compassion towards us.

13. We have been desirous of escaping from them, that we might fly away, and be at rest; but we have found no place to which we could fly, and be secure from them. We have sought an asylum with princes in our distress, and have cried out to those who were devouring us; but our cry has not been regarded, nor have they been disposed to hear our voice;

14. But rather to assist those who plunder and devour us; those who diminish us, and hide their oppression; who remove not their yoke from us, but devour, enervate, and slay us; who conceal our slaughter, nor remember that they have lifted up their hands against us.

[a] *to see life.* [b] *food for sinners.*

CHAP. CIV.

1. I swear to you, ye righteous, that in heaven the angels record your goodness before the glory of the mighty One.

2. Wait with patient hope; for formerly you have been disgraced with evil and with affliction; but now shall you shine like the luminaries of heaven. You shall be seen, and the gates of heaven shall be opened to you. Your cries have cried for judgment; and it has appeared to you: for an account of all your suffering shall be required from the princes, and from every one who has assisted your plunderers.

3. Wait with patient hope; nor relinquish your confidence; for great joy shall be yours, like that of the angels in heaven. Conduct yourselves as you may, still you shall not be concealed in the day of the great judgment. You shall not be found like sinners; and eternal condemnation shall be far from you, so long as the world exists[a].

4. And now fear not, ye righteous, when you see sinners flourishing and prosperous[b] in their ways.

5. Be not associates with them; but keep yourselves at a distance from their oppression; be you associated with the host of heaven. You, ye sinners, say; All our transgressions shall not be taken account of, and be recorded. But all your transgressions shall be recorded daily.

[a] *during every generation of the world.* [b] *strong and worthy.*

6. And be assured by me[a], that light and darkness, day and night, behold all your transgressions. Be not impious in your thoughts; lie not; surrender not the word of uprightness; lie not against the word of the holy and the mighty One; glorify not your idols; for all your lying and all your impiety is not for righteousness, but for great crime.

7. Now will I point out a mystery; Many sinners shall turn and transgress against the word of uprightness.

8. They shall speak evil things; they shall utter falsehood; execute great undertakings[b]; and compose books in their own words. But when they shall write all my words correctly in their own languages,

9. They shall neither change nor diminish them; but shall write them all correctly; all which from the first I have uttered concerning them.

10. Another mystery also I point out. To the righteous and the wise shall be given books of joy, of integrity, and of great wisdom. To them shall books be given, in which they shall believe;

11. And in which they shall rejoice. And all the righteous shall be rewarded, who from these shall acquire the knowledge of every upright path.

CHAP. CIV.[c]

1. In those days, saith the Lord, they shall call

[a] *I will shew you.* [b] *create a great creation.* [c] This chapter occurs twice.

to the children of the earth, and make them listen to their wisdom. Shew them that you are their leaders;

2. And that remuneration *shall take place* over the whole earth; for I and my Son will for ever hold communion with them in the paths of uprightness, while they are still alive[a]. Peace shall be yours. Rejoice, children of integrity, in the truth.

CHAP. CV.

1. After a time[b], my son Mathusala took a wife for his son Lamech.

2. She became pregnant by him, and brought forth a child, the flesh of which was white as snow, and red as a rose; the hair of whose head was white like wool, and long; and whose eyes were beautiful. When he opened them, he illuminated all the house, like the sun; the whole house abounded with light.

3. And when he was taken from the hand of the midwife, opening also his mouth, he spoke to the Lord of righteousness. Then Lamech his father was afraid of him; and flying away came to his own father Mathusala, and said; I have begotten a son, unlike *to other children*[c]. He is not human; but, resembling the offspring of the angels of heaven, is of a different nature *from ours*, being altogether unlike to us.

[a] *we will for ever mix with them in the paths of uprightness in their lives.* [b] *after days.* [c] *a changed son.*

4. His eyes are *bright* as the rays of the sun; his countenance glorious, and he looks not as if he belonged to me, but to the angels.

5. I am afraid, lest something miraculous should take place on earth in his days.

6. And now, my father, let me entreat and request you to go to our progenitor Enoch, and to learn from him the truth; for his residence is with the angels.

7. When Mathusala heard the words of his son, he came to me at the extremities of the earth; for he had been informed that I was there: and he cried out.

8. I heard his voice, and went to him, saying; Behold I am *here*, my son; since thou art come to me.

9. He answered and said; On account of a great event have I come to thee; and on account of a sight difficult *to be comprehended* have I approached thee.

10. And now, my father, hear me; for to my son Lamech a child has been born, who resembles not him; and whose nature is not like the nature of man. His colour is whiter than snow; he is redder than the rose; the hair of his head is whiter than white wool; his eyes are like the rays of the sun; and when he opened them he illuminated the whole house.

11. When also he was taken from the hand of the midwife, he opened his mouth, and blessed the Lord of heaven.

12. His father Lamech feared, and fled to me, believing not that *the child* belonged to him, but that he resembled the angels of heaven. And behold I am come to thee, that thou mightest point out to me the truth.

13. Then I, Enoch, answered and said; The Lord will effect a new thing upon the earth. This have I explained, and seen in a vision. I have shewn thee that *in* the generations of Jared my father, those who were from heaven disregarded the word of the Lord. Behold they committed crimes; laid aside their class, and intermingled with women. With them also they transgressed; married with them, and begot children.

14. A great destruction therefore shall come upon all the earth; a deluge, a great destruction, shall take place in one year.

15. This child which is born to you shall survive on the earth, and his three sons shall be saved with him. When all mankind who are on earth shall die, he shall be safe.

16. And his posterity shall beget on the earth giants, not spiritual, but carnal. Upon the earth shall a great punishment be inflicted, and it shall be washed from all corruption. Now therefore inform thy son Lamech, that he who is born is his child in truth; and he shall call his name Noah, for he shall be to you a survivor. He and his children shall be saved from the corruption which shall take place in the world; from all the sin and from all the ini-

quity which shall be consummated on earth in his days. Afterwards shall greater impiety take place than that which had been before consummated on the earth; for I am acquainted with holy mysteries, which the Lord himself has discovered and explained to me; and which I have read in the tablets of heaven.

17. In them I saw it written, that generation after generation shall transgress, until a righteous race shall arise; until transgression and crime perish from off the earth; until all goodness come upon it.

18. And now, my son, go, tell thy son Lamech,

19. That the child which is born is his child in truth; and that there is no deception.

20. When Mathusala heard the word of his father Enoch, who had shewn him every secret thing, he returned with understanding[a], and called the name of that child Noah; because he was to console the earth on account of all its destruction.

21. Another book, which Enoch wrote for his son Mathusala, and for those who should come after him, and preserve their purity of conduct[b] in the latter days. You, who have laboured, shall wait in those days, until the evil doers be consumed; and the power of the guilty be annihilated. Wait, until sin pass away; for their names shall be blotted out of the holy books; their seed shall be destroyed, and their spirits slain. They shall cry out and lament

[a] *seeing.* [b] *their state of life.*

in the invisible waste, and in the bottomless fire shall they burn[a]. There I perceived, as it were, a cloud which could not be seen through; for from the depth of it I was unable to look upwards. I beheld also a flame of fire blazing brightly, and, as it were, glittering mountains whirled around, and agitated from side to side.

22. Then I inquired of one of the holy angels who was with me, and said; What is this splendid *object?* For it is not heaven, but a flame of fire alone which blazes; and *in it there is* the clamour of exclamation, of wo, and of great suffering.

23. He said; There, into that place which thou beholdest, shall be thrust the spirits of sinners and blasphemers; of those who shall do evil, and who shall pervert all which God has spoken by the mouth of the prophets; all which they ought to do. For respecting these things there shall be writings and impressions above in heaven, that the angels may read them, and know what shall happen both to sinners and to the spirits of the humble; to those who have suffered in their bodies, but have been rewarded by God; who have been injuriously treated by wicked men; who have loved God; who have been attached neither to gold nor silver, nor to any good thing in the world, but have given their bodies to torment;

24. To those who from the period of their birth[b]

[a] *in the fire shall they burn, where there is no earth.* [b] *from the time they were.*

have not been covetous of earthly riches; but have regarded themselves as a breath passing away.

25. Such has been their conduct[a]; and much has the Lord tried them; and their spirits have been found pure, that they might bless his name. All their blessings have I related in a book; and He has rewarded them; for they have been found to love heaven with an everlasting aspiration. *God has said;* While they have been trodden down by wicked men, they have heard from them revilings and blasphemies; and have been ignominiously treated, while they were blessing Me. And now will I call the spirits of the good from the generation of light, and will change those who have been born in darkness; who have not in their bodies been recompensed with glory, as their faith may have merited.

26. I will bring them into the splendid light of those who love my holy name; and I will place each of them on a throne of glory, of glory *peculiarly* his own, and they shall be at rest[b] during unnumbered periods. Righteous is the judgment of God;

27. For to the faithful shall He give faith in the habitations of uprightness[c]. They shall see those, who having been born in darkness into darkness shall be cast; while the righteous shall be at rest. Sinners shall cry out, beholding them, while they

[a] *And this have they kept.* [b] ወዩተወሀወሁ፡ See Remarks. [c] *of upright ways.*

exist in splendor and proceed forwards to the days and periods prescribed to them[d].

Here ends the vision of Enoch the prophet. May the benediction of his prayer, and the gift of his appointed period, be with his beloved! Amen.

[a] *written down for them.*

EXTRACTS

FROM THE

BOOK OF ENOCH,

TRANSLATED FROM THE ETHIOPIC INTO LATIN, BY M. DE SACY.

[*See Magasin Encyclopédique An.* VI. (1800.) *Tom.* I. p. 382.]

CAP. I.[a]

SERMO benedictionis Enochi, quomodo benedixit electis et 1
justis, qui futuri sunt in die afflictionis ad expellendum (i. e.
quando expelletur) omnem improbum et impium. Locutus est,
et dixit Enoch, vir justus, qui a Domino (venit), quo tempore
oculi ejus aperti sunt, et vidit visionem sancti qui in cœlis est,
quem ostenderunt mihi Angeli, et audivi ab eis omnia, et novi 2
ego illud quod vidi, et non est (i. e. non esse) futurum, in hac
generatione, sed in generatione quæ ventura est (hominum) longe
dissitorum, propter electos. Dixi et locutus sum propter eos, 3
cum (eo) quod exibit[b] sanctus et magnus de tabernaculo suo, et
deus mundi: et inde calcabit super montem Sina, et videbitur in 4
tabernaculo suo, et manifestabitur in fortitudine virtutis suæ de
cœlo, et pavebunt omnes, et commovebuntur vigiles, et capiet eos 5
timor et tremor magnus usque ad fines terræ, et consternabuntur 6
montes excelsi, et deprimentur colles sublimes, et liquescent[c]

[a] The order of chapters is here made conformable with that which is adopted in the Bodleian MS.

[b] *Mysla zayywatsa.* Si on lisoit *mysâla*, on pourroit traduire *parabolam* (*illam*) *quod*, etc.

Yytmaschawou. Je lis *yytmahawou*, que le sens exige.

sicut mel favi præ æstu, et submergetur terra, et omnia quæ
in ea sunt peribunt, et erit judicium super omnes, et super justos;
7 quoad justos autem, pacem faciet eis, et servabit electos, et erit
8 clementia super eos, et omnes erunt Dei (τοῦ Θεοῦ) et erunt felices[a], et benedicentur, et splendor Dei lucescet eis.

CAP. II.

Et venit cum myriadibus sanctorum, ut faciat judicium super eos, et perdat impios, et litiget cum omnibus carnalibus, pro omnibus quæ fecerunt et operati sunt contra eum, peccatores et impii[b].

CAP. III.

1 Norunt omnes qui sunt in cœlis opus eorum, quomodo non
2 mutant vias suas luminaria quæ sunt in cœlo, quemadmodum
unumquodque oritur et occidit regulariter, unumquodque in tempore suo, et non transgrediuntur mandata sua (quæ acceperunt): vident terram, intelliguntque constitutum, quod super ea observa-
3 tur ab initio usque ad finem ejus, quomodo non immutatur omne
opus suum deo, quando apparet: (i. e. quando tempus apparendi advenit, nempe tempestatibus anni, germinationi, floribus etc.) vident æstatem et hyemem, quomodo dies aquarum, nubes roris,

[a] *Yyscherhou.* Ce mot, qui devroit être écrit par un *Saut* (S) et un *Harm* (H), est écrit par un *Schat* (Sch) et un *Haut* (H). Il y a de semblables fautes d'orthographe presque à chaque ligne.

[b] C'est le fameux passage cité dans l'Epître de Saint Jude: Ἰδοὺ ἦλθε Κύριος *ἐν μυριάσιν ἁγίαις (al. ἁγίαις ἀγγέλων vel ἁγίων ἀγγέλων) αὐτοῦ, ποιῆσαι κρίσιν κατὰ πάντων, καὶ ἐξελέγξαι πάντας τοὺς ἀσεβεῖς αὐτῶν περὶ πάντων τῶν ἔργων ἀσεβείας αὐτῶν ὧν ἠσέβησαν, καὶ περὶ πάντων τῶν σκληρῶν ὧν ἐλάλησαν κατ' αὐτοῦ ἁμαρτωλοὶ ἀσεβεῖς.* Plusieurs écrivains anciens et modernes ont tiré, de cette citation, des conséquences contre l'authenticité de l'Epître de Saint Jude. Ce n'est pas ici le lieu d'entrer dans l'examen de cette discussion. On peut seulement remarquer que ce reproche, s'il étoit fondé, seroit commun à plusieurs autres lettres des Apôtres; car Origène et Saint Jérôme ont observé avec raison que l'on trouve, dans les écrits des Apôtres, plusieurs passages tirés de divers livres apocryphes. Voy. J. E. Grabe, *Præfat. ad testam.* 12. *Patriarch.* dans le *Codex pseudepig. Veter. Test. de Fabricius.* Au reste, on pourroit supposer que l'auteur du livre d'Enoch auroit emprunté ce passage de Saint Jude.

et pluvia super omnem terram requiescant (*vel forte*, omnem terram refocillent.)

CAP. VII.

Factum est autem cum multiplicati essent filii hominum in illis 1
diebus, natæ sunt eis pulchræ filiæ et formosæ, videruntque illas 2
angeli filii cœlorum, concupiveruntque illas, et dixerunt inter se:
venite, seligamus nobis uxores ex progenie hominum, et procree-
mus nobis filios. Tunc ait ad illos Samyâzâ, qui erat princeps 3
eorum: timeo ne forte nolitis confici hoc negotium, et ego solus 4
hujus peccati gravissimi pœnas luere cogar. Locutique sunt 5
omnes et dixerunt: juremus omnes, nosque mutuo anathemate 6
constringamus, nos non immutaturos illud consilium, istudque
propositum opere completuros. Tunc juraverunt omnes, mutuo- 7
que anathemate sese invicem constrinxerunt in id: erant autem
omnes ducenti, descenderuntque in Ardis quod est cacumen mon-
tis Armon. Istum vero montem Armon nominaverunt, quia in 8
illo juraverant, et sese mutuo anathemate devinxerant[a]. Hæc 9
sunt autem nomina principum ex eis: Samyâzâ, qui erat prin-
ceps eorum, Ourâcabarameel, Akibeel, Tamiel, Râmouel, Dânyel,
Azkeel, Sarâkouyal, Asâel, Armoris, Batrâal, Anânyou, Zawebe,
Samsâweel, Irtael, Touryel, Yomyael, Arâzyâl. Hi erant præ-
fecti eorum, ducentorum nempe angelorum, et alii omnes cum
eis[b].

Et acceperunt sibi uxores, elegeruntque sibi singuli singulas, et 10

[a] Le nom de Hermon s'écrit en Hébreu par un *Heth*, et il vient de la racine *Haram*, qui signifie *dévouer, consacrer à Dieu par une sorte d'anathême*. Dans l'Ethiopien, la lettre aspirée, qui devroit commencer ce mot, est omise, ce qui prouve que ce livre a été traduit en Ethiopien, d'apès un original Grec, et non sur un texte Hébreu. Dans la Chronique Syriaque de Grégoire Bar-Hebræus (p. 3), on lit: *Tempore Sethi, quando filii ejus beatam vitam paradisi recordati sunt, in montem Hermon secesserunt, et vivebant moribus* (et non *in deserto*, comme on lit dans la traduction imprimée) *puris et sanctis, a matrimoniis abstinentes, unde vocati sunt vigiles et filii Dei*. Cette tradition semble être due aussi à l'interprétation du mot *hermon*, dérivé de *haram, mettre hors de l'usage commun, consacrer*. Peut-être *haram* est-il l'origine du Grec ἔρημος.

[b] Dans le fragment conservé par le Syncelle, ces mots appartiennent à la phrase suivante: οὗτοι καὶ οἱ λοιποὶ πάντες . . . . . ἔλαβον ἑαυτοῖς γυναῖκας.

cœperunt accedere ad eas, mixtique sunt cum illis, et docuerunt
eas pharmaca et incantationes, succidere quoque radices et arbo-
11 res docuerunt eas. Illæ vero conceperunt, et pepererunt gigantes
12 magnos, quorum statura erat trecentorum cubitorum; hi vorave-
runt omnem laborem hominum, donec impossibile factum est eis
13 alere homines (*forte*, impossibile fuit hominibus alere eos); con-
14 versique sunt gigantes adversus homines, ut eos vorarent, et cœ-
perunt male facere avibus, et feris, et reptilibus, et piscibus, car-
nemque suam invicem comedebant, et sanguinem bibebant ex
15 illa. Tunc conquesta est terra contra injustos.

CAP. VIII.

1 Porro Azazyel docuit homines facere gladios, et cultros, et
scuta, et loricas pectoris, et fecit eos videre quod post se erat
(edocuit artem specula faciendi), institutumque illorum sunt ar-
millæ et ornatus, et stibio uti, et superciliis decus addere, et lapi-
des ex quocumque lapide pretioso et electo, omnesque tincturæ
2 simul; et immutatus est mundus, factaque est impietas magna, et
multiplicata est fornicatio, erraveruntque et corruperunt omnes
3 vias suas. Amazârâk edocuit omnes incantatores et succisores ra-
4 dicum; Armaros (docuit) solvere incantationes; Barkâyâl (do-
5 6 cuit) astrorum observatores, Kobabyel characteres[a] (magicos);
7 Tamiel docuit astronomiam: Asaradyel docuit motum lunæ[b]. Et
8 propter perditionem hominum (homines) clamaverunt, pervenit-
9 que vox eorum ad cœlum.

CAP. IX.

1 Tunc respexerunt Michaël et Gabryel, Râfâel, et Souryân et
Ouryan de cœlo, et viderunt multitudinem sanguinis qui effunde-
batur in terra, et omnem iniquitatem quæ fiebat super terram, et

[a] Ou *Signa*. On lit daus le Grec: *τὰ σημεῖα τῆς γῆς . . . . τὰ σημεῖα τοῦ ἡλίου.* Ceci paroît avoir été abrégé par le traducteur Ethiopien.

[b] On lit ici, dans le Grec, une ou deux phrases qui semblent nécessaires pour lier ce qui suit avec le récit précédent. *Μετὰ δὲ ταῦτα ἤρξαντο οἱ γίγαντες κατεσθίειν τὰς σάρκας τῶν ἀνθρώπων, καὶ ἤρξαντο οἱ ἄνθρωποι ἐλαττοῦσθαι ἐπὶ τῆς γῆς . . . .*

dixerunt inter se : vox clamorum eorum ascendit : clamor terræ 2
usque ad ostium cœli (pervenit), et nunc apud vos, ô sancti cœ- 3
lorum, queruntur animæ hominum, dicentes : inducite nobis ju-
dicium apud Excelsum. Et dixerunt domino suo regi, quia (tu
es) dominus dominorum, et deus deorum, et rex regum, et thro-
nus gloriæ tuæ in omni generatione sæculi, et nomen tuum san-
ctum et gloriosum in omni generatione sæculi. Tu benedictus et
gloriosus fecisti omnia, et potestas omnium tecum est, omniaque 4
sunt patentia et manifesta coram te. Tu vides omnia, et non est
qui possit abscondi a te. Vidisti quæ fecit Azâzyel, quomodo do- 5
cuit omnem iniquitatem super terra, et manifestavit omnia arcana
mundi quæ fiunt in cœlis. Docuit quoque incantationes Samyâzâ, 6
cui tu dedisti potestatem, ut imperet iis qui una cum eo sunt,
elegeruntque inter filias hominum simul, dormieruntque cum illis,
cum illis, inquam, mulieribus, immundique facti sunt, et nota fe- 7
cerunt eis ista peccata. Mulieres vero pepererunt gigantes, et 8
ob id impleta est terra omni sanguine et iniquitate. Et nunc 9
ecce clamant animæ eorum qui mortui sunt, et queruntur usque 10
ad portam cœli, et ascendit gemitus eorum, et non possunt exire[a] 11 12
a facie injustitiæ quæ fit super terram. Tu scis omnia cum non-
dum sunt, et tu nosti hæc, et quæ ab illis facta sunt, et non est 13
quod dicas nobis (*vel* et nihil dicis nobis) : quid ergo convenit ut 14
faciamus illis propter hoc ?

CAP. X.

Tunc Excelsus magnus et sanctus locutus est, et misit Ar- 1
sayalalyor ad filium Lamechi dicens ei : dic ad eum in nomine 2 3
meo : Operi caput tuum : tum manifesta ei finem qui venturus 4
est, quia peribit omnis terra, et aquæ diluvii futuræ sunt super
omnem terram, peribuntque quæcumque sunt in ea ; et nunc 5
edoce eum quo pacto salvus evadet, sedebitque semen ejus super
omnem terram. Rursusque dixit Dominus Raphaeli : Liga Azâ- 6

a Dans le Grec, on lit : *καὶ οὐ δύναται (ὁ στεναγμὸς αὐτῶν) ἐξελθεῖν ἀπὸ προσώπου τῶν ἐπὶ τῆς γῆς γινομένων ἀδικημάτων.* Je crois donc qu'il faut substituer *potest* à *possunt.*

zyelis manus et pedes, et projice illum in tenebras, aperique deser-
7 tum, qui est in Dondael, et illuc projice eum: injiceque in eum
8 lapides tortos et acutos, obtege eum tenebris, et ibi mansurus est
9 in sæculum: obtegeque faciem ejus, ut non videat lucem, et in
10 die magno judicii (erit) ut mittatur in ignem. Vivifica (sana)
11 terram quam corruperunt angeli, vitamque terræ annuntia, et non
pereant omnes filii hominum, in mysterio omnium quæ palam
12 fecerunt vigiles[a], et docuerunt filios suos, et corrupta est omnis
terra in doctrina operis[b] Azazyelis, et omne peccatum in eum
13 scribe. Gabrieli vero dixit Dominus: Vade ad . . . et ad re-
probos, et ad filios fornicationis, perdeque filios fornicationis, filios
vigilum, de medio hominum. Exire fac eos, mitteque illos inter
se, in hos et in illos (committe eos mutuo certamine); occisione
14 pereant, quia diuturnitas dierum non erit eis. Omnes illi te roga-
bunt, et non erit patribus eorum propter eos (jus intercedendi[c]),
quia sperant vitam æternam, et ut vivant vitam æternam, unus-
15 quisque quingentos annos. Michaeli vero dixit Dominus: Nun-
tia Samyazæ, et aliis qui cum eo sunt, qui conjuncti sunt cum
mulieribus, ad corrumpendum se cum illis in omni immunditia
earum, quando jugulati fuerint omnes filii eorum, et quando vide-
rint perditionem dilectorum suorum, liga eos in 70 generationes
sub collibus terræ, usque in diem judicii eorum, et consumma-
tionis eorum, donec consummetur judicium, quod est in sæcula
16 sæculorum. Et in diebus illis deducent eos in infima loca ignis,
in cruciatus, et in carcerem, ut concludantur in sæculum sæculi.
17 Et illico comburetur et peribit (Samyaza) ab hoc nunc cum ipsis
simul: vincientur usque ad consummationem generationis gene-
18 rationum. Perde omnes animas ludo deditas, et filios vigilum,
19 qui oppresserunt homines. Perire fac omnem oppressorem a
20 facie terræ, et omne opus malum absumatur, et appareat planta

[a] Il y a dans l'Ethiopien *katalou*, *occiderunt*. C'est visiblement une faute. Peut-être faut-il lire *bahalou*, *dixerunt*. J'ai suivi le Grec, où on lit: εἶπον.

[b] Ou plutôt *in operibus doctrinæ*, comme on lit dans le Grec: ἐν τοῖς ἔργοις τῆς διδασκαλίας Ἀζαήλ.

[c] Il y a dans le Grec ἐρώτησις.

justitiæ et rectitudinis, et sit in benedictionem opus justitiæ et 21
rectitudinis. In sæculum cum lætitia plantabuntur. Et tunc 22
sancti omnes confitebuntur, et erunt viventes, usque dum genera- 23
verint mille (filios), et omnes dies adolescentiæ eorum et sabbata
eorum consummabuntur in pace. Et in diebus illis operabitur
omnis terra in justitia, omnis terra plantabitur arboribus, et im-
plebitur benedictione: omnis arbor exultationis plantabitur in
ea, conserentur in ea vineæ, et vinea, quæ plantata fuerit in ea, 24
faciet fructum ad satietatem; omne semen, quod in ea seminabi-
tur, faciet pro una mensura mensuras mille, et una mensura oli-
varum [a] faciet decem mensuras olei. Et tu munda terram ab 25
omni oppressione, et ab omni injustitia, et ab omni peccato, et
ab omni impio, et ab omni immunditia, quæ fit super terram.
Disperde illos a terra, et erunt omnes homines terræ justi, et om- 26
nes gentes Deum me habebunt, et benedicent mihi; omnes me
adorabunt, et mundabitur terra ab omni corruptione, et ab omni 27
peccato, et ab omni plaga, et ab omni dolore, et non erit iterum
ut mittam in eam diluvium, in generationem generationis, et us-
que in sæculum. In diebus illis aperiam thesauros benedictionis 28
qui sunt in cœlo, ut descendere faciam eos super terram, et super
opera eorum (hominum), et super laborem eorum. Filiis ho- 29
minis pax et æquitas sociæ erunt in omnibus diebus sæculi, et in
omni generatione sæculi.

CAP. XII. SECT. III.

Ante vero omnem rem (istam) absconsus fuerat Enoch, et non 1
fuit e filiis hominum qui sciret ubi absconsus erat, et ubi fuerat,
et quid factus fuerat, et omne opus ejus cum sanctis et cum vigi- 2
libus in diebus ejus. Ego Enoch benedicebam Domino magno 3
et regi sæculi, et ecce vigiles appellabant me Enochum scribam. 4
Et dixit mihi (Dominus): Enoch, scriba justitiæ, vade, et nuntia 5
vigilibus cœli, qui deseruerunt cœlum excelsum, et stationem san-
ctam, quæ est in sæculum, et cum mulieribus corrupti sunt, et 6
fecerunt quemadmodum faciunt filii hominum, et uxores sibi ac-

[a] On lit dans l'Ethiopien *Elyas;* c'est un mot Grec.

7 ceperunt, et magna corruptione super terram corrupti sunt, pa-
cem et remissionem peccati haud unquam futuram eis in terra;
quoniam non gaudebunt in filiis suis; occisionem dilectorum
suorum videbunt, et de interitu filiorum suorum gement, et de-
precabuntur in sæculum, et non erit eis misericordia, neque
pax.

CAP. XIII.

1 Pergens vero Enoch Azazyeli dixit: Non erit tibi pax. Mag-
2 num judicium egressum est contra te. Vinciet te, nec erit tibi
remissio, neque deprecatio, neque misericordia, quia docuisti op-
3 pressionem, et propter omne opus blasphemiæ, et oppressionis, et
4 peccati, quod ostendisti filiis hominum. Tunc abiens ego locutus
5 sum omnibus illis simul, omnesque timore timuerunt, et tremor
6 corripuit eos, et rogaverunt me, ut memoriale facerem petitionis
eorum, utque pro ipsis scriberem, ut esset eis remissio, et ut ascen-
dere facerem memoriale deprecationis eorum ad Dominum cœli,
quia jam non liceret eis ex hoc nunc loqui, nec oculos ad cœlum
7 tollere præ confusione delicti sui, cujus rei judicati fuerant. Tunc
scripsi memoriale deprecationis eorum, et supplicationis eorum,
et pro spiritu eorum, et pro unoquoque operum ipsorum, et pro
8 eo quod rogabant, nempe ut esset eis remissio et quies. Et per-
gens ego steti super aquas Dan, in Dan quod est a dextra occasus
Armon, legens memoriale deprecationis eorum, donec obdormivi.
9 Et ecce somnium venit ad me, et visiones factæ sunt super me:
cecidi, et vidi visionem plagæ, ut eam narrarem filiis cœlorum, eos-
que verbis arguerem. Experrectusque veni ad illos: omnes vero
congregati stabant lugentes in Oubilsalâyel, qui locus est inter
10 Libanon et Seneser, opertis faciebus; locutusque sum coram eis
11 cunctas visiones quas videram, et somnium meum, et cœpi pro-
loqui hæc verba justitiæ, et verbis coarguere vigiles cœli.

CAP. XIV.

Hic est liber sermonum justitiæ, et reprehensio vigilum qui
1 sunt a sæculo, quemadmodum præcepit sanctus et magnus in hac
visione. Ego vidi in somnio meo, quia ego jam loquebar in lin-

gua mea carnali, et in spiritu meo, quem dedit Excelsus in os ho-
minibus, ut cum hominibus colloquantur in eo, et corde intelli- 2
gant. Quemadmodum creavit deditque hominibus, ut intelligant
vocem intellectus, mihi quoque creavit et dedit verbis arguere vi-
giles filios cœli. Ego rogationem vestram scripsi, et in visione
mea sic apparuit, quia id quod petitis non erit vobis omnibus die-
bus sæculi, judiciumque consummatum est super vos: non erit 3
vobis (petitio vestra). A nunc non ascendetis in cœlum usque 4
in omne sæculum, et in terra locutus est ut vinciat vos (vosque
dixit in terra vinctos futuros) omnibus diebus sæculi. Ante hæc 5
vero videbitis interitum filiorum vestrorum dilectorum, et non
erunt vobis in possessionem, sed cadent coram vobis gladio, et 6
rogatio vestra pro eis non erit, nec pro vobis. Vos autem, flentes 7
supplicantesque, haud commemorabimini; hæc sunt verba ex libro 8
quem scripsi. Mihi autem hujusmodi visio apparuit: Ecce nubes 9
in visione amplectebantur me, et nubecula involvebat me, et cur-
sus stellarum fulguraque sollicitum me tenebant, premebantque
(metu) et spiritus[a] volare me faciebant, et sollicitum tenebant:
abstuleruntque me sursum in cœlum, et veni usque dum appropin- 10
quarem ad murum, qui ædificatus erat lapidibus grandinis, lingua-
que ignis circumdabat eum; tum cœpit timor me apprehendere,
intravique in linguam ignis, et appropinquavi ad domum mag- 11
nam, quæ ædificata erat lapidibus, grandinis: mœniaque hujus do- 12
mus, sicut et pavimentum ejus, erant tabulæ e lapidibus grandinis,
et terra ejus grando; tectum ejus stellæ discurrentes et fulgura,
et inter illa cherubim[b] ex igne, quorum cœlum erat aqua; ignis
ardens circum mœnia ejus, et porta ejus igne ardebat. Intravique
in domum istam, et ipsa calida erat sicut ignis, et frigida sicut
grando. Nullum oblectamentum, nec vita est in ea. Timor ob-
texit me, et tremor cepit me, vehementerque commotus et tre- 13
mens cecidi in faciem meam. Vidique in visione mea, et ecce do- 14
mus alia major (priori), et omnes portæ ejus apertæ coram me,
et ædificata erat lingua ignis, et in omnibus abundabat, in gloria, 15

[a] C'est-à-dire, *venti vehementes* : c'est un Hébraïsme.

[b] Il y a dans le texte *Kiroubel*.

in magnificentia, et in magnitudine, ita ut impossibile sit narrare
16 vobis gloriam ejus et magnitudinem ejus. Terra ejus ignis, et de-
super fulgur et stellæ discurrentes, tectumque illius ignis ardens;
17
18 respiciensque vidi in ea thronum excelsum, cujus aspectus sicut
19 pruina, et circuitus ejus sicut sol lucens, et vox cherubim, et de
20 sub throno magno exibant flumina ignis ardentis, nec erat possi-
21 bile contueri eum. Gloria magnus sedebat super eum, et pallium
22 ejus lucebat magis quam sol, et albentius erat omni grandine, et
23 non poterat nec ullus angelorum ingredi, et contueri faciem ejus,
magnifici illius nempe et gloriosi. Non poterat ullus carnalis vi-
24 dere eum. Ignes ignium ardentium circa eum, magnusque stabat,
et ignis coram eo. Non erat qui appropinquaret ad eum ex iis
qui erant circa ipsum: myriades myriadum coram illo. Ipsi au-
tem opus non erat concilio sanctitatis: sanctique, qui ad illum
accedebant, non discedebant nocte ac die, nec ab eo recedebant.
Ego autem accessi usque ad eum, velo faciem tectus, tremens-
que. Dominus autem ore suo vocavit me, et dixit mihi: Ac-
25 cede huc, Enoch, et ad vocem meam sanctam; sustulitque me,
et ad portam usque accedere fecit: facies autem mea deorsum
dejecta erat.

CAP. XV.

1 Et alloquens me dixit mihi voce sua: Audi, ne timeas Enoch,
vir juste, et scriba justitiæ: accede huc, et audi vocem meam.
Vade, et dic vigilibus cœli, qui te miserunt, ut deprecareris pro
eis: Vos decebat deprecari pro hominibus, non vero homines
2 pro vobis. Quare dereliquistis cœlum excelsum et sanctum, quod
est in sæculum, et cum mulieribus dormiistis, et cum filiabus ho-
minum coinquinati estis, et vobis uxores accepistis, et sicut filii
3 terræ fecistis, et filios procreastis gigantes? Vos autem spirituales,
sancti, viventes vitam quæ est in sæculum, cum mulieribus coin-
quinati estis, et in sanguine carnali genuistis, et in sanguine ho-
4 minum concupivistis, et fecistis, sicut ipsi faciunt, caro et sanguis.
5 At illi moriuntur, ideoque dedi eis uxores, ut in illis semen de-
ponant, et nascantur filii per eas, ut similiter opus fiat super ter-
6 ram. Vos vero ab initio facti estis spirituales, viventes vitam quæ

est in sæculum, nec morituri in omni generatione sæculi. Pro- 7
pterea non feci vobis uxores, quia spirituales eratis, quorum man-
sio in cœlo. Nunc vero gigantes, qui nati sunt ex spiritu et 8
carne, spiritus mali vocabuntur super terra, et in terra erit habi-
tatio eorum; et spiritus mali exierunt ex carne eorum, quia ex
desuper creati sunt, ex sanctis vigilibus fuerunt primordia eorum,
primumque fundamentum. Spiritus mali ipsi erunt super ter-
ram, et spiritus malorum vocabuntur: Spiritus cœli, in cœlo erit
habitatio eorum; spiritus vero terræ, qui nati sunt super terra, in
terra erit mansio eorum; spiritus gigantum (erunt, sicut) nubes, 9
quæ opprimient, corrumpent, cadent, pugnabunt, et conterent
super terram, et luctum inducent: nihil erit quod comedant, 10
frumentum, et sitient; et occulti erunt, et non [a] insurgent spiri-
tus illi super filios hominum et mulieres, quia venerunt (ab eis [b]).
Ab diebus occisionis et stragis.

CAP. XVI.

Et mortis gigantum qui ....[c] similiter peribunt, usque ad 1
diem judicii magni a sæculo, magni (quod) consummabitur a
vigilibus et impiis. Nunc vigilibus, qui te miserunt, ut depreca- 2
reris pro eis, qui ab initio in cœlo fuerunt, (dic): Et nunc vos 3
autem in cœlo fuistis, et arcana jam non manifesta erunt vobis,
et vile mysterium cognovistis, et illud narrastis mulieribus in 4
duritie cordis vestri, et per illud mysterium multiplicabunt ho-
mines et mulieres mala super terram. Dic eis: Itaque non erit 5
vobis pax.

SECT. V. CAP. XXII.

..... Vidi animas filiorum hominum, qui mortui sunt, et vox earum usque ad cœlum pertingebat, et querebatur. Tunc inter-

[a] Cette négation est vraisemblablement de trop; elle ne se lit point dans le Grec. En général, la fin de ce chapitre et le chapitre suivant sont remplis de fautes, et peu intelligibles.

[b] Je supplée ces mots d'après le Grec: ὅτι ἐξ αὐτῶν ἐξεληλύθασι. Mais le traducteur Ethiopien a lié le mot *venerunt* avec les mots *à diebus*, comme le prouve la division du chapitre.

[c] Je passe ici une ou deux lignes dont on ne peut tirer aucun sens.

rogavi Raphael angelum, qui mecum erat, dicens : Quænam est anima hæc, cujus vox ita pertingit, et queritur ? Responditque, et dixit mihi : Hæc est anima, quæ exiit de Abel, quem occidit Cain frater ejus, et de eo queritur, usque dum deleatur progenies ejus a facie terræ, et pereat a sobole hominum semen ejus. . . .

CAP. XXXI.

1 Post hæc respexi versus aquilonem, suspiciens desuper montes ;
et vidi tres montes plenos nardo aromatica pura, et arboribus sua-
2 veolentibus, et cinnamomo et papyro. Inde respexi desuper sum-
mitates illorum montium, qui sunt procul ad orientem, et transii
super mare Erythræum [a], longeque ab eo fui, et transii desuper
angelum Zetiel, et veni in hortum justitiæ, et vidi ibi inter illas
3 arbores, arbores multas et magnas, quæ germinabant ibi, quarum
odor erat bonus, magnus, et elegantes valde et admirabiles ; et
arborem scientiæ, ex qua quicumque comedit, magnam acquirit
4 scientiam. Arbor illa similis est fabæ Græcæ [b], et fructus ejus,
sicut uva vineæ, valde bonus : fragrantiaque hujus arboris ibat et
pertingebat longe, et dixi : O pulchram arborem, et quam bonus
5 et lætus aspectus ejus ! Responditque mihi angelus Raphael, qui
6 erat mecum, et dixit mihi : Hæc est arbor scientiæ, ex qua man-
ducaverunt pater tuus senex et mater tua Hebræa [c] qui fuerunt
ante te ; scientiamque cognoverunt, et aperti sunt oculi eorum,
noveruntque se nudos esse, et ex horto pulsi sunt.

[a] Il y a dans le texte *Erytri*.

[b] Le mot employé ici répond, dans la version Ethiopienne du N. T. en S. Luc. ch. xv. ver. 16. au mot Grec τῶν κερατίων. Ludolf dit que les Ethiopiens entendent par là une sorte de tamarin. V. le Dict. Eth. de Ludolf, édition de Londres, 1661. col. 28 et 435.

[c] Cette expression présente un anachronisme remarquable.

EXTRACTS

FROM THE

CHRONOGRAPHIA

OF

GEORGIUS SYNCELLUS,

AS QUOTED BY FABRICIUS IN HIS CODEX PSEUDEPIGRAPHUS VETERIS TESTAMENTI, Vol. I. p. 179—198.

Georgius Syncellus in Chronographia, p. 11. ed. Par. 1652.

Ἐκ τοῦ πρώτου βιβλίου Ἐνὼχ, περὶ τῶν Ἐγρηγόρων.

I. ΚΑΙ ἐγένετο, ὅτε ἐπληθύνθησαν οἱ υἱοὶ τῶν ἀνθρώπων, ἐγεννήθησαν αὐτοῖς θυγατέρες ὡραῖαι, καὶ ἐπιθύμησαν αὐτὰς οἱ Ἐγρήγοροι, καὶ ἀπεπλανήθησαν ὀπίσω αὐτῶν, καὶ εἶπον πρὸς ἀλλήλους, ἐκλεξώμεθα ἑαυτοῖς γυναῖκας ἀπὸ τῶν θυγατέρων τῶν ἀνθρώπων τῆς γῆς. καὶ εἶπεν Σεμιαζᾶς ὁ ἄρχων αὐτῶν πρὸς αὐτούς· Φοβοῦμαι μὴ οὐ θελήσετε ποιῆσαι τὸ πρᾶγμα τοῦτο, καὶ ἔσομαι ἐγὼ μόνος ὀφειλέτης ἁμαρτίας μεγάλης. καὶ ἀπεκρίθησαν αὐτῷ πάντες, καὶ εἶπον. ὀμόσωμεν ἅπαντες ὅρκῳ, καὶ ἀναθεματίσωμεν ἀλλήλους, τοῦ μὴ ἀποστρέψαι τὴν

Ex libro primo Enoch, de Egregoris.

I. Hominum vero in immensum crescente numero, filiæ natæ sunt illis speciosissimæ, in quas exarserunt Egregori, et earum amore capti in varios errores abducti sunt. Mutuis itaque sermonibus sese adhortantes: Eligamus, inquiunt, nobis uxores ex hominum terræ filiabus. Dixit autem Princeps eorum Semiazas: Vereor, ne hoc adimplere nolitis, et ego solus gravis hujus peccati reus agar. Responderunt autem ei omnes, dixeruntque: Jurejurando firmemus cuncti propositum hocce nostrum, dirisque invicem devoveamus nos, a sententia, donec opere perficiatur, nusquam discessuros.

γνώμην ταύτην, μέχρις οὗ ἀποτελέσωμεν αὐτήν. τότε πάντες ὤμοσαν ὁμοῦ, καὶ ἀνεθεμάτισαν ἀλλήλους. ἦσαν δὲ οὗτοι διακόσιοι οἱ καταβάντες ἐν ταῖς ἡμέραις Ἰαρὲδ εἰς τὴν κορυφὴν Ἑρμονιεὶμ ὄρους. καὶ ἐκάλεσαν τὸ ὄρος Ἑρμῶν, καθότι ὤμοσαν, καὶ ἀνεθεμάτισαν ἀλλήλους ἐν αὐτῷ. καὶ ταῦτα τὰ ὀνόματα τῶν ἀρχόντων αὐτῶν. α'. Σεμιαζᾶς ὁ ἄρχων αὐτῶν. β'. Ἀταρκούφ. γ'. Ἀρακιήλ. δ'. Χωβαβιήλ. ε'. Ὀραμμαμή. ς'. Ῥαμιήλ. ζ'. Σαμψίχ. θ'. Ζακιήλ. θ'. Βαλκιήλ. ι'. Ἀζαλζήλ. ια. Φαρμαρός. ιβ'. Ἀμαριήλ. ιγ'. Ἀναγημᾶς. ιδ'. Θαυσαήλ. ιε'. Σαμιήλ. ις'. Σαρινᾶς. ιζ'. Εὐμιήλ. ιη'. Τυριήλ. ιθ'. Ἰουμιήλ. κ'. Σαριήλ.

Juramento tunc devinxere se cuncti, maledictisque sibi invicem imprecati sunt. Erant autem hi numero ducenti, qui in diebus Jared in montis Ermonim verticem profecti sunt. Montem autem dixerunt Ermon, ex jurejurando, quo se invicem constrinxerunt, et maledictis, quibus se sponte subjecerunt. Hæc porro sunt Principum illorum nomina. 1. Semiazas princeps eorum. 2. Atarcuph. 3. Araciel. 4. Chobabiel. 5. Horammame. 6. Ramiel. 7. Sampsich. 8. Zaciel. 9. Balciel. 10. Azalzel. 11. Pharmarus. 12. Amariel. 13. Anagemas. 14. Thausacl. 15. Samiel. 16. Sarinas. 17. Eumiel. 18. Tyriel. 19. Jumiel. 20. Sariel.

II. Οὗτοι, καὶ οἱ λοιποὶ πάντες, ἐν τῷ χιλιοστῷ ἑκατοστῷ ἑβδομηκοστῷ ἔτει τοῦ κόσμου ἔλαβον ἑαυτοῖς γυναῖκας, καὶ ἤρξαντο μιαίνεσθαι ἐν αὐταῖς, ἕως τοῦ κατακλυσμοῦ. καὶ ἔτεκον αὐτοῖς γένη τρία· πρῶτον γίγαντας μεγάλους. οἱ δὲ γίγαντες ἐτέκνωσαν Ναφηλείμ. καὶ τοῖς Ναφηλεὶμ ἐγεννήθησαν Ἐλιούδ· καὶ ἦσαν αὐξανόμενοι κατὰ τὴν μεγαλειότητα αὐτῶν καὶ ἐδίδαξαν ἑαυτοὺς, καὶ τὰς γυναῖκας ἑαυτῶν φαρμακείας καὶ ἐπαοιδίας.

II. Isti, cæterique cuncti, acceperunt sibi uxores anno mundi millesimo, centesimo septuagesimo, et ad diluvium usque in eas insanierunt. Hæ vero pepererunt eis tria genera: quorum primum gigantes, homines proceri: gigantes autem Naphelim procreaverunt: ex Naphelim porro Eliudæi orti sunt. Cæterum juxta corporis eorum molem auctus est quoque numerus, ac sese uxoresque suas veneficia et incantationes mutuo docuerunt. Pri-

πρῶτος ᾿Αζαὴλ, ὁ δέκατος τῶν ἀρχόντων, καὶ ἐδίδαξεν ποιεῖν μαχαίρας, καὶ θώρακας, καὶ πᾶν σκεῦος πολεμικὸν, καὶ τὰ μέταλλα τῆς γῆς, καὶ τὸ χρυσίον πῶς ἐργάσωνται, καὶ ποιήσωσιν αὐτὰ κόσμια ταῖς γυναιξὶν, καὶ τὸν ἄργυρον. ἔδειξεν δὲ αὐτοῖς καὶ τὸ στίλβειν, καὶ τὸ καλλωπίζειν, καὶ τοὺς ἐκλεκτοὺς λίθους, καὶ τὰ βαφικά. καὶ ἐποίησαν ἑαυτοῖς οἱ υἱοὶ τῶν ἀνθρώπων καὶ ταῖς θυγατράσιν αὐτῶν, καὶ παρέβησαν, καὶ ἐπλάνησαν τοὺς ἁγίους. καὶ ἐγένετο ἀσέβεια πολλὴ ἐπὶ τῆς γῆς, καὶ ἠφάνισαν τὰς ὁδοὺς αὐτῶν. ἔτι δὲ καὶ ὁ πρώταρχος αὐτῶν Σεμιαζᾶς ἐδίδαξεν εἶναι ὀργὰς κατὰ τοῦ νοὸς, καὶ ῥίζας βοτανῶν τῆς γῆς. ὁ δὲ ἑνδέκατος Φαρμαρὸς ἐδίδαξεν φαρμακείας, ἐπαοιδίας, σοφίας, καὶ ἐπαοιδῶν λυτήρια. ὁ ἔννατος ἐδίδαξεν ἀστροσκοπίαν. ὁ δὲ τέταρτος ἐδίδαξεν ἀστρολογίαν. ὁ δὲ ὄγδοος ἐδίδαξεν ἀεροσκοπίαν. ὁ δὲ τρίτος ἐδίδαξεν τὰ σημεῖα τῆς γῆς. ὁ δὲ ἕβδομος ἐδίδαξεν τὰ σημεῖα τοῦ ἡλίου. ὁ δὲ εἰκοστὸς ἐδίδαξεν τὰ σημεῖα τῆς σελήνης. πάντες οὗτοι ἤρξαντο ἀνακαλύπτειν τὰ μυστήρια ταῖς γυναιξὶν αὐτῶν, καὶ τοῖς τέκνοις αὐτῶν.

mus Azael (*supra Azalzel*) in ordine Principum decimus, qui gladios, thoracas, et omne bellicum instrumentum, et terræ metalla conflare docuit, nec non aurum et argentum qua tractarent arte, ornatum muliebrem compositur: instruxit et ostendit insuper, quomodo polire, et electis lapidibus nitorem adjicere, et colores fucare possent. Ista sibi filiabusque suis comparaverunt filii hominum, et violato Dei mandato sanctos in errorem inpulerunt; ac tandem perversis justitiæ semitis ingens terram universam pervagata est impietas. Animo insuper odia fovere, et herbarum radicibus aliis damna parare, Semiazas eorum dux aperuit: Pharmarus Princeps undecimus veneficia, incantationes, præstigias et incantationum impedimenta: Nonus astrorum cursus: quartus astrologiam: octavus aëris inspectionem: tertius terræ: septimus solis: vicesimus lunæ signa exposuit: singuli denique arcana hæc uxoribus filiisque suis revelaverunt.

III. Μετὰ δὲ ταῦτα ἤρξαντο οἱ γίγαντες κατεσθίειν τὰς σάρκας τῶν ἀνθρώπων, καὶ ἤρξαντο οἱ ἄνθρωποι ἐλαττοῦσθαι ἐπὶ τῆς γῆς. οἱ δὲ λοιποὶ ἐβόησαν εἰς τὸν οὐρανὸν περὶ τῆς κακώσεως αὐτῶν, λέγοντες εἰσενεχθῆναι τὸ μνημόσυνον αὐτῶν ἐνώπιον Κυρίου.

III. Gigantes postmodum carnes humanas vorare cœperunt. Hinc hominum numerus minor indies fieri, ac pene deficere visus: tum reliqui quique tantæ nequitiæ pertæsi, vocem extulerunt in cœlum, et sui memoriam ad Dei conspectum deferri precati sunt.

Idem, p. 24.

IV. Καὶ ἀκούσαντες οἱ τέσσαρες μεγάλοι ἀρχάγγελοι, Μιχαὴλ, καὶ Οὐριὴλ, καὶ Ῥαφαὴλ, καὶ Γαβριὴλ, καὶ παρέκυψαν ἐπὶ τὴν γῆν ἐκ τῶν ἁγίων τοῦ οὐρανοῦ· καὶ θεασάμενοι αἷμα πολὺ ἐκκεχυμένον ἐπὶ τῆς γῆς, καὶ πᾶσαν ἀσέβειαν καὶ ἀνομίαν γενομένην, εἰσελθόντες εἶπον πρὸς ἀλλήλους· ὅτι τὰ πνεύματα καὶ αἱ ψυχαὶ τῶν ἀνθρώπων στενάζουσιν ἐντυγχάνοντα καὶ λέγοντα, ὅτι εἰσαγάγετε τὴν κρίσιν ἡμῶν πρὸς τὸν ὕψιστον, καὶ τὴν ἀπώλειαν ἡμῶν ἐνώπιον τῆς δόξης τῆς μεγαλοσύνης, ἐνώπιον τοῦ Κυρίου τῶν Κυρίων πάντων τῇ μεγαλοσύνῃ. καὶ προσελθόντες οἱ τέσσαρες ἀρχάγγελοι εἶπον τῷ Κυρίῳ τῶν αἰώνων· σὺ εἶ ὁ Θεὸς τῶν θεῶν, καὶ Κύριος τῶν κυρίων, καὶ Βασιλεὺς τῶν βασιλευόντων, καὶ Θεὸς τῶν ἀνθρώπων· καὶ ὁ θρόνος

IV. His auditis quatuor archangeli magni, Michael, Uriel, Raphael, et Gabriel, de sanctis cœli prospexerunt in terram, et viso plurimo sanguine super terram effuso, et universa impietate et iniquitate cognita, regressi dixerunt ad invicem: Spiritus et animæ hominum suspirant, dicentes: inducite ad Altissimum orationem nostram, internecionemque nostram ad gloriam Majestatis, ad Dominum dominorum omnium in Majestate. Tum Deum interpellantes quatuor archangeli dixerunt: Tu es Deus Deorum, et Dominus dominorum, regum Rex, et hominum Deus: thronus gloriæ tuæ in omnes sæculorum generationes perseverat, et no-

τῆς δόξης σου εἰς πάσας τὰς γενεὰς τῶν αἰώνων, καὶ τὸ ὄνομά σου ἅγιον καὶ εὐλογημένον εἰς πάντας τοὺς αἰῶνας. σὺ γὰρ εἶ ὁ ποιήσας τὰ πάντα, καὶ πάντων τὴν ἐξουσίαν ἔχων, καὶ πάντα ἐνώπιόν σου φανερὰ καὶ ἀκάλυπτα, καὶ πάντα ὁρᾷς, καὶ οὐκ ἔστιν ὃ κρυβῆναι (δυνηθῇ). ὁρᾷς ὅσα ἐποίησεν Ἀζαὴλ, ὅσα εἰσήνεγκεν, καὶ ὅσα ἐδίδαξεν, ἀδικίας καὶ ἁμαρτίας ἐπὶ τῆς γῆς, καὶ πάντα δόλον ἐπὶ τῆς ξηρᾶς. ἐδίδαξε γὰρ τὰ μυστήρια, καὶ ἀπέκαλυψε τῷ αἰῶνι τὰ ἐν οὐρανῷ. ἐπιτηδεύουσι δὲ τὰ ἐπιτηδεύματα αὐτοῦ, εἰδέναι τὰ μυστήρια (τολμῶσιν) οἱ υἱοὶ τῶν ἀνθρώπων. τῷ Σεμιαζᾷ τὴν ἐξουσίαν ἔδωκας ἔχειν τῶν σὺν αὐτῷ ἅμα ὄντων, καὶ ἐπορεύθησαν πρὸς τὰς θυγατέρας τῶν ἀνθρώπων τῆς γῆς, καὶ συνεκοιμήθησαν μετ' αὐτῶν, καὶ ἐν ταῖς θηλείαις ἐμιάνθησαν, καὶ ἐδήλωσαν αὐταῖς πάσας τὰς ἁμαρτίας, καὶ ἐδίδαξαν μίσητρα ποιεῖν. καὶ νῦν ἰδοὺ αἱ θυγατέρες τῶν ἀνθρώπων ἔτεκον ἐξ αὐτῶν υἱοὺς γίγαντας· κίβδηλα ἐπὶ τῆς γῆς ἐκκέχυται, καὶ ὅλη ἡ γῆ ἐπλήσθη ἀδικίας. καὶ νῦν ἰδοὺ τὰ πνεύματα τῶν ψυχῶν τῶν ἀποθανόντων ἀνθρώπων ἐντυγχάνουσι, καὶ μέχρι τῶν πυλῶν τοῦ οὐρανοῦ ἀνέβη ὁ στεναγμὸς

men tuum Sanctum et benedictum per omnia sæcula. Tu enim omnia condidisti, et omnium tua est potestas, cuncta tibi sunt aperta et manifesta; prospicis universa, nec est quod te possit latere. Vides quæ fecerit Azael, illata ab eo damna, invectam ab eo criminum luem, quas fraudes, quæ crimina super terram induxerit, artes, dolosque, quibus aridam corrupit. Secreta palam fecit, et ista, quæ in cœlis occlusa erant, sæculo revelavit. Genium ejus student assequi, et arcana quæque perscrutari non verentur hominum filii. Omnium sibi conjunctorum et familiarum Semiazæ contulisti potestatem. Illi vero ad filias hominum terræ diverterunt, et cum eis dormierunt: polluti cum mulieribus, nihil non facinorosum eis aperuerunt, et exosa quæque perpetrare edocuerunt. En insuper prolem giganteam ex eis pepererunt hominum filiæ: tetra corruptionis labes super terram omnem grassata est, et totus orbis injustitia plenus est. En adstant Spiritus animarum hominum morte jam functorum, et ad portas usque cœli suspiria eorum pertigerunt, nec

αὐτῶν, καὶ οὐ δύναται ἐξελθεῖν ἀπὸ προσώπου τῶν ἐπὶ τῆς γῆς γινομένων ἀδικημάτων· καὶ σὺ αὐτὰ οἶδας πρὸ τοῦ αὐτὰ γενέσθαι, καὶ ὁρᾷς αὐτοὺς, καὶ ἐᾷς αὐτοὺς, καὶ οὐδὲν λέγεις. τί δεῖ ποιῆσαι περὶ τούτου;

V. Τότε ὁ ὕψιστος εἶπεν, καὶ ὁ ἅγιος ὁ μέγας ἐλάλησε. καὶ ἔπεμψε τὸν Οὐριὴλ πρὸς τὸν υἱὸν τοῦ Λάμεχ, λέγων· πορεύου πρὸς τὸν Νῶε, καὶ εἰπὸν αὐτῷ τῷ ἐμῷ ὀνόματι· κρύψον σεαυτόν· καὶ δήλωσον αὐτῷ τέλος ἐπερχόμενον, ὅτι ἡ γῆ ἀπόλλυται πᾶσα. καὶ εἰπὸν αὐτῷ, ὅτι κατακλυσμὸς μέλλει γίνεσθαι πάσης τῆς γῆς, ἀπολέσαι πάντα ἀπὸ προσώπου τῆς γῆς. δίδαξον τὸν δίκαιον, τί ποιήσει, τὸν υἱὸν Λάμεχ, καὶ τὴν ψυχὴν αὐτοῦ εἰς ζωὴν συντηρήσει, καὶ ἐκφεύξεται δι' αἰῶνος. καὶ ἐξ αὐτοῦ φυτευθήσεται φύτευμα, καὶ σταθήσεται πάσας τὰς γενεὰς τοῦ αἰῶνος.

VI. Καὶ τῷ Ῥαφαὴλ, εἶπεν· πορεύου Ῥαφαὴλ, καὶ δῆσον τὸν Ἀζαὴλ, χερσὶ καὶ ποσὶ συμπόδισον αὐτὸν, καὶ ἔμβαλλε αὐτὸν εἰς τὸ σκότος· καὶ ἄνοιξον τὴν ἔρημον τὴν οὖσαν ἐν τῇ ἐρήμῳ Δουδαὴλ, καὶ ἐκεῖ πορευθεὶς βάλε αὐτὸν, καὶ ὑπόθες αὐτῷ λίθους ὀξεῖς, λίθους τραχεῖς, καὶ ἐπικάλυψον αὐτῷ σκότος, καὶ οἰκειωσάτω ἐκεῖ εἰς

propter scelerum in terris commissorum gravitatem discedere queunt. Tu tamen, antequam fiant, illa nosti, vides, permittis, nec verbum eloqueris? Quid rei nunc agendum?

V. Respondit Altissimus, et Sanctus excelsus loquutus est: et misit Uriel ad filium Lamech, dicens: Vade ad Noe, et dic ei meo nomine: Absconde temetipsum: et eventurum finem illi denuncia, quoniam terra peribit universa. Et dic ei: Totius terræ futurum est diluvium, ut e superficie terræ cuncta dispereant, et deleantur. Edoce justum filium Lamech quid agere debeat, et animam suam servabit incolumem, et per sæculum perniciem evadet. Ejus quoque industria novum germen pullulabit, et coletur, et per omnes sæculi generationes consistet.

VI. Et Raphaeli dixit: Vade Raphael, et Azaelem liga, manus et pedes ejus vinculis constringe, et in tenebras mitte; aperi deserti Dudael desertum, et profectus illuc eum conjice: et suppositis ei lapidibus acutis et asperis, induc super eum tenebras, quas in æternum incolat, visum desuper obstrue, nec lumen respiciat, ut in die

τὸν αἰῶνα· καὶ τὴν ὄψιν αὐτοῦ πώμασον, καὶ φῶς μὴ θεωρείτω· καὶ ἐν τῇ ἡμέρᾳ τῆς κρίσεως ἀπαχθήσεται εἰς τὸν ἐμπυρισμὸν τοῦ πυρός. καὶ ἴασαι τὴν γῆν, ἣν ἠφάνισαν οἱ Ἐγρήγοροι. καὶ τὴν ἴασιν τῆς πληγῆς δήλωσον, ἵνα ἰάσωνται τὴν πληγὴν, καὶ μὴ ἀπόλωνται πάντες οἱ υἱοὶ τῶν ἀνθρώπων ἐν τῷ μυστηρίῳ ὃ εἶπον οἱ Ἐγρήγοροι, καὶ ἐδίδαξαν τοὺς υἱοὺς αὐτῶν, καὶ ἐρημώθη πᾶσα ἡ γῆ ἐν τοῖς ἔργοις τῆς διδασκαλίας Ἀζαήλ. καὶ ἐπ' αὐτῇ γράψον πάσας τὰς ἁμαρτίας.

judicii incendio consumendus abducatur. Terram vero ab Egregoris corruptam sana; plagæ cicatricem manifesta, ut curetur hæc eorum plaga, ne arcanis ab Egregoris revelatis, quorum peritia posteri eorum sunt imbuti, et ex quibus universa terra operum, quæ Azael docuit, pravitate deserta est, omnes hominum filii funditus intereant: et omnia hucusque perpetrata scelera super eam describe.

VII. Καὶ τῷ Γαβριὴλ εἶπεν. πορεύου, Γαβριὴλ, ἐπὶ τοὺς γίγαντας, ἐπὶ τοὺς κιβδήλους, ἐπὶ τοὺς υἱοὺς τῆς πορνείας, καὶ ἀπόλεσον τοὺς υἱοὺς τῶν Ἐγρηγόρων ἀπὸ τῶν υἱῶν τῶν ἀνθρώπων, πέμψον αὐτοὺς εἰς ἀλλήλους ἐξ αὐτῶν εἰς αὐτοὺς, ἐν πολέμῳ καὶ ἐν ἀπωλείᾳ, καὶ μακρότης ἡμερῶν οὐκ ἔσται αὐτοῖς, καὶ πᾶσα ἐρώτησις οὐκ ἔστιν τοῖς πατράσιν αὐτῶν, ὅτι ἐλπίζουσιν ζῆσαι ζωὴν αἰώνιον, καὶ ὅτι ζήσεται ἕκαστος αὐτῶν ἔτη πεντακόσια.

VII. Et Gabrieli dixit: Tu Gabriel ad Gigantes, spurios, ex adulteriis ortos proficiscere: filios Egregororum a filiis hominum disperde: bellis excitatis partem eorum in sibi adversam excita, conserant invicem exercitus, ut cædibus, et mutua internecione conficiantur, resecetur diuturnior eorum vita, nec sit patribus eorum inquirendi locus: promittant sibi licet æternitatem vitæ, et ad quingentos usque annos luminis visum.

VIII. Καὶ τῷ Μιχαὴλ εἶπεν· πορεύου Μιχαὴλ, δῆσον Σεμιαζᾶν, καὶ τοὺς ἄλλους σὺν αὐτῷ, τοὺς συμμιγέντας ταῖς

VIII. Et Michaeli dixit: Vade Michael, Semiazam aliosque filiabus hominum commixtos, et immunditiis eorum inquinatos

θυγατράσι τῶν ἀνθρώπων τοῦ μιανθῆναι ἐν αὐταῖς ἐν τῇ ἀκαθαρσίᾳ αὐτῶν· καὶ ὅταν κατασφαγῶσιν οἱ υἱοὶ αὐτῶν, καὶ ἴδωσιν τὴν ἀπώλειαν τῶν ἀγαπητῶν αὐτῶν, δῆσον αὐτοὺς ἐπὶ ἑβδομήκοντα γενεὰς εἰς τὰς νάπας τῆς γῆς, μέχρι ἡμέρας κρίσεως αὐτῶν, μέχρι ἡμέρας τελειώσεως τελεσμοῦ, ἕως συντελεσθῇ κρίμα τοῦ αἰῶνος τῶν αἰώνων. τότε ἀπενεχθήσονται εἰς τὸ χάος τοῦ πυρὸς, καὶ εἰς τὴν βάσανον, καὶ εἰς τὸ δεσμωτήριον τῆς συγκλείσεως τοῦ αἰῶνος. καὶ ὃς ἂν κατακριθῇ καὶ ἀφανισθῇ ἀπὸ τοῦ νῦν μετ' αὐτῶν, δεθήσεται μέχρι τελειώσεως γενεᾶς αὐτῶν.

vinculorum nexibus coërce; et mactati fuerint eorum filii, dilectorumque sibi stragem viderint, abduc eos in extremos terræ recessus usque ad septuaginta generationes, ad judicii eorum terminum, ad consummationis eorum finem, usque dum sæculi sæculorum judicium absolvatur. Tunc in ignis confusum chaos, in tormenta, et æterni carceris vincula rapientur: quivis autem cum eis nunc damnatus et suppliciis adjudicatus, ad consummatum usque generis eorum finem compedibus vinctus concludetur.

Καὶ μεθ' ἕτερα.

IX. Καὶ νῦν οἱ Γίγαντες, οἱ γεννηθέντες ἀπὸ πνευμάτων καὶ σαρκὸς, πνεύματα πονηρὰ ἔσονται, τὰ πνεύματα ἐξεληλυθότα ἀπὸ τοῦ σώματος τῆς σαρκὸς αὐτῶν, διότι ἀπὸ τῶν ἀνθρώπων ἐγένοντο, καὶ ἐκ (τῶν ἁγίων) τῶν Ἐγρηγόρων ἡ ἀρχὴ (τῆς) κτίσεως αὐτῶν, καὶ ἀρχὴ θεμελίου. πνεύματα πονηρὰ ἐπὶ τῆς γῆς ἔσονται, τὰ πρῶτα τῶν Γιγάντων νεμόμενα, ἀδικοῦντα, ἀφανίζοντα, ἐμπίπτοντα, καὶ συμπαλαίοντα, καὶ ῥίπτοντα ἐπὶ τῆς γῆς, καὶ δρόμους ποιοῦντα,

Et aliis quibusdam interjectis.

IX. Gigantes deinceps, a Spiritus et carnis copula procreati, erunt Spiritus nequam, Spiritus e corpore carnis suæ deflectentes, eo quod ex hominibus nati sunt, et ex sanctis Egregoris ortus eorum principium ac fundamenti exordium fuit deductum: scelerati Spiritus erunt super terram, inter Gigantes præcipui, hinc populabuntur, cædent, et vastabunt; illinc insilient, colluctabuntur, in terram prosternent,

καὶ μηδὲν ἐσθίοντα, ἀλλὰ ἀσιτοῦντα, καὶ φάσματα ποιοῦντα, διψῶντα, καὶ προσκόπτοντα. καὶ ἐξαναστήσονται τὰ πνεύματα ἐπὶ τοὺς υἱοὺς τῶν ἀνθρώπων, καὶ τῶν γυναικῶν, ὅτι ἐξ αὐτῶν ἐξεληλύθασι. καὶ ἀπὸ ἡμέρας καιροῦ σφαγῆς, καὶ ἀπωλείας καὶ θανάτου τῶν Γιγάντων, Ναφιλεὶμ καὶ ἰσχυροὶ τῆς γῆς, οἱ μεγάλοι ὀνομαστοὶ, τὰ πνεύματα τὰ ἐκπορευόμενα ἀπὸ τῆς ψυχῆς αὐτῶν, ὡς ἐκ τῆς σαρκὸς, ἔσονται ἀφανίζοντα χωρὶς κρίσεως, οὕτως ἀφανίσουσι μέχρις ἡμέρας τῆς τελειώσεως, ἕως τῆς κρίσεως τῆς μεγάλης, ἐν ᾗ ὁ αἰὼν ὁ μέγας τελεσθήσεται, ἐφ' ἅπαξ ὁμοῦ τελεσθήσεται.

et incursibus alios impetent: absque ullo cibo victitabunt, immittent spectra, sitient ipsi, et in alios irruent. Et in filios virorum et mulierum, ceu ex iisdem prognati, insilient. A primo cædis, internecionis, et Gigantum mortis momento fiet, ut Naphilim et robusti terræ, proceres celebres, Genii ab animis suis digressi, quasi carne compacti, cuncta absque delectu devastent, hoc pacto cuncta susque deque mittent usque ad consummationis diem, ad magnum usque judicium, quo sæculum illud magnum absolvetur, et semel ac simul ultimo claudetur fine.

Καὶ αὖθις.

X. Περὶ δὲ τοῦ ὄρους, ἐν ᾧ ὤμοσαν καὶ ἀνεθεμάτισαν πρὸς τὸν πλησίον αὐτῶν, ὅτι εἰς τὸν αἰῶνα οὐ μὴ ἀποστῇ ἀπ' αὐτοῦ ψύχος καὶ χιὼν, καὶ πάχνη, καὶ δρόσος, οὐ μὴ καταβῇ εἰς αὐτὸ, εἰ μὴ εἰς κατάραν καταβήσεται ἐπ' αὐτὸ, μέχρις ἡμέρας κρίσεως τῆς μεγάλης. ἐν τῷ καιρῷ ἐκείνῳ κατακαυθήσεται, ταπεινωθήσεται, καὶ ἔσται κατακαιόμενον καὶ τηκόμενον ὡς κηρὸς ἀπὸ πυρὸς, οὕτω κατακαήσεται περὶ πάντων τῶν

Et rursus.

X. A monte vero, in quo juramento sese invicem adstrinxerunt, ac ubi se diris mutuo devoverunt, nusquam deficient frigora, vel nives; pruina, vel ros, ad diem usque judicii magni nusquam, nisi forte in perniciem, delabentur. Ardebit, et deprimetur in illo tempore, horrenda fœdabitur adustione, liquefiet ad instar ceræ, et omnes ejus fructus arescent. Nunc vero vobis filiis hominum edico; Magna

ἔργων αὐτοῦ. καὶ νῦν ἐγὼ λέγω ὑμῖν υἱοῖς ἀνθρώπων· ὀργὴ μεγάλη καθ' ὑμῶν, (καὶ) κατὰ τῶν υἱῶν ὑμῶν, καὶ οὐ παύσεται ἡ ὀργὴ αὕτη ἀφ' ὑμῶν, μέχρι καιροῦ σφαγῆς τῶν υἱῶν ὑμῶν. καὶ ἀπολοῦνται οἱ ἀγαπητοὶ ὑμῶν, καὶ ἀποθανοῦνται οἱ ἔντιμοι ὑμῶν ἀπὸ πάσης τῆς γῆς ὅτι πᾶσαι αἱ ἡμέραι τῆς ζωῆς αὐτῶν ἀπὸ τοῦ νῦν οὐ μὴ ἔσονται πλείω τῶν ἑκατὸν εἴκοσι ἐτῶν· καὶ μὴ δόξητε ἔτι ζῆσαι ἐπὶ πλείονα ἔτη· οὐ γὰρ ἔστιν ἐπ' αὐτοῖς πᾶσα ὁδὸς ἐκφεύξεως ἀπὸ τοῦ νῦν διὰ τὴν ὀργὴν, ἣν ὠργίσθη ὑμῖν ὁ Βασιλεὺς πάντων τῶν αἰώνων. μὴ νομίσητε ὅτι ἐκφεύξησθε ταῦτα.

vobis et filiis vestris pernicies instat: et usque ad filiorum vestrorum internecionem non deficiet. Dilecti vestri peribunt, et præcipuo honore digniores habiti tollentur e terra: eo quod ab hoc momento dies vitæ eorum non nisi centum et viginti annorum sint futuri: diuturniorem vitam ne vobis ipsis polliceamini; a data siquidem hoc momento sententia nullus defensionis aut effugii dabitur locus, propter iram, qua sæculorum omnium Rex motus est, a qua deflectendi spes vana est et fallax.

Καὶ ταῦτα μὲν ἐκ τοῦ πρώτου βίβλου τοῦ Ἐνὼχ περὶ τῶν Ἐγρηγόρων.

Et hæc quidem ex primo libro Enoch, de Egregoris.

I have pointed out where the *first two* of these extracts occur, namely, between the first verse of chapter vii. and the sixteenth verse of chapter x: and also where the *third* occurs; viz. between the eighth verse of chapter xv. and the second verse of chapter xvi. But I can nowhere discover where the *fourth* extract is to be found. Syncellus himself remarks, that he has taken all from the first book of Enoch respecting the Watchers: and it is marked in the "Codex" of Fabricius as the *tenth* chapter.

REMARKS.

CHAP. I.

VER. 1. *he saw a holy vision in the heavens.*] M. De Sacy translates the words ወይሬኢ፡ ራእየ፡ ቅዱሰ፡ ዘበሰማያት "vidit visionem sancti, qui in cœlis "est." But he appears to have overlooked the vowel in the letter ሰ, which is the short *a*, and not the short *e* ስ, so that the word ቅዱሰ being an adjective in construction seems clearly to agree with the preceding substantive ራእየ also in construction, after the verb ይሬኢ. I should add, that the Paris MS., as transcribed by Woide, and the Bodleian, both read ቅዱሰ, not ቅዱስ.

CHAP. VII.

Ver. 8. *That mountain therefore was called Armon, because they had sworn upon it and bound themselves by mutual execrations.*] This derivation of the word *Armon* [*Hermon*] proves that the book was originally composed in Hebrew. The verse is thus expressed in the Greek; καὶ ἐκάλεσαν τὸ ὄρος Ἑρμῶν, καθότι ὤμοσαν, καὶ ἀνεθεμάτισαν ἀλλήλους ἐν αὐτῷ. In Hebrew this mountain is termed חֶרְמוֹן *Chermon* or *Hermon:* an appellation which, in conformity with the sense of the passage, can only be referred to the root חרם; which, when used in the conjugation Hiphil in Hebrew, and Aphel in Chaldee and Syriac, signifies to *anathematize* or *devote*. On the supposition therefore, that the book was written in Hebrew, or in either of the kindred languages, the passage would be in itself sufficiently explicit, and the derivation of the word apparent; but on the supposition that the book was written in Greek, it would be absolutely unintelligible without some further explanation; or at least without a notice, that the term was derived from a foreign language.

Ver. 9. *These are the names of their chiefs*] These names are expressed differently in the Greek; but variety on such occasions is by no means unusual. To two of the apostate angels here mentioned, Jonathan Ben Uziel in his Targum on the Law distinctly refers. On the expression הנפילים, *giants*, Genes. vi. 3, he has the following remark: שמחזאי ועזיאל הינן נפילין מן שמיא והוו בארעא ביומיא האינון *Samchazai and Uziel fell from heaven and were upon earth in those days. Samchazai* and *Uziel* appear to be the names of the first and ninth angel in the list of apocryphal Enoch, according to the Ethiopic version. In the Greek they are the first and tenth; and are there thus written, Σεμιαζᾶς, [Σεμιεξᾶς Scaliger] Ἀζαλζήλ. Upon the last name Fabricius gives the following note; "Infra Ἐξαὴλ et "Ἀζαήλ. Cedreno quoque et Judæis *Azael*."

CHAP. IX.

Ver. 1, 2. It is *the voice of their cries; the earth deprived* of her children *has cried even to the gate of heaven.*] M. De Sacy mistakes this passage: in the Ethiopic it is thus expressed ቃለ፡ ጽራኃቲሆሙ፡፡ ዕራቃ፡ ጸርሐት፡ ምድር፡ እስከ፡ አንቀጸ፡ ሰማይ, which he translates in the following manner, "Vox clamo-" rum eorum *ascendit:* clamor terræ usque ad osti-" um cœli (pervenit)." The adjective ዕራቃ, *orba, denudata,* he seems to have confused with the verb ዐርገ, *ascendit;* and the verb ጸርሐት, *clamavit,* (third person singular feminine,) he conceived to be the substantive ጽራሕ, *clamor.* Hence arose the inaccuracy of his translation; in which he mistook an adjective for a verb, and a verb for a substantive; an inaccuracy, which likewise compelled him to make sense of the latter clause by supplying from conjecture the supposed ellipsis of another verb, viz. *pervenit.* Besides, had ጸርሐት been a substantive, which it is not, the vowel connected with the letter ት shews that it could not be in construction with the other substantive ምድር, *terra.* I should however observe, that although both the Bodleian and Paris MSS. agree in the words, they do not agree in the stops; for after ጽራኃቲሆሙ፡፡ in the Bodl. MS. there is a full stop, (where indeed the verse ends;) but in the Paris MS. no such stop occurs; so that the first word in the second verse ዕራቃ may be incautiously referred to the preceding verse.

Ver. 6. *They have gone together to the daughters of men*] ወሖሩ፡ ኀበ፡ አዋልደ፡ ሰብእ፡ ኅቡረ. M. De Sacy renders this passage; "*elegerunt*que inter filias "hominum simul; mistaking the verb ሖሩ, *iverunt*, for ሐርዩ or ኀርዩ, *elegerunt*. The Greek text here reads, καὶ ἐπορεύθησαν πρὸς τὰς θυγατέρας τῶν ἀνθρώπων τῆς γῆς, *et profecti sunt ad filias hominum terræ.*

CHAP. X.

Ver. 13. *Go to the biters*] ለመንዝራን. M. De Sacy does not translate this word at all. The root ነዘረ occurs neither in Ludolf nor in Castellus. It is again used in chap. lxxxv. 7. Happening however to possess an Ethiopic MS. which contains the greatest part of the Minor Prophets, I have accidentally found the word in Micah iii. 5. "Thus saith "the Lord," exclaims Micah, "concerning the pro-"phets, that make my people err, እለ፡ ይነዝርዎ "ሙ፡ በስነኒሆሙ, *that bite with their teeth.*" Perhaps the *biters* may mean the *destroyers* of mankind. But in the Greek the word is κιβδήλους, *spurios.*

Ver. 24. *one measure of olives shall produce ten presses of oil*] The word translated olives is ኤልያስ, which is not to be found in the Lexicons, except as answering to the proper name *Elias.* M. De Sacy correctly remarks, that it is a Greek word. It is indeed nothing more than ἐλαίας the genitive case of ἐλαία, *oliva.* Perhaps the Greek expression was preserved, because in Ethiopic there is no distinction between the *olive berry*, and the *oil* extracted from that berry; the same word, ዘይት, signifying both. For it is evident that if ዘይት had been used for *olives* in the former part of the sentence, as it necessarily was for *oil* in the latter part of it, considerable obscurity of meaning must have taken place. The retention however of the Greek term renders the passage perhaps not much more intelligible to the mere Ethiopic reader.

Instead of "*presses* of oil," M. De Sacy has "*measures* of oil," mensuras olei. This is a little oversight; for the word is not መስፈርት, *measures*, but ምክያዳት, *presses*.

CHAP. XIV.

Ver. 9. *clouds and a mist invited me*] The verb in the Ethiopic is ይጸውዑኒ, *did call*, or *invite*. It occurs twice. This M. De Sacy translates *amplectebantur* in the first instance, and *involvebat* in the second. Certainly however he gives not the sense of the verb as it stands in both the MSS. Perhaps he conjectured that instead of ይጸውዑኒ, *did invite*, it should have been written ይጸንዑኒ, *did prevail over me*; a sense not very different from that which he has given; and indisputably a preferable sense. But a preferable sense is not always the most correct one. In the present instance however, the conjecture, if so bold a one be allowable, seems probable.

Ib. *winds assisted my flight*] This passage is thus translated by M. De Sacy, "spiritus volare me faci-

o 2

" ebant;" who remarks in a note upon the word *spiritus*, that it means *strong winds*, and is a Hebraism. But the expression in both MSS. is ነፋሳት, *naphasat venti*, and not ነፍሳት, *naphsat spiritus*; between which words in Ethiopic there is a marked difference; ነፋስ, *naphas*, signifying *wind*, and ነፍስ, *naphs*, *the soul*, or *spirit*; so that this distinction in the vowels indicates a distinction in the sense of the respective words.

CHAP. XV. XVI.

xv. 10. —*for they came forth during the days of slaughter and destruction.* xvi. 1. *And as to the death of the giants, wheresoever their spirits depart from their bodies, let their flesh, that which is perishable, be without judgment. Thus shall they perish, until the day of the great consummation of the great world. A destruction shall take place of the Watchers and the impious.*] እስመ፡ ወፅኡ፡ ሖመ፡ መዋዕለ፡ ቀትል፡ ወሙስና። ወሞተ፡ ረዓይትኒ፡ እንተ፡ ኀበ፡ ወፅአ፡ መንፈሳት፡ እምነፍስት፡ ለሥጋሆሙ፡ ለይኩን፡ ዘይማስን፡ ዘእንበለ፡ ኵነኔ፡ ከማሁ፡ ይማስኑ፡ እስከ፡ ዕለተ፡ ተፍጻሜት፡ ዐቢይ፡ እምዓለም፡ ዓቢይ፡ ይትፌጸም፡ እምተጉሃን፡ ወረሲዓን. M. De Sacy considers this passage as obscure and dislocated; and therefore only translates it in part. I have nevertheless attempted to give the whole of it; that too great an hiatus in the sense might not occur. The following is his translation; —" quia venerunt (ab eis). Ab " diebus occisionis et stragis, (chap. xvi.) Et mor-

" tis gigantum qui ..... similiter peribunt, usque " ad diem judicii magni a sæculo, magni (quod) " consummabitur a vigilibus et impiis." I will here add the Greek of the passage as preserved by G. Syncellus: *ὅτι ἐξ αὐτῶν ἐξεληλύθασι. καὶ ἀπὸ ἡμέρας καιροῦ σφαγῆς, καὶ ἀπωλείας καὶ θανάτου τῶν γιγάντων, Ναφιλεὶμ καὶ ἰσχυροὶ τῆς γῆς, οἱ μεγάλοι ὀνομαστοὶ, τὰ πνεύματα τὰ ἐκπορευόμενα ἀπὸ τῆς ψυχῆς αὐτῶν, ὡς ἐκ τῆς σαρκὸς, ἔσονται ἀφανίζοντα χωρὶς κρίσεως, οὕτως ἀφανίσουσι μέχρις ἡμέρας τῆς τελειώσεως, ἕως τῆς κρίσεως τῆς μεγάλης, ἐν ᾗ αἰὼν ὁ μέγας τελεσθήσεται, ἐφ' ἅπαξ ὁμοῦ τελεσθήσεται.*

CHAP. XIX.

Ver. 2. ***their wives also shall be*** judged, ***who led astray the angels of heaven that they might salute them.***] In the Ethiopic the whole sentence is thus expressed: እስመ፡ በዕለተ፡ ዐቢይ፡ ኵነኔ፡ በዘይትኰነኑ፡ እስከ፡ ይትፌጸሙ፡ ወአንስቲያሆሙኒ፡ ለስሒቶን፡ መላእክተ፡ ሰማይ፡ ከመ፡ ሰላማውያን፡ ይከውና::

CHAP. XXII.

Ver. 2. ***very smooth***] ለሙጽ from the verb ለምጸ, which Ludolf thus explains: " ***planum et leve*** red- " didit id, quod asperum fuit. Sic quidem Æthiops " meus exposuit. At mihi ***durum*** vel ***asperum*** signi- " ficare videtur." But the context in this place demonstrates, that Gregory, the Abyssinian interpreter, was right, and that Ludolf was wrong, in the respective significations which they attributed to this word.

CHAP. XXVIII.

Ver. 2. *choice trees, particularly* those which produce *the sweet smelling drugs, frankincense and myrrh*] ዕፀወ: ኵነኔ: ፈድፋደ: ቍስቍስ: መዓዛ: ለሰ ኂን: ወከርቤ. I am not perfectly satisfied with the sense which I have given to this passage; but I have not been able to discover a more probable one. The expression ዕፀወ: ኵነኔ, *trees of judgment*, seems singular; perhaps my own interpretation of it may be a little doubtful. I should add, that the word ቍስቍስ, which I have rendered *drugs*, is thus explained by Ludolf; "*supellex* omnis generis." Gen. xxxi. 37.

CHAP. XXXI.

Ver. 1. *After these things, surveying the entrances of the north, above the mountains*] The word አፈወ, which I have translated *entrances*, as the plural of እፍ, *ostium, ingressus*, M. De Sacy translates *respexi;* "Post hæc *respexi* versus aquilonem, suspiciens desuper montes." The Paris and Bodleian MSS. read alike. I cannot find out any sense of the word resembling that which M. De Sacy gives to it.

Ver. 5. *thy aged mother*] The version of M. De Sacy is, "mater tua *Hebræa*," upon which he observes in a note, that the expression, "*Hebrew* mother," presents a remarkable anachronism. But the Ethiopic certainly contains no anachronism whatsoever. The word which he translates *Hebrew*, and I translate *aged*, is ዕቤራዊት, *eberavit*, both in the Paris and Bodleian MSS. Now this word (changing the ዕ into an እ, which letters are in almost every page put indifferently for each other) signifies *widowed*, or *aged*, from the substantive እቤር, *an old woman*, or *widow*; but M. De Sacy appears to have mistaken it for ዑብራዊት, *Ebravit*, which indisputably signifies *Hebrew*; overlooking the vowel *e* long in the second letter; a vowel which constitutes the distinction between the two words. This error was probably occasioned by his not recollecting at the moment, that the first letter, ዕ, might have been written (as is the case perpetually) for እ; so that his attention was directed to a word commencing with a wrong letter; with a letter, the same indeed in pronunciation as that for which it was substituted, but very different in figure, and in its alphabetical station.

I have alluded to these inadvertencies of M. De Sacy with less reserve, because the reputation of that profound Oriental Scholar is too highly, and justly established, to be at all injured by them. Besides, it should be recollected, that in the translation of a work which is but little known, and which is found in a language but little cultivated, a language likewise, the means of cultivating which are so greatly circumscribed, lapses of this description may, perhaps I might say must, occasionally occur.

CHAP. XLI.

Ver. 7. *Nor does the angel prevent this*] What angel is here alluded to, it seems difficult to conjecture; unless indeed we suppose him to be the angel whose peculiar office it is, according to the Jewish creed, to conduct the souls of men from this world to the next.

CHAP. XLVIII.

Ver. 2, 3. *In that hour was the Son of man invoked before the Lord of spirits, &c.*] As this passage is strongly illustrative of Jewish opinion upon an important point of doctrine, before the appearance of Christ upon earth, I shall here give it in Ethiopic.

2. ወበይእቲ፡ ሰዓት፡ ተጸውዓ፡ ዝኩ፡ ወልደ፡ ሱብእ፡ በኀበ፡ እግዚእ፡ መናፍስት፡ ወስሙ፡ መቅድመ፡ ርእሰ፡ መዋዕል።

3. ወዘእንበለ፡ ይትፈጠር፡ ፀሐይ፡ ወተኣምር፡ ዘእንበለ፡ ይትገበሩ፡ ከዋክብተ፡ ሰማይ፡ ወስሙ፡ ተጸውዓ፡ በቅድመ፡ እግዚእ፡ መናፍስት፡ ውእቱ፡ ይከውን፡ በትረ፡ ለጻድቃን፡ ወቅዱሳን፡ ከመ፡ ቦቱ፡ ይትመርጐዙ፡ ወኢይደቁ፡ ወውእቱ፡ ብርሃን፡ አሕዛብ።

The following is a literal translation into Latin:

2. Et in illa hora invocatus est hic Filius hominis apud Dominum spirituum, et nomen ejus coram antiquo dierum.

3. Et antequam creabatur sol, et signa, antequam faciebantur stellæ cœli, nomen ejus invocatum est

coram Domino spirituum. Ille erit baculus justorum et sanctorum, ut in eo innitantur, et non cadant; et ille [erit] lux gentium.

Ver. 5. *Therefore the Elect and the Concealed one existed in his presence before the world was created, and for ever.*] ወበእንተዝ: ኮነ: ኅሩየ: ወኅቡእ: በቅድሜሁ: እምቅድመ: ይትፈጠር: ዓለም: ወእስከ: ለዓለም. Igitur fuit [or factus est] Electus, et Occultus, coram eo, antequam creabatur mundus, et usque ad secula seculorum.

CHAP. LI.

Ver. 2. *a mountain of fluid metal*] To the word ነጥብጥብ, which I have rendered *fluid metal*, Ludolf affixes the signification of *gutta, stilla*, a drop; the same as he likewise affixes to ነጥብ. But as it is evidently derived from a verb of the *ninth* conjugation, it seems to signify something more than a *mere drop*: that is, *an active continuation of drops*, or *a series of droppings*. And indeed he himself remarks upon an example adduced by him in the way of illustration, that the subject there alluded to is, *de copiosis et densis guttis tanquam imbrium.*

As therefore all the other mountains here spoken of are mountains of metal, I have given to this word the sense of *dropping*, or *fluid metal*, that is, of *Quicksilver*, a metal, which Aristotle terms ἄργυρος χυτὸς, "*fluid silver*."

CHAP. LV.

Ver. 1. ***After this I beheld another army of chariots***] The army here alluded to was probably the Roman, coming "***from the east, from the west, and from the south.***"

In the preceding chapter "the chiefs of the east "among ***the Parthians and Medes***" are mentioned; who, with the Romans, divided the whole empire of the world at that period, when it is most probable that the book was written. But as the Parthian power was perhaps the nearest, as well as the most formidable, to the country in which the author lived, he naturally represented this in the first place, as the great object of terror to the impious monarchs of the earth.

CHAP. LVIII.

Ver. 7. ***At that time a separation was made between two monsters***] To the Jewish fable of the Leviathan and the Behemoth I have alluded in my remarks upon the first book of Ezra, p. 308. 8°. 1819. The fable is too trite among the Jews to require repetition.

I have translated the word አናብርት, ***monsters.*** Ludolf gives ***tigres, tigers,*** as the only signification of it. But as the Leviathan and Behemoth were evidently never considered as belonging to the species of *tigers,* I have adopted a more general term, although without authority.

Ver. 12. *that the punishment of God may not be in vain.*] The Bodleian MS. omits here the verb ኢይኩን, *may not be,* which occurs in the Paris MS., and which is absolutely necessary to constitute that negative assertion in the sentence, which the sense of it requires.

CHAP. LIX.

Ver. 6, 7. *That every division is divided; that the lightning flashes, &c.*] There is much obscurity in these verses. The sixth verse is differently expressed in the two MSS. The Bodleian reads thus; ወኵሉ: ክፍል: ይትከፈል: በመብረቅ: ከመ: ይብርቅ. *Et omnis divisio dividitur; fulgure quod fulgurat.* The Paris MS. thus, at least according to Woide's transcript; ወኵሉ: ክፍል: ይትከፈል: ወነጐድጓድ: በ በመደቃቲሆሙ: ወለኵሉ: ክፍል: ዘይትከፈል: ከመ: ይብርቅ: በመብረቅ. *Et omnis divisio dividitur; et tonitru [tonitrua] in singulis suis casibus; et in omni divisione, qua dividitur, quod fulgurat fulgure.* The last passage may perhaps, with a little latitude of expression, be rendered into English in the following manner: *That every division is divided; the thunderings in each of their falls; and that at every division which takes place, the lightning flashes.* But I should observe, that the word መደቃት, (the plural of መደቅ,) which I translate *casus, falls,* as derived from the root ወድቀ, *to fall,* is not to be found in Ludolf. Its form however is a legitimate form of substantives derived from verbs defective in the first radical ወ; as ሙሉድ, *locus nativitatis*, or *patria*, comes from ወለደ, *genuit;* so that it seems necessarily referable to the root ወደቀ. Our Lexicons in this language are too incomplete to preclude significations of such a description. The noise of thunder, I conceive, is here compared with the resounding crash of a falling edifice.

The transcriber of the Bodleian MS. seems to have overlooked, and consequently omitted, all the words between the first occurrence of the verb ይትከፈል and its second occurrence with the prefix H. The Paris MS. therefore appears in this instance to be more correct. As I cannot however implicitly rely upon the accuracy of Woide's transcript, I have not ventured to introduce the words, thus apparently omitted, into the text.

Nor is the first clause of the next verse much more clear; ወተዐይንቶሙ: ከሙ: ፍጡነ: ይሰምዑ *et castra* [or *exercitus*] *eorum quod protinus obediunt,* or *audiunt. That their troops* [or *their host*] *immediately obey.* The *troops,* or *host,* here alluded to, are awkwardly referred to *the lightning,* according to the Bodleian MS.; for the Ethiopic substantive has a pronoun affix in the *plural* number connected with it. Perhaps the allusion is better in the Paris MS. as referring to the plural noun *thunderings,* which is immediately followed by a substantive in connection with the very same pronoun affix.

CHAP. LX.

Ver. 11. *in the word of the name of the Lord of spirits*] በነገረ፡ ስሙ፡ እግዚአ፡ መናፍስት, *in sermone nominis Domini spirituum.* But it is well known, that the prefix በ in the word በነገረ often indicates the mere *instrumentality* of the substantive to which it is prefixed, expressed in Latin by the ablative case alone; as well as bears the signification of the preposition *in.* I am doubtful whether I have ascertained the precise meaning of the sentence.

Ver. 13, 14. *He shall call to every power of the heavens, to all the holy above, and to the power of God. The Cherubim, the Seraphim, and the Ophanim, and all the angels of power, and all the angels of the Lords, namely, of the Elect one, and the other Power, who* was *upon earth over the water on that day, shall raise their united voice, &c.*] ወይጼውዕ፡ ኵሎ፡ ኃይለ፡ ሰማያት፡ ወኵሎ፡ ቅዱሳን፡ ዘመልዕልተ፡ ወኃይለ፡ እግዚአብሔር፡ ኪሩቤል፡ ወሱራፌል፡ ወኦፋኒን፡ ወኵሉ፡ መላእክተ፡ ኃይል፡ ወኵሉ፡ መላእክተ፡ አጋእዝት፡ ወኅሩይ፡ ወከልዕ፡ ኃይል፡ እለ፡ ወስተ፡ የብስ፡ ዲበ፡ ማይ፡ በይእቲ፡ ዕለት። ይነሥኡ፡ ዐ፡ ቃለ, &c. *Et vocabit omnem potestatem cælorum, et omnes sanctos, qui* sunt *supra, et potestatem Dei. Cherubim, et Seraphim, et Ophanim, et omnes angeli potestatis, et omnes angeli Dominorum, nempe Electi, et alterius Potestatis, quæ* erat *in terra super aquam illo die, tollent unam vocem, &c.*

That all the nouns in the first sentence of this passage are governed by the verb ይጼውዕ, *he shall call to*, is apparent from the vowel in the noun ኵሎ; a vowel which distinctly indicates, that it is in that state of construction with the verb, which is in Latin denominated the accusative case. But the words which follow, that is, ኪሩቤል፡ ሱራፌል፡ ኦፊ ኒን, *Cherubim*, *Seraphim*, *Ophanim*, as well as the same noun ኵሉ, which occurs twice, prove by their respective vowels that they are all in the nominative case: I have therefore placed a full stop after the words, *and to the power of God*.

Upon my mode likewise of translating another part of this important passage, it is necessary to be a little particular. Instead of the version, which I have given in these words; "—all the angels of the "Lords, *namely*, *of the Elect one*, *and of the other* "*Power*, who upon earth were over the water on "that day, shall raise, &c.;" another version may perhaps occur to the following effect; "—all the an-"gels of the Lords, *and the Elect one*, *and the other* "*Power*, who upon earth were over the water on "that day, shall raise, &c." But the latter appears to me incorrect, as leaving the phrase "angels of "the *Lords*" perfectly unintelligible; that is, as not explaining, what otherwise must be inexplicable, to whom the character of *Lords*, requiring the attendance of angels, appropriately belongs. In point of grammar both translations are admissible; but the one which I have chosen, for the reason assigned, seems to me preferable.

In proof that the conjunction ወ has the meaning of *nempe, namely,* although no such meaning is ascribed to it by Ludolf, I shall refer to Hebrews ii. 14. "That through death he might destroy him "that had the power of death, *that is,* the devil." The Greek is thus expressed; ἵνα διὰ τοῦ θανάτου καταργήσῃ τὸν τὸ κράτος ἔχοντα τοῦ θανάτου, τουτέστι, τὸν διάβολον. But this in the Ethiopic version is translated in the following manner; ከመ፡ በውእቱ፡ ሞት፡ ይስዐሮ፡ ለመልአከ፡ ሞት፡ ወለሰይጣን, ut per ipsam mortem aboleret angelum mortis, *nempe,* Satanam. Here it is evident that the Greek expression τουτέστι, *that is,* is rendered by the Ethiopic conjunction ወ.

CHAP. LXI.

Ver. 10. *for from the beginning the Son of man existed in secret*] The expression እምቀዲም, which I have translated *from the beginning,* Ludolf thus explains; "*a principio,* id est, *ab æterno.*"

CHAP. LXXI.

Ver. 4. *six* gates were *at the rising, and six at the setting of the sun.*] The system of astronomy, detailed in this and in the subsequent chapters, is precisely that of an untutored, but accurate observer of the heavens. He describes the eastern and western parts of heaven, where the sun and moon rise and set, as divided each into six different gates, through which those orbs of light pass at their respective periods. In the denomination of these gates he begins with that, through which the sun passes at the winter solstice; and this he terms the *first* gate. It of course answers to the sign *Capricornus;* and is the southernmost point to which the sun reaches both at rising and at setting. The next gate, at which the sun arrives in its progress towards the east at rising, and towards the west at setting, and which answers to the sign *Aquarius,* he terms the *second* gate. The next, in continuation of the same course of the sun, which answers to the sign *Pisces,* he terms the *third* gate. The *fourth* gate in his description is that which is situated due east at sun-rising, and due west at sun-setting, and which, answering to the sign *Aries,* the sun enters at the vernal equinox. With this *fourth* gate he commences his account of the sun's annual circuit, and of the consequent change in the length of day and night at the various seasons of the year. Verse 12, &c. His *fifth* gate is now to be found in the sun's progress northwards; and answers to the sign *Taurus.* And his *sixth* gate is situated still further north: which, answering to the sign *Gemini,* concludes at the most northern point of heaven, to which the sun arrives, and from which it turns at the summer solstice, again to measure back its course southwards.

Hence it happens, that the same gates which answer to the six signs alluded to in the sun's passage from the winter to the summer solstice, necessarily also answer to the remaining six of the twelve signs of the zodiac in its passage back again; viz. the *sixth* gate answers to *Cancer*, as before it did to *Gemini*; the *fifth* to *Leo*, as before to *Taurus*; the *fourth* to *Virgo*, as before to *Aries*; the *third* to *Libra*, as before to *Pisces*; the *second* to *Scorpio*, as before to *Aquarius*; and the *first* to *Sagittarius*, as before to *Capricornus*.

The *turning* of the sun both at the winter and summer solstices, the first at the most southern, the last at the most northern, point of its progress, must have always struck the eye of those who contemplated the variety as well as splendor of its daily appearance. The astronomy of apocryphal Enoch was perhaps formed in this respect upon the same principles as the astronomy of Homer, who places the situation of the island Συρίη or Σῦρος under the *turnings of the sun*, ὅθι τροπαὶ ἠελίοιο, Odyss. lib. xv. ver. 404. By translating the word τροπαὶ, *tropics*, the geography of the place has been strangely confused. Wood, in his Essay on the Genius and Writings of Homer, has given a better sense to the passage; and even argued from it that *Chios* was the birthplace of Homer. "Let us suppose," he remarks, "the Ionians looking southwest from the "heights of *Chios* at the winter solstice. They "would see the sun set behind Tenos, and towards "*Syros*, the next island in the same direction; and "having observed that when he advanced thus far,

" he ***turned back***, they would fix the ***turnings*** (*τροπαὶ*) " of the sun to this point." p. 17. It seems difficult to determine which is most striking; the simplicity or ingenuity of this explanation.

Ver. 25. *is made equal*] ይትዔረይ, Paris MS. The Bodleian MS. has incorrectly ይትሬአይ, *is seen*.

CHAP. LXXII.

Ver. 6. *Half of it &c.*] As I may have mistaken the sense of this passage, I subjoin the original; ወመንፈቁ፡ ርኁቅ፡ ፯፡ ለደ፡ ፩፡ ወኵሉ፡ ክበበ፡ ዚአሁ፡ በከ፡ ዘአልቦ፡ ብርሃን፡ ዘእንበለ፡ ሱብዓት፡ እደ፡ እም፡ ፲፡ ወ፬፡ እደ፡ ብርሃን፡ ወበዕለት፡ ይነሥእ፡ ፯፡ እደ፡ ወ መንፈቀ፡ ብርሃኑ፡ ይከውን፡ ብርሃኑ፡ ፯፯፡ እደ፡ ለሐቲ፡ ወመንፈቃ፡ ወየዓርብ፡ ምስለ፡ ፀሐይ.—The disk or face of the moon seems here to be considered as being divided into *fourteen* portions, that is, each half of it into *seven* portions; so that in its increase or decrease one of these fourteen portions becomes enlightened or darkened every day, when there are only *fourteen* days between the new and full moon, or vice versa; but so that in the last two days one *half* only of a fourteenth portion becomes enlightened or darkened each day, when there are *fifteen* days between the new and full moon.

Ver. 9. in ***its fourteen portions, that is,*** in each ***half***] ፯፡ ወ፯፡ እደ፡ ወንፋቃ.

Ver. 10. ***its light increases to fourteen portions.***] ወይበርህ፡ ፯፡ ወ፯፡ እደ.

CHAP. LXXIII.

Ver. 4. *In each of its two seven portions it completes all its light at rising and at setting.*] Between the words በምሥራቅ, *at rising*, and በምዕራብ, *at setting*, the Paris MS. inserts ወበበጊ፡ ጊ፡ እዴ፡ ይፈጽም፡ ኵሎ፡ ጽልመቶ, *and in each of its two seven portions it completes all its darkness*, that is, at setting.

Ver. 5. *In two* gates *the moon sets with the sun*, viz. *in those two gates which are in the midst, in the third and fourth gates.*] The meaning seems to be, that when the sun is in the third and fourth gates, that is, about the periods of the vernal and autumnal equinoxes, the *full* moon, as well as *new* moon, rises and sets in the *same gates*, or *parts, of the heavens* as the sun; which cannot be the case at other times; for, except about these periods, the place of the *full* moon being always *six* signs distant from that of the sun, the two luminaries must then necessarily rise and set in different parts of the heavens. Thus, when the sun enters *Cancer*, it rises and sets in the utmost *northern* point of its deviation from the east and west; but the full moon at that time rises and sets in the utmost *southern* points of its deviation from the same quarters.

I should add, however, that the two instances given in the text solely relate to the periods when the sun enters *Libra*, at the autumnal equinox, one only of the signs appropriated to the *third* gate; and when it enters *Aries*, at the vernal equinox, one only of the signs appropriated to the *fourth* gate.

Ver. 6. *Then it declines from the sun, and enters in eight days into the sixth gate, from which the sun goes forth.*] Here there appears a manifest omission in both MSS. For from the full to the new moon only *eight* days are enumerated, instead of *fifteen*; and the sun, which before was clearly stated to proceed from the third or fourth gate, is made to go forth from the *sixth* gate, "*into the sixth* "*gate*, from which the sun goes forth." I suspect that after the words, በስድስ፡ ኆኅት, *into the sixth gate*, the following have been omitted; ወይገብእ፡ ሰቡዐ፡ መዋዕለ፡ በኆኅት፡ ሣልስ, *and returns in seven days to the third gate*. This insertion therefore, distinguished by Italic letters, I have ventured to make.

Ver. 11. *there is an excess of thirty days belonging to the sun in five years*] The ancient year, according to the general computation, consisted of only *three hundred and sixty days*. Hence, as the lunar year was but *three hundred and fifty-four*, the solar year exceeded it by *six* days in one, and by *thirty* days in five years.

Ver. 13. *that the years may be changed with correct precision in three hundred and sixty-four days.*] Having given the excess of the solar above the lunar year, according to the vulgar computation, the author now adverts to what he conceives to be the true computation; that is, he reckons the solar year at three hundred and sixty-*four* days. The detail of the sun's progress through the different gates of heaven, and of the exact time during which it remains in each, he had already given in chap. lxxi. 10—42; and by this it appears, that he adds his four supernumerary days to the four quarters of the year, *viz.* at the vernal equinox, the summer solstice, the autumnal equinox, and the winter solstice.

Had he been conversant with the wisdom of the Egyptians, he would not have computed the year at three hundred and sixty-four days; for long before his time Herodotus records, that in Egypt it was computed at three hundred and sixty-five days; ἐπάγουσι ἀνὰ πᾶν ἔτος πέντε ἡμέρας πάρεξ τοῦ ἀριθμοῦ, *they add every year five supernumerary days*[a].

CHAP. LXXV.

Ver. 9. *the north, which is called the sea*] I have already remarked, in the Preliminary Dissertation, from the account given of the longest day in the year, that the country of the author must have been situated in a high latitude. The denomination here affixed to the *north*, the same which in Judæa was affixed to the *west*, seems to be a corroboration of that remark. In Judæa the term ים, *sea*, was applied to the *west*, because the Mediterranean sea is so situated with respect to that country. For the same reason perhaps the term *sea* is here applied

[a] Herodot. II. cap. 4. pag. 105, edit. Wesseling.

to the *north;* because the author, and those with whom he lived, believed, that the region north of them was wholly occupied by an immense ocean. This persuasion indeed, that the great Northern ocean approached much nearer to the Euxine and Caspian seas than it really does, appears to have been general among the ancients. For Strabo, in his description of the country lying between those two seas, calls it a *peninsula,* the northern part of which is bounded by the ocean; ἐκ δὲ τῶν ἄρκτων τῷ ὠκεανῷ[a]. So also again alluding to the same country he states, that a wandering tribe of Scythians inhabits the first part of it, *of those parts which are towards the north and the ocean,* ἐκ μὲν τῶν πρὸς ἄρκτον μέρων, καὶ τὸν ὠκεανόν[b].

CHAP. LXXVI.

Ver. 6. *Seven rivers I beheld upon earth, greater than all rivers*] From the brief account here given it is perhaps difficult to discover the names of the seven great rivers alluded to. The first is said to take its course from the west, and to flow into a great sea. This probably is the *Danube,* which flows into the Euxine sea at between forty-six and forty-seven degrees of latitude. Two others begin their course in the north, and are emptied into the Erythræan sea on the east. I apprehend that these are the *Ganges* and *Indus.* And of the remaining four flowing in the cavity of the north, two are

[a] Geograph. lib. xi. p. 491. ed. 1620. [b] Ib. p. 492.

stated to be poured into the Erythræan sea, and two others into a great sea, where it is said that there is a desert. The former two of these four I conceive to be the *Euphrates* and *Tigris;* the latter the *Don* and *Volga,* one of them being poured into the *Euxine,* the other into the *Caspian* sea; seas which the ancients generally believed to have a secret union [a]. I should add, that the word **መድበር**, *desert,* (which, by the way, as Ludolf observes, is *Hebrew,* מדבר, not *Ethiopic,* and certainly not *Greek,*) seems to signify an uninhabited region; and that the course of the *Don* and *Volga* was through a country altogether unknown to the ancients.

Seven appears to be a favourite number with the author. Here, besides the rivers, are seven high mountains, and seven great islands. It is impossible however to guess at these without some more definite description.

CHAP. LXXVIII.

Ver. 3. *its decrease is effected in the sixth gate in its period, until a hundred and seventy-seven days are completed*] The meaning seems to be, that the moon always passes the most *northern* point of its rising, or the turning point of the sixth gate, at some time during *its wane,* in one hundred and seventy-seven days, or half of the lunar year. The part of the year alluded to is from the *longest*

[a] Strabo, p. 509.

to the *shortest* day of the year. This must necessarily prove to be the case; because the place of the full moon, from which *its wane commences*, as being always opposite to that of the sun, *falls short*, during the period mentioned, of the sign Cancer, the turning point of the sixth gate.

The reverse holds good during the other half of the year, while the sun is proceeding from the *shortest* to the *longest* day. Of this an account is given, at chap. lxxvii. 19, 20.

Ver. 4. Its period *is less than that of the sun, according to the ordinance of the stars, by five days in one half year*] The lunar year being three hundred and fifty-four days, it is of course ten days shorter than the solar year (as computed in this book); so that its half year must consequently be five days shorter than the solar half year.

CHAP. LXXIX.

Ver. 6. *and barrenness shall take place in the borders of the great chariots in the west*] ወይበጽሕ፡ ዓበር፡ በጸንፈ፡ ሰረገላት፡ ዓቢይ፡ በመዕራብ. The borders of the great chariots in the west seem to designate the Roman territory; the territory of a power, which, with the Parthians in the east, at the period when the book was composed, divided the empire of the world.

CHAP. LXXXIV.

Ver. 2. *And behold a white cow sprung forth*

from the earth] The allegorical allusions to scriptural history contained in this vision are in general too obvious to require a minute detail. I have made however an occasional reference of the kind in the notes.

CHAP. LXXXIX.

Ver. 20. *to break the horn of the dabela*] No such word as ደቤላ, *dabela*, is to be found in Ludolf's Ethiopic Lexicon. But in his Amharic Lexicon the word ዶኩላ, *dekula*, occurs, which he says bears the signification of *ibex*, a species of *wild goat*, or some such animal. Perhaps the Dabela, by whatsoever appellation we may distinguish him, is introduced to represent *Alexander the Great*, who is described by Daniel[a] as a he-goat, which "had *a* "*notable horn* between his eyes," and of which also it is said, that "he waxed very great; and, when he "was strong, *the great horn was broken*[b]." Alexander seems to be the *sixteenth* of the *twenty-three* shepherds mentioned in ver. 7, who intervened between the period of the captivity, and the rise of the Maccabæan dynasty. The *last twelve* shepherds, the computation of whom commences with the Maccabees, are not alluded to until the 25th verse.

Ver. 45. *were alarmed at him*] ይፈርህዎ with a *masculine* affix. The Ethiopic word ላህም, *a cow*, seems a generic term, like the English word *a sheep*.

[a] Chap. viii. 5. [b] Ibid. ver. 8.

Ver. 47. *the first,* who *was in the midst of them, spoke, when that word became a large beast*] ቀዳማዊ፡ በማእከሎሙ፡ ኮነ፡ ነገረ፡ ወውእቱ፡ ነገር፡ ኮነ፡ ሶርዊ፡ ዐቢየ. The literal sense, "*the first in the* "*midst of them became a word, and that word be-* "*came a large beast,*" seems not very intelligible. Perhaps I have not rendered it much more so.

CHAP. XCII.

Ver. 4. *I have been born the seventh in the first week*] In the mode of reckoning here adopted, it is evident that *a day* stands for *a hundred years;* so that consequently a week is made to express a period of seven hundred years. The chronology however, thus established, does not always accord with that which has been deduced from the Bible, in consequence of the necessity of computing from the uncertain æra of creation. This is the case when we attempt to assign dates to the different events alluded to in the first *six* weeks. But at the latter end of the sixth week an event is recorded, the precise date of which can be ascertained. The destruction of the temple of Solomon is mentioned as having taken place at that period. Now this occurrence happened fifty-two years before the going forth of the commandment to rebuild Jerusalem in the first year of Cyrus; and we know that from the first year of Cyrus to the birth of Christ there were exactly 536 years. Such has been the certainty afforded by the celebrated Canon of Ptolemy, in which the duration of the intermediate reigns of the respective monarchs are distinctly marked. Assuming, therefore, that the destruction of the temple of Solomon took place in the 588th year before Christ, we may consider the 500th year of the same æra as the end of the *sixth*, and the commencement of the *seventh* week.

During the interval between the destruction of the temple and the birth of Christ, but at a period approximating to the latter time, the Book of Enoch, as I have already endeavoured to demonstrate, evidently seems to have been written. As then the author of it lived antecedently to the conclusion of the *seventh* week, his reference to the events of that conclusion must have been solely conjectural, and is therefore probably erroneous. That it is so, I apprehend, little doubt can be entertained. For although he is correct in his allusion to the first part of this week, when he remarks, that an active and perverse generation will arise in it; yet is he completely mistaken in his allusion to the latter part of it; a period which he did not himself live to see. In it, he says, "the righteous, "selected from the plant of everlasting righteous-"ness, *shall be rewarded;* and to them shall be "given sevenfold instruction respecting every part "of creation." Now when it is recollected, that the *seventh* week closed with the second century of the Christian æra, and that towards the end of the preceding, or first, century of that æra, Jerusalem was irrecoverably captured and destroyed, its inhabitants massacred by thousands, and the very name of the Jewish people blotted out from the list of independent nations;—when these things are recollected, we cannot but admit the total irrelevancy of the pseudo-prophet's allusion. Never also can it be supposed, that he would have mentioned only the demolition of the *first* temple, and the Babylonian captivity, had he witnessed that more calamitous event, that complete annihilation of national character and consequence, which took place at the demolition of the *second* temple.

Nor is he more fortunate in his subsequent conjectures; for in the *eighth* week he foretells, that there shall be given to it *a sword* to execute judgment and justice against "all oppressors; that sin-"ners shall be delivered up into the hands of the "righteous, who during its completion shall ac-"quire habitations by their righteousness; and that "the house of the great King shall be built up for "ever." Now as this week comprehends the period between the commencement of the third, and that of the tenth century after Christ, it is evident that here again his prophecy completely fails; for the very reverse of what he states actually happened, as the Jews still continued to suffer from the sword of their oppressors; as they were so far from acquiring habitations by their righteousness, that they were more widely scattered over the face of the whole earth; and as the house of the great

King still remained in its previous state of total demolition.

A similar remark also may be applied to his notice of the *ninth* week, embracing the period between the years 900 and 1600. A. D. in which he prophesies, that "the judgment of righteousness "shall be revealed to the whole world; every work "of the ungodly shall disappear from every part of "the earth; the world shall be marked for destruc-"tion; and all men shall be on the look-out for in-"tegrity." Respecting these events, at any part of the time alluded to, the page of history exhibits a perfect blank.

Upon the occurrences of the *tenth* week, it is impossible to make any satisfactory observation; because these occurrences will not take place till the last day of that week, that is, till the period commencing with the year 2200, and ending with that of 2300. A. D.; a period which is not yet arrived.

CHAP. XCV.

Ver. 2. *into the cavities*] በንድላታት. No such root as ንደለ occurs in Ludolf's Ethiopic Lexicon; but in his Amharic Lexicon he gives the signification of *foramen* to the substantive ነደሉ. This signification I have adopted.

The passage seems to be taken from Isaiah ii. 21, which is thus expressed in the Septuagint; Τοῦ εἰσελθεῖν εἰς τὰς τρώγλας τῆς στερεᾶς πέτρας, καὶ εἰς τὰς σχισμὰς τῶν πετρῶν, *to enter into the cavities of the solid rocks, and into the clefts of the rocks.* The words adopted by the Ethiopic translator of Isaiah, to express the latter clause of the sentence, are precisely the same as in the Book of Enoch; *viz.* ንቅዓታተ፡ ኰኵሕ, *the clefts of the rocks.*

Ver. 2. *like hares*] ከመ፡ ግሔ. Ludolf renders ግሔ, *lepus, a hare;* he adds, however, "Sed *cunicu-* "*lum* interpretabatur Æthiops meus." The latter sense seems to be best adapted to the context.

Ver. 3. *Who shall groan over you, and weep like sirens.*] The word which I have translated *groan* is ይነዕኩ: Ludolf however had not met with it as a verb; but he gives this meaning to it as a substantive, under the form of ፃእክ.

There is also another word in this verse, ጺጸናታት, which Ludolf translates *fauni*, referring to Isaiah xiii. 21, which I have translated *sirens*. In the passage of Isaiah referred to, the Septuagint reads thus; καὶ ἀναπαύσονται ἐκεῖ σειρῆνες, καὶ δαιμόνια ἐκεῖ ὀρχήσονται, *and sirens shall rest there, and demons shall dance there.* This is thus rendered into Ethiopic; ወየዐርፉ፡ ወስቴታ፡ ጺጸናታት፡ ወይዘፍኑ፡ በሀየ፡ አጋንንት. Here the Greek word σειρῆνες, *sirens,* is evidently interpreted by the Ethiopic word ጺጸናታት.

CHAP. CV.

Ver. 26. *and they shall be at rest*] ይተወሀወሁ. I am doubtful whether I have given the correct meaning of this word. I consider its root to be ነወኀ, or ነወሀ with a duplication of the last two letters, so as to form the quinque-literal verb ነወንወን. This, in the sixth conjugation, would make ይትነወሀወሁ. But the transcriber of the MS. must have in this case carelessly omitted the radical letter ን, *n*. Ludolf gives the sense of ***requievit*** to the verb ነወን, in conformity with the Hebrew verb נוח. Hence I have deduced the preceding sense of the quinque-literal verb.

THE END.